Garden Guide

to the Lower South
New Revised Edition

Green
Survival
it's something
you do.

Trustees' Garden C
member of
The Garden Club of Americ
National Council of State Garden Clubs,
The Garden Club of Georgia, Inc.

D1294517

by
ciation
of Nurserymen

Proceeds from the sale of **Garden Guide to the Lower South** will be used to support projects of The Trustees' Garden Club. These projects include civic beautification and horticultural and conservation education.

First Edition – Copyright 1986

First Printing	5000 copies	October 1986
Second Printing	5000 copies	February 1988

Second Edition

First Printing	5000 copies	July 1991
Second Printing	5000 copies	February 1994
Third Printing	5000 copies	January 1999

Third Edition

First Printing	5000 copies	October 2006

Additional copies may be obtained by addressing:
Trustees' Garden Club
P.O. Box 24215
Savannah, Georgia 31403-4215

For your convenience, order blanks are
included in the back of the book.

Library of Congress Catalog Card Number
ISBN 0-9617508-2-0
978-0-9617508-2-4

Third Edition Copyright 2006 by the Trustees' Garden Club, Savannah, Georgia. All rights reserved, including the right to reproduce this book or parts thereof in any form, except for the inclusion of brief quotation in a review.

WIMMER
COOKBOOKS

A CONSOLIDATED GRAPHICS COMPANY

800.548.2537 wimmerco.com

TABLE OF CONTENTS

PREFACE

The new and revised sections of this 2006 edition of the **Garden Guide to the Lower South** reflect our growing concern for the environment and introduce additional information, as well as plants, for the informed gardener. Since its first publication in 1986, The **Garden Guide to the Lower South** has been an immensely successful book. As we celebrate the 80th year of the Trustees' Garden Club, we hope that we bring further knowledge and enjoyment to your garden days.

We are mindful of the fact that each chapter should reflect the growing need to care for the environment. Thus environmental concerns are highlighted in new chapters on invasive plants, gardening with less water (xeriscaping), and gardening for pollinators (hummingbirds, butterflies and bees). In addition, the chapters on native plants, grasses and lawns have been updated to emphasize these concepts.

Recognizing the growing popularity and availability of orchids, succulents and gingers, we have added new chapters on those plants, as well as making additions to many of the other plant lists. Azalea and rose growers have introduced excellent new hybrids, and the expanded list of perennials may prove to be a happy surprise. Don't miss the latest information on growing the best tomatoes in the chapter on vegetables. Finally, we have a chapter on basic landscaping and one on container gardening.

Conflicting information about plants contributes to confusion for the gardener. We hope that this book will solve some of these dilemmas for you, and also will introduce you to the wonderful world of unusual and lesser-known plants suitable for the lower south.

We know that many plants either will not grow in the south or must be grown differently. We have made certain that every plant discussed is suitable for growing in the U.S. Department of Agriculture Hardiness Zones indicated on the map (page 7) as changing weather patterns have made it necessary to reconsider the use of certain plant materials, their drought tolerance, hardiness and maintenance. New to our book is the Heat Zone Map introduced by the American Horticultural Society in 1997 (page 8). By using both of these maps, a wide array of unexpected plants may be enjoyed.

The information gathered here is the fruit of years of experience by a group of Savannah gardeners, who by trial and error have learned which plants can be grown successfully in our region. These are not armchair gardeners, but rather a hands-on group, who hope that you may benefit from their mistakes and triumphs, tears and enchantment. Advice of experts, both professional and amateur, has been sought where needed. The last word about growing things has yet to be written, but we hope that this book will enlighten while it challenges, make the timid more daring and the brave even more adventurous, while bringing the immense fulfillment that comes from successful gardening.

Our aim is to provide a wealth of new information to the seasoned gardener and to be an inspiration to the novice. We hope to make your choices easier, to encourage you to forget your fingernails and fears and to get in the dirt as you delve into that happiest of hobbies – gardening.

ACKNOWLEDGEMENTS

We are grateful to Mr. Henry Clay, University of Georgia Extension Horticulturist and Mr. Ed Poenicke, Chatham County Extension Agent for review of the horticultural material.

For general advice, encouragement and help, we would like to thank Miss Clermont Lee, Mr. Jack M. Jones, Mr. Bob Upson and Miss Cynthia White.

For invaluable help with specific sections, we acknowledge Dr. John Angell, Col. Albert Sidney Britt, Jr., Mr. Woodford Brown, Mr. Frank A. Chisholm, Mr. Gustave R. Dubus, Jr., Mr. Frank Dunn, Mr. Stewart Forbes, Dr. Donald Gardner, Miss Nellie Miller, Mrs. Mary Helen Ray, Mr. John Schaaf, Mrs. A.D. Strobhar and Professor and Mrs. William A. Wood.

We appreciate the special advice and technical assistance of Mr. J. Wiley Ellis, Dr. Robert Gongaware and Mr. Robert B.Hallock.

For horticultural advice in the 1991 revision of the **Garden Guide**, we would like to thank in addition to those listed above, Vivian Anderson, Betty Eisenhart, Dr. Phillip Flexon, Patty Hartman, Carolyn Hyman, John McEllen, Frances Parker, Carolyn Sartor, and Marshall Stone. In addition we would like to thank Thomas Angell, Henry M. Cathey, Dr. Thomas Perry and Louise G. Smith for their contributions, and David Ellis, American Horticulture Society, for his assistance.

Many of those listed above participated in this 2006 revision of the Garden Guide. We thank them along with Kathrine Clark, Stacy Fordham, John Gray, Gail Matthews, Jason Toole and Grover Zipperer.

Cover art is a reproduction of an oil painting by Chip Goldsmith titled "Trustees' Garden".

Graphic designs for the title page and certain chapter dividers are by Christi Williby courtesy of Cunningham, Tallman, Pennington, Inc. and by Andrea Rhangos. Photographs are by Tim Hall and Harris Lewis.

Hortus III has been used as the source for spelling of botanical names.

Title page design is *Gloriosa superba 'Greeneae'*. The late Mrs. Carl Espy, of Savannah, was solely responsible for propagating and distributing this unique and highly desirable "Climbing Lily" to American horticulture.

THE TRUSTEES GARDEN CLUB
A HISTORY

The Trustees' Garden Club, formed in February 1926, took its name from the first public garden in Georgia, established at Savannah in 1733 to assess the viability of growing indigo and mulberry trees for silkworms by the Trustees of the Georgia Colony.

Early Club projects included planting the grounds of the Sunshine Unit of the Chatham County Home for Tubercular Children, printing a monthly garden calendar and publishing a translation of extracts from the journal of naturalist, Andre Michaux. In 1932 the Club began the first of what would become over three-quarters of a century of challenging preservation projects with the landscaping of the historic Bethesda Home for Boys, an orphanage founded in 1740. One thousand trees and shrubs were planted; a plant nursery begun and the addition of an entrance gateway and outdoor theatre were coordinated. Work at Bethesda continued for 25 years.

During the 1930's and 1940's, Club members actively supported the preservation of Savannah's historic squares against encroaching traffic, advocated the addition of azaleas on Victory Drive, planted areas of Hunter Field Army Air Base, furnished flowers to the local military hospitals and sponsored horticulture lectures.

In 1957, at the request of the City's Park and Tree Commission, the Club began its rescue and revitalization of Emmett Park, once the commons land of the Georgia Colony. This ten-year task, financed in part by local businessmen, produced a twelve-block oasis of plants, shrubs, lawns, brick walks, iron fencing and the planting of 13,950 bulbs!

A three-year project, the restoration of Colonial Park Cemetery, Georgia's second oldest burial ground, soon followed. Members researched ironwork, colonial plantings, and tombstone and brick repair. Much of the latter work, they performed themselves. With community financial assistance, the Club refurbished the Cemetery with new watering systems, tabby walks and decorative iron gates creating an inner-city retreat for Savannahians and visitors alike. To this day, members provide maintenance.

The beautification and restoration of Columbia Square, originally laid out in 1799 as part of Savannah's town plan, was initiated in 1970. Beginning with a landscape design that included brick walks, a center pool and a memorial fountain, the members planted dozens of annuals each spring and maintained the square for the next seven years.

As a bicentennial endeavor, the Club, in concert with Historic Savannah Foundation, committed itself to the creation of a parterre garden for the 19th century Isaiah Davenport House Museum. The design turned a sandy lot into an attractive period garden, whose walkways and shaded benches host thousands of Savannah's visitors each year. More recently this garden has been re-designed and re-planted with help from Club members.

In 1980 the Historic Savannah Foundation approached the Trustees' Garden Club to design and landscape a formal yet functional garden for its headquarters at the William Scarbrough House, a National Historic Landmark. Thirty thousand dollars was raised for the major groundwork of grading and installing sprinkler and drainage systems. The garden, featuring a terrace with complementing shrubs, walks, benches, a pavilion and a pool, took five years to complete.

The Club has actively participated in the restoration of Forsyth Park. In 2002, the Park's playground areas were landscaped; brick walkways and benches were added. Working with other community groups, the walled Fragrant Garden for the Blind has been totally re-landscaped. Trustees' financial commitment in Forsyth has thus far amounted to over forty thousand dollars. Volunteer hours for this and other projects are incalculable.

A garden at the Historic Railroad Shops adjacent to the Revolutionary War Battle Park was landscaped and dedicated in 2005. The Club also has been involved in a wide variety of other landscape projects: the grounds of the Savannah Science Museum, the Georgia Historical Society, the Telfair Academy of Arts, the YMCA, the entrance to the original Talmadge Bridge, the Spanish American War Memorial at the Laurel Grove Cemetery, projects for Hospice Savannah, and creation of a native plant garden at the Savannah Botanical Center. In addition, the Club has funded the salary of a Georgia Endangered Plant Stewardship Network Intern at the Georgia Botanical Garden and various horticultural and conservation scholarships.

In addition to civic projects, Club members engage in flower arranging and horticulture training, attending educational meetings throughout the country. Trustees' sponsors Garden Club of America sanctioned flower shows, which are open to the public. Conservation is an increasingly important focus for the Club. Each year Trustees' hosts a public meeting on an environmental issue of local or national concern. The Club worked toward the enactment of both a City and County tree ordinance.

Club projects are funded by a Christmas Greenery Sale held each year since 1991 and by proceeds from this book, published for the first time in 1986. Our first two editions have sold 25,000 copies, an amazing feat for a small club of 50 members. This third edition and first major revision of the **Garden Guide to the Lower South** honors the 80th anniversary of the Trustees' Garden Club.

As this book goes to the publisher, the Club's on-going project study committee continues its charge of finding new and rewarding projects to benefit the community.

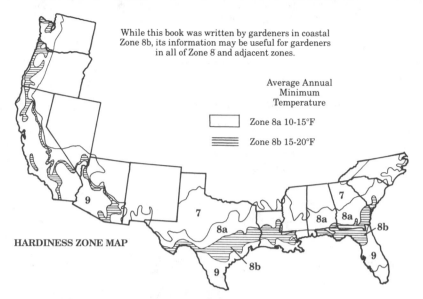

While this book was written by gardeners in coastal Zone 8b, its information may be useful for gardeners in all of Zone 8 and adjacent zones.

Average Annual Minimum Temperature

Zone 8a 10-15°F

Zone 8b 15-20°F

HARDINESS ZONE MAP

USDA PLANT HARDINESS ZONE MAP
AHS PLANT HEAT ZONE MAP

Henry M. Cathey, Director
U.S. National Arboretum

Most gardeners are familiar with the U.S. Department of Agriculture's Plant Hardiness Zone Map. By using the map to find the zone in which you live, you can determine which plants will "winter over" in your garden and survive for many years. Most American reference books, nursery catalogs and gardening magazines describe plants using the USDA zones.

But as we all know, cold isn't the only factor determining whether our plants will survive and thrive. In 1997, the American Horticultural Society (AHS) introduced the AHS Heat Zone Map, which was created by analyzing daily maximum temperatures from National Weather Service stations across the country. Heat has a significant impact on our plants, particularly during seasons of drought. Although there is still disagreement in the scientific community on this issue, many believe that our planet is becoming hotter because of changes in the atmosphere.

The effects of heat damage often are subtler than those of extreme cold, which will kill a plant immediately. Heat damage can first appear in many different parts of the plant: Flower buds may wither; leaves may droop or become more attractive to insects; chlorophyll may disappear so that leaves appear white or brown; roots may cease growing. Plant death from heat is slow and lingering. The plant may survive in a stunted or chlorotic state for several years. When desiccation reaches a high enough level, the enzymes that control plant growth are deactivated and the plant dies.

USING THE MAPS

To use the AHS Heat and USDA Hardiness Zone Maps, you must first locate your town or city on the maps. The hardiness zones reflect the average annual minimum temperatures. The heat zones indicate the average number of days each year that a given region experiences temperatures over 86 degrees. That is

7

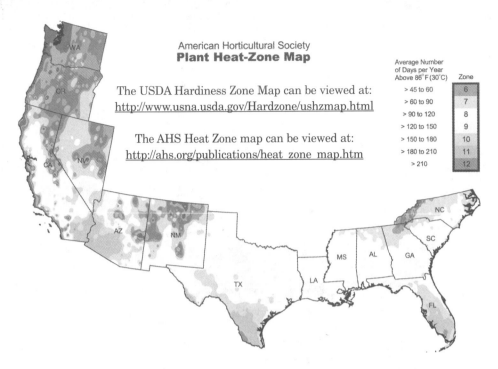

American Horticultural Society
Plant Heat-Zone Map

The USDA Hardiness Zone Map can be viewed at:
http://www.usna.usda.gov/Hardzone/ushzmap.html

The AHS Heat Zone map can be viewed at:
http://ahs.org/publications/heat_zone_map.htm

Average Number of Days per Year Above 86°F (30°C)	Zone
> 45 to 60	6
> 60 to 90	7
> 90 to 120	8
> 120 to 150	9
> 150 to 180	10
> 180 to 210	11
> 210	12

the point at which plants begin suffering physiological damage from the heat.

Most ornamental plants have been coded for cold hardiness over the last few decades, and thousand of plants have now been coded for heat tolerance. Many catalogs, books, magazines and plant tags now use a four-zone coding system that includes both hardiness and heat codes.

For example, a tulip may be numbered Zones 3-8, 8-1. The first two numbers are the range of hardiness zones in which that tulip will thrive and the second two numbers are the range of heat zones in which it will do well. If you live in USDA Zone 7 and AHS Zone 7, you will be able to leave tulips outdoors in your garden year round. An ageratum may be coded 10-11,12-1. It can withstand summer heat throughout the United States, but will over winter only in our warmest zones, 10 and 11. An English wallflower may be 5-8, 6-1. It is relatively cold hardy, up to USDA Zone 5, but cannot tolerate extreme summer heat beyond AHS Zone 6.

Many of the plants that we consider annuals, such as petunias, coleus, snapdragons and vinca, are capable for living for years in a frost-free environment. The AHS Heat Map differs from the USDA Hardiness Map because it assigns codes to annuals, including vegetables and herbs as well as flowering plants.

Despite all this information, the maps are not intended to account for unusually low or extended periods of abnormally high temperatures. Under such conditions, plants of borderline hardiness or heat tolerance may be harmed. Other factors also affect performance, including lack of adequate water, surrounding structures, light, day length, humidity and air movement. Older plants tend to survive better than young ones. The zone ratings are guidelines. Used wisely a wide array of unexpected plants may be enjoyed.

There is also a handy searchable database where gardeners can find their AHS Heat Zone by entering their zip codes.

Garden Care

SOIL AND ITS IMPROVEMENT

For good growth, plants require a fertile soil with adequate water. The soil is constantly changing as nutrients are used by the plants, and decaying organic materials put nutrients back into the soil.

We can improve the soil, but to do this we need to know something about our soil. We need to know its physical and its chemical characteristics as well as the requirements of the plants.

SOIL TYPES AND DRAINAGE:

An ideal soil would consist of 45% solid particles, 5% organic matter, 30% air and 20% water. Air and water vary as water is added. As water drains, it pulls in fresh air providing oxygen to the roots.

When the soil particle size is large, as with sand, the pore spaces for air and water are large, and the water drains out like a sieve. Adequate moisture, in this situation, is hard to maintain. When the soil particle size is too small, as with clay, the very small pore spaces act as a reservoir for water. Thus, clay soils hold excessive amounts of water and air is not available to the plant roots. Excessive water promotes disease and root rot. Ideally, the soil contains particles of all sizes.

The addition of organic material, such as peat moss, manure, or compost increases the soil's ability to hold nutrients. Organic materials should be added regularly to maintain good soil conditions in clay or sandy soils.

After a rain or after sprinkling, if the soil stays wet and mushy instead of just moist, there is probably a drainage problem. Raised beds may be a solution to questionable drainage situations. Professional help may be required to improve a poorly-drained site. Preferably, this is done before building or planting.

SOIL pH:

The pH refers to the acidity or alkalinity of the soil. Finding the pH of the soil is like reading a thermometer. The scale contains 14 points; 7.0 is the neutral point. Below pH 7 is acid; above is alkaline. Most plants thrive at a pH that is slightly acid between 6.0 and 6.9, but will tolerate a wider range. Azaleas, camellias, and certain broad-leaved evergreens require a more acid soil (pH 5.0 to 6.0). Most annual and perennial flowers, herbs and vegetables prefer a neutral or slightly acid soil. Soil in this area tends to be acid. In order to determine the pH, an analysis should be obtained. This is done through the county extension agent. Small samples should be taken from just below the surface to a six inch depth from several spots in the garden and combined to give about a pint for analysis. There are also soil testing kits available. Soil should be tested at least every two years.

If the soil is too acid, the pH may be raised by adding lime. The response to dolomitic lime is slow, requiring 2 to 4 months before a change in the pH is noted. Hydrated lime works more rapidly, but may cause damage. Since decaying organic material provides an acidic environment, and the soil is constantly changing, lime may be required at intervals.

If a more acid soil is required, as for azaleas, camellias, and blueberries, aluminum sulfate and/or peat moss may be added. Oyster shells and building rubble or plaster will tend to make soils alkaline.

FERTILIZATION:

The major nutrient elements required by any plant are nitrogen (N), phosphorus (P), and potassium (K). Fertilizers will indicate the relative amounts of each on the package. Thus, this NPK analysis may be 8-8-8 or 10-10-10, indicating an equal amount of each. Or the analysis may be 6-12-12 or 5-10-10, indicating twice as much phosphorus and potassium as nitrogen. 5-10-15 contains 5% nitrogen, 10% phosphorus, and 15% potassium. An analysis of your soil, as discussed under pH will indicate the N-P-K analysis to use.

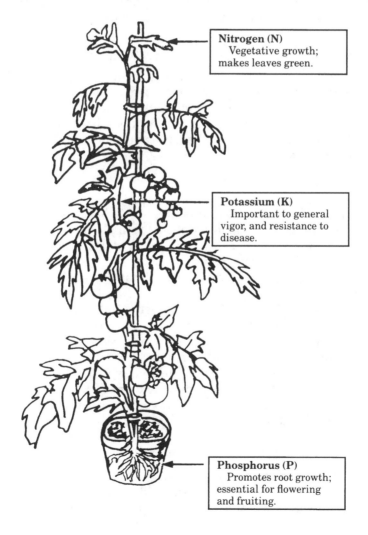

Nitrogen (N)
Vegetative growth; makes leaves green.

Potassium (K)
Important to general vigor, and resistance to disease.

Phosphorus (P)
Promotes root growth; essential for flowering and fruiting.

Other mineral elements required by plants include calcium, magnesium, sulfur, iron, manganese, zinc, molybdenum, copper, boron, and chlorine. These are referred to as minor or trace elements. Premium grade fertilizers will contain these nutrients as indicated on the label.

The major elements are needed in relatively large amounts. Nitrogen provides healthy vegetative growth. Phosphorus promotes root growth and is essential for good flowering and fruiting. Potassium is important to general vigor, root formation and resistance to disease. The other elements are required in lesser amounts. They are present in most soils, and may occur as impurities in fertilizers and in the breakdown of organic matter.

The availability of the elements is strongly affected by pH. Iron deficiency indicated by chlorosis or yellowing of the young foliage between the leaf veins, often occurs where the pH is too high from over liming or from construction mortar in the soil. In this situation the iron is in the soil, but the high pH results in poor uptake by the roots.

TYPES OF FERTILIZERS:

Organic fertilizers come from plant and animal sources. Their major advantage is the slower release of nutrients, which reduces the chance of plant injury. Because the organic fertilizers are most costly and not easily available, they are used less often.

Inorganic fertilizers come from mineral and other non-living sources. Some are mined, while others are manufactured. Their greatest advantage is lower cost.

Organic fertilizers commonly used:
1. Blood meal–High in nitrogen. May deter squirrels.
2. Bone meal–Analysis approximately 2-28-0. More expensive with few advantages over superphosphote to supply phosphorus.
3. Compost–Analysis varies with organic material. Useful as a soil conditioner. See section below.
4. Cottonseed meal–Analysis approximately 6-2-1. Relatively inexpensive.
5. Fish emulsion–Analysis 5-1-1. Excellent to alternate with chemical fertilizers on houseplants.
6. Manure–Good fertilizer, analysis varies. Fresh is excellent if available, but must be used judiciously, as it may injure plants if not well rotted. Dehydrated manure, in which weed seeds have been killed, causes less risk of injury to plants. This may be bought in bags at garden stores, but is relatively expensive.
7. Peat moss–Good soil conditioner. Has acid reaction.
8. Wood ashes–High in phosphorus (P), and potassium (K). Alkaline reaction. Use in vegetable or flower beds.

Inorganic fertilizers commonly used:
Inorganic or chemical fertilizers are sold under a number of trade names. The proportions of the three major elements are written on the

package. Trace elements are also listed. Inorganic fertilizers are available in different forms. They may be granular, or may be liquid or powder to be dissolved in water.

All fertilizers must be used as directed. Frequent light applications will produce better results than too much at once. Pelleted, slow release fertilizer works well in beds. Specific amounts and/or preferences are given in the feature sections, and in Gardening Month by Month.

COMPOST

Compost is a substance made up of a variety of decomposed or rotted organic waste materials and is adaptable to use as a fertilizer. Compost is "brown gold". It is an excellent soil conditioner, and is made from waste products of the garden or kitchen.

Those with smaller yards may feel they haven't the room for a compost pile. Not so. Compost may be made in a modified plastic garbage can, a wooden tub with drainage holes, or even a large plastic bag. Ready-made bins are available that reduce the time required to produce compost. If more space is available, a bin may be made to the desired dimensions, using poultry wire attached to metal posts. It should be 3 to 4 feet high and of any desired dimensions.

Compost is made using layer upon layer of organic matter, soil, lime and manure or fertilizer. Vegetable matter may include kitchen refuse (except meat products), leaves and grass clippings. The pile should be kept moist (pile in a concave manner), and turned every two weeks.

The compost is ready when the substances are not recognizable, or when they fall apart easily when handled. Keep covered so that heavy rains will not leach out nutrients. If made in the fall, most piles will be ready in the spring. Use about one shovelful per square yard.

MULCH:

A mulch is any material used around the roots of plants for the following purposes:

1. To conserve moisture by slowing evaporation.
2. To save weeding and cultivating. Since sunlight cannot get to the soil under the mulch, many weed seeds will not germinate.
3. To moderate soil temperature, keeping it cooler in summer and warmer in winter.
4. To add organic matter and nutrients to the soil as they decompose.
   After settling, the mulch should only be 2 to 4 inches deep. A deeper mulch may result in poor aeration and soggy soil.

In general, mulch does not need to be removed each season. Clean mulch may be added as the materials decompose. A light winter mulch around perennials, and fall-planted annuals is useful to protect them from severe cold.

Mulch does not have to be removed or pulled back in order to fertilize. Simply scatter fertilizer on top of the mulch and water.

There are a number of different materials that may be used for mulch. Some are more attractive than others.

1. Pine straw–Because of availability, pine straw is the most widely used mulch in our area. It is attractive and long-lasting. Pine straw is acid upon decomposition so it is particularly useful around azaleas and camellias.

2. Grass clippings–Grass clippings are readily available, but may pack down (poor aeration) and decompose rapidly. Do not use fresh clippings or those that have recently been sprayed with an herbicide.

3. Leaves–Oak leaves make a particularly good mulch, as they do not pack down and are acid on decomposition. Other fall leaves work better if shredded or allowed to decompose first. Do not use pecan or walnut leaves as they contain growth inhibiting enzymes.

4. Straw–Straw from various grains makes a good mulch except for the untidy appearance and the introduction of weed seeds.

5. Gravel–Crushed stone and pebbles are become more popular as mulch and ground covering. Gravel serves as a permanent mulch, but may reflect too much heat for some plants, and is difficult to clean.

6. Evergreen boughs–Evergreen boughs are easy to place and allow air to circulate. They are particularly useful in protecting perennials and fall-planted annuals from freezing temperatures.

7. Landscape fabric–Landscape fabric, available at garden centers, may be used as a much denser mulch, but must be removed to fertilize. It may be placed on top of the soil and holes made to insert the plants. This fabric should be covered with a mulch to retard decomposition of the fabric.

8. Bark–By-products (shredded, clipped or nuggets) of various sizes from the pulp industry may be used for mulch. Cypress bark is recommended if an acid soil is not desired as with flowers, herbs and vegetables.

9. Newspapers and wood chips may be included in the long list of possible mulches.

10. Hay–Bermuda hay is usually weed free. It is inexpensive and decomposes to add nutrients to the soil.

11. Sawdust–Sawdust may be used as a mulch. If incorporated into the soil, it may utilize nitrogen for decomposition at the expense of the plants.

WATERING

Water is an ingredient essential to the success of any garden. All nutrients must be absorbed by plants in a soluble form. Draining water also works as a siphon to pull in air, also an essential ingredient for root growth. Either too much or too little water may be devastating.

Watering should be done thoroughly and infrequently. A good rule of thumb is 1 to 2 inches each week. If this is not provided by rainfall, it should be done by sprinkling. This may be measured by placing wide-mouthed containers (coffee cans) at several points under the sprinkler. It is ineffective to sprinkle for a few minutes with a hand-held hose. The watering will be superficial, promoting shallow growth of roots and weak plants. Water early in the spring and through the fall. The fall often is a time of drought and the roots will require moisture.

Ideally, watering is best done in the morning. In the heat of the day, more water evaporates than goes into the soil. Moisture left on the leaves in the evening promotes disease. Adequate water, however is more important than either of these considerations.

An efficient method of watering is by drip irrigation. The black "leaky pipe" is an innovation and is available at garden centers. It can be laid on the surface, under mulch or underground. It puts water where it is needed, at the roots, and conserves water.

PRUNING

Regular pruning in the garden is as important as fertilizing, weeding, or any other garden chore. It should be started when the plant is young and continued on a yearly basis at least.

Pruning is no mystery. No cut should be made without good reason and without an understanding of what the results might be.

Where you make the cut on your plant determines how it will grow. A limb or branch cut back to its origin will not stimulate new growth; the plant will be thinned. A cut between the tip and the point of origin will stimulate new growth from the dormant buds below the cut. The plant will become bushier.

WHY PRUNE:

1. The first reason to prune is obvious: all dead and diseased limbs should be removed. Cut back to healthy wood above a bud, or at the origin of the branch or limb. Do not leave a stub. Crossed-rubbing wood should be removed to prevent disease.

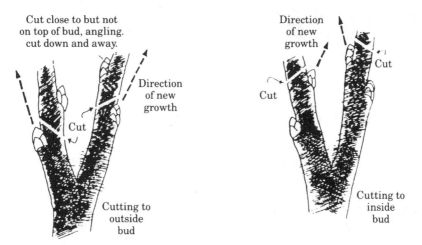

Cut close to but not on top of bud, angling. cut down and away.

Direction of new growth

Cut

Cutting to outside bud

Direction of new growth

Cut

Cut

Cutting to inside bud

2. Prune to shape your shrub or tree. Prune back ungainly shoots (as on eleagnus and pyracantha) to the origin at any time. To form a taller, more narrow shrub, prune back to a bud facing into the plant. Prune to an outward-facing bud for more lateral growth (make your cut inside the plant). Rarely should a shrub be sheared. This is appropriate only for formal shrubs such as boxwood, and in very formal gardens.

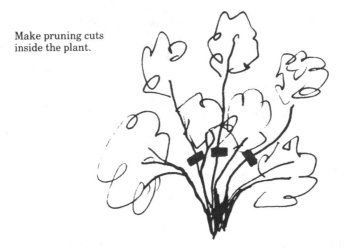

Make pruning cuts inside the plant.

Hedges should be trimmed so that the bottom is wider than the top. This will allow the sun to penetrate to all branches and prevent a leggy look.

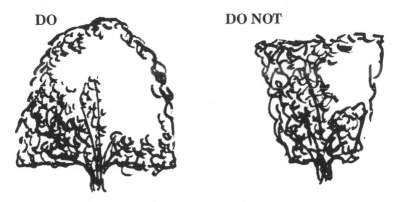

DO   DO NOT

Always remove suckers (growth from the base of a tree) and water sprouts (vertical growth from a horizontal branch). These are unsightly, do not produce good flowers or fruit, and compete with more valuable growth.

3. Prune to increase flowering or fruiting. We can see this result when we pinch back petunias or snapdragons–more flowers develop. It is also true that the best production of flowers and fruit is on one and two year old wood. The older the wood is, the less productive it becomes. Annual removal of some of the old wood encourages new growth.

4. Finally, we prune to rejuvenate shrubs and trees. Annual pruning, as suggested above, will keep a tree or shrub blooming and growing well for years. Occasionally, however, a shrub becomes too large for its site. Overgrown, multi-stemmed shrubs may be controlled with a three year renewal plan. In the winter/spring of the first year one third of the oldest branches should be cut back to the base of the shrub. In the second year another third should be removed, and again, a third in the third year. By the fourth year, you should have a new shrub of a more manageable size.

On occasion, a shrub will be so overgrown or freeze damaged that you will want to cut it back to within 10 to 12 inches of the ground. Most will come back rapidly. In June vigorous shoots should be topped to promote branching. Boxwoods recover very slowly.

Trees may also at times need major pruning for rejuvenation. The help of a professional should be sought for all but the smallest trees. Never top a tree. Prune branches back to an inner crotch to thin and reduce size.

TOOLS:

The basic tools you need are a pair of clippers, a pair of loppers, and a pruning saw. The tools should be of good quality, as you will want to make good, clean cuts. Scissor-type shears will produce a closer, neater cut than the anvil type. Keep the tools sharpened and cleaned.

OTHER RULES:

Always make your cuts on a slant ¼ inch above the bud.

If the limb is heavy, take care that it will not rip the bark from the main trunk as it falls. Do this by cutting through the bark opposite your cut.

The experts debate the necessity of pruning paint. There is no evidence that it harms, though it may not prevent disease as suggested.

Most conifers do not respond to heavy pruning, because they do not have adventitious (bypassed) buds on older wood. Consequently, they do not send out new shoots. That is why old pfitzer junipers do not recover after heavy pruning.

WHEN TO PRUNE:

A list of general guidelines follows, but for more specific suggestions, see individual chapters.

In the South, light pruning may be done at almost any time. Do not hesitate to pinch or cut out the tips of new growth during the growing season. This will stimulate branching. Do this with perennials as well as shrubs.

Spring flower shrubs (azalea, spirea) can be pruned immediately after flowering.

Summer bloomers (buddleia, althea) should be pruned in late winter before growth begins.

Major pruning should be done in late winter so that the plant has the maximum amount of time to recover.

Early fall pruning is discouraged as the growth that is stimulated may be killed back by cold weather.

Water sprouts, suckers and other ungainly growth may be cut back to the origin at any time.

Removing spent flowers (deadheading) is an important form of pruning. Even crape myrtles may be encouraged to bloom a second time, if the first bloom is removed.

ESPALIER:

The original definition of an espalier is a trellis against which a plant or tree has been pruned in such a way that it has been forced to grow on one plane. In common usage, espalier refers to any plant that is pruned or trained on one plane whether supported by a trellis, a wall or other structure. The best espaliers have a pattern. Advantages are the conservation of space and the decorative appearance. An espalier is ideal for small city gardens if one has the patience to prune continuously. Pruning must be done in spring, winter and all during the growing season. New shoots should be pruned back as they appear.

A number of plants are conducive to this training including *Camellia sasanqua,* elaeagnus, pyracantha and dwarf fruit trees.

PESTS AND DISEASES

There is nothing more aggravating to a gardener than to see a tender plants with its leaves stripped, or deformed and discolored. Control of damaging insect pests and diseases is a continuing problem. We are learning that control, not elimination, is the answer. There have been tremendous changes in the recommendations over the last few years. No longer are we told to spray regularly every two weeks, but rather to keep a close surveillance and take care of the problems as they appear.

The development of newer, stronger pesticides has taught us that we can not fully eradicate the pests. Many species adapt and become resistant to pesticides. Spraying and dusting eliminates natural predators as well as beneficial insects. For these reasons continuous and preventative sprays are losing favor particularly in the home garden. We are now looking to more natural and biological controls being developed.

GENERAL MEASURES:

When an infestation is recognized early, there are measures which may be taken without resorting to poison. They are certainly easier to manage in a small gardening location.

1. The first step toward prevention is buying and maintaining healthy plants. When buying plants at a nursery, look carefully at the

foliage for signs of disease or pests. Look underneath the leaves and at the new growth.

2. Maintain a healthy garden with appropriate fertilizing and watering practices. Poor drainage and wet conditions promote disease. Water early enough in the day so that the leaves can dry. Excess moisture at night encourages fungal diseases.

3. Keep your yard clean. Pick up, destroy, and remove diseased plant materials. Attract birds and appreciate lizards, frogs and nonpoisonous snakes which prey on insect pests.

4. Use disease-free and disease-resistant plants in your garden. If one plant seems to attract problems, get rid of it. Native plants are, in general, good selections to reduce pest problems. Particularly in vegetable gardening, many varieties are selected for their resistance; use those varieties. Strong smelling plants, such as herbs and marigolds, when inter-planted, confuse insect pests.

INSECTICIDES:

There is no doubt that at times we must resort to insecticides. If you cannot identify the problem, your county extension agent or nurseryman can help you with identification and with appropriate treatment. For the greatest safety, use the following rules:

1. Use the safest pesticide available. Safety is noted by the LD 50. The higher the accompanying number, the safer the spray.

2. Use a specific insecticide for a specific insect problem. Broad-spectrum agents will kill the beneficial as well as the harmful.

3. Read the entire label and follow directions, measuring carefully. Use only on plant species that are specified.

4. Dilute the spray as directed. Cover the plant uniformly being careful to spray the underside of leaves.

5. Wear gloves and protective clothing.

6. Minimize drift by spraying in the early morning or evening, when there is little breeze.

7. When finished, wash out the sprayer carefully.

8. Do not harvest vegetables too soon after spraying. Follow recommendations on the label. Use only insecticides specified for vegetables, and observe the waiting period before harvest.

Some insecticides act locally. When the leaf is washed off, the insecticide is washed off as well. Sticking ability may be improved by adding a few drops of detergent to the spray jar. Systemic insecticides are absorbed by the plant and travel through the entire system of the plant. They have, therefore, a longer lasting effect, but also are more toxic.

Many insects build up a resistance to a particular chemical. Different types may have to be used.

BIOLOGICAL CONTROLS:

Extensive research is being done in the development of biological controls. Work is being done with pest diseases, viruses and protozoa, to use against the pests in our gardens. Insect sterilization and growth regulation are also areas being developed. Currently predator insects and bacterial insecticides are available commercially.

1. Predator insects include lady bugs and praying mantis. Methods to induce their settling in your garden are being developed.

2. The microbial insecticide *Bacillus thuringiensis* (Dipel, Thuricide) is available. It is a bacterium which infects the larvae of caterpillars and worms, and is non-toxic to other living things.

SAFE INSECTICIDES:

Recognizing that spraying is easy and convenient, it is fortunate that there are a few botanical and mechanical insecticides that are relatively safe as well as effective.

Pyrethrum is a botanical insecticide made from the dried flowers of *Chrysanthemum cinerariifolium*. It is very safe (LD 50 of 1500 mg/kg), as well as effective against a large number of insects. Thus, it would seem to be the perfect insecticide. Unfortunately, the paralzyed pest may recover so it must be used with other agents. It is frequently used in sprays for household pests.

Rotenone is another widely used botanical insecticide that is relatively safe (LD 50 350 mg/kg). It is effective against caterpillars, aphids, spider mites and leafhoppers, as well as a number of other pests. Its disadvantages are its short life after application and its toxicity to fish.

Oil sprays, (both dormant and warm season), suffocate pests such as scale, whitefly larvae, mites, mealy bugs, and some aphids. The dormant spray is a heavier spray to be used during January and February. More commonly, we use the lighter oil in fall and spring. The oils must be used at the appropriate temperatures. Read the label carefully.

The fatty acids in soaps kill insects by disrupting the metabolism. They cause no plant injury and are harmless to other organisms. Diluted dishwashing detergents may be used, but some fatty acids are being especially blended and packaged for use on plants.

Lime sulfur may be used as a dormant spray with the oils or alone. It is particularly effective against over-wintering fungal disease spores as well as against some insects. It is used most extensively in rose gardens and on fruit trees.

PROBLEM IDENTIFICATION:

The following are a few brief paragraphs, with pointers, describing some of the most common, almost inevitable, diseases or insect problems. The type of damage will often help in identification of the offender. Because there are so many problems, and the remedies are so often changed, it is wise to ask your county agent or nurseryman to help you. Carry the damaged leaves, the dead plant (with roots), the infected branch, or even the bug in with you for the most accurate diagnosis.

CHEWING PESTS:

Pests that do their damage by chewing, leave holes in leaves. They may even strip the leaf to the central vein or chew a young plant off at the ground. Use recommended chemical dusts and sprays.

Caterpillars: Foliage is eaten. May be hand-picked or use the biological control *Bacillus thuringiensis*.

Cutworms: Frequently cut young tender plants at the ground. Place a cardboard collar loosely around the stem, pushing it into the soil 1 to 2 inches.

Slugs and snails: Slimy pests that do their damage at night. Sand or wood ashes spread on the ground will deter them. Sink a saucer with beer to ground level. The slugs will be attracted to it and will drown. Baits are available.

Nematodes: These small eel worms feed on roots causing knots on the roots. French marigold roots will trap these pests and are, therefore, interplanted for control. Crops should be rotated to aid on control.

SUCKING PESTS:

A large number of pests cause damage by sucking the sap and cell contents from the plant. This causes deformed foliage, flowers or fruit, and mottling or yellowing of the leaves. A strong spray of water, soap, pepper, or garlic may discourage these insects. Recommended chemicals are also effective.

Aphids: Tiny, soft-bodied insects that frequently feed on new growth. They excrete a sticky substance called honeydew that attracts ants, and also acts as a medium for a fungus growth called black sooty mold. Aphids may transmit plant viruses. Aphids are attracted to yellow. Yellow paint on a board covered with oil will attract and trap these insects. A sharp spray of water also aids control.

Leaf miners: These larvae of certain flies make a long serpentine tunnel in the leaf. The flies, when swarming, may be killed by using an insecticide. Once the tunnel is visible the affected leaves must be removed.

Mealy bugs: These small oval insects are identifiable by their covering of powdery white wax. They tend to cluster in axils and on the undersides of leaves, but may be found in the soil. They multiply rapidly. Since houseplants are most susceptible, it is practical to use non-spray methods. If touched with alcohol-soaked cotton swab, or sprayed with alcohol (make a mister out of the alcohol bottle) the insects will shrivel. An outdoor vacation under the trees often helps.

Spider mites: These minute insects are found on the undersides of leaves. Small webs may be on the underside of leaves, or a red streak may be seen when the leaf is pulled between the fingers. The mites themselves may require a magnifying glass to become visible. Miticides may be used, but the pests rapidly become resistant. Repeated sharp sprays of cold water are often the best control.

Scale: There are a number of different scales. They feed on the underside of leaves causing yellow spots and, eventually, leaf drop. Sooty mold may grow in the excreted honeydew. Scale is best controlled with an oil spray, which may be mixed with other chemicals. Take care to use oil sprays at the designated temperatures, or the plant may be defoliated. Systemic insecticides are recommended for summer applications.

Thrips: These are tiny insects that may be light yellow to black. Their mouth-parts have rasping, sucking parts that rasp the surfaces of new growth, causing them to become disfigured. These are very difficult to control even with insecticides.

Whiteflies: The name describes these small bothersome insects. They secrete a honeydew upon which a black sooty mold feeds and grows. Frequent forceful water sprays may help but one usually resorts to chemical sprays. Like aphids, white flies may also be attracted to, and trapped by oil applied to a board painted yellow.

DISEASES:

Plant diseases are caused by fungi, bacteria and viruses. Fungal diseases are more common and fortunately are much easier to treat. Fungicides may be used. The major deterrent to bacterial and viral problems has been the development of resistant varieties of susceptible plants.

Blackspot: As the name implies, infection is indicated by black spots on the leaves. The black spots ultimately become larger, killing the leaf and defoliating the plant. Good air circulation to decrease humidity helps in prevention.

Damping off: This is a dreaded fungal disease for those who propagate their own plants. It causes seedlings and young cuttings to rot at soil level. To prevent this use sterilized soil, treat seeds with a fungicide and avoid excessive moisture. A layer of sphagnum moss will prevent damping off.

Downy mildew: This fungal disease causes a powdery white, mold-like growth on leaves, buds and twigs, which stunts growth. Crape myrtle and roses are particularly susceptible. Start treatment early with a fungicide.

LARGER PESTS:

Moles and voles are small animals, grey to black in color, that cause damage to lawns and plants by their tunneling. They feed on grubs, slugs and other insects. The best means of eliminating moles is by getting rid of the insects upon which they feed (insecticides, worked into the soil will discourage these insects). Traps may be helpful.

Deer are beautiful, yet damaging to the planted landscape. As their habitat becomes less plentiful, deer are becoming less fearful of humans. There are a number of products on the market that will repel deer when used regularly; most are non-toxic. In addition, a pulse sprinkler, activated by motion, is available as are various other devices. Ask your nurseryman, peruse garden catalogs and search the web for the latest in the battle against these four footed pests. One should also attempt to use plants that are not attractive to these animals. Native plants are generally safe, as are lantana and holly fern. Petunias repel deer.

PROPAGATION

Once you begin to enjoy gardening, really digging in the dirt, it won't be long before you realize what fun it is to propagate your own plants. You may start with division of a few daylilies, whose clumps have grown too large, or the planting of a few tomato seeds. However you begin, curiosity and awe will soon make you want to try other methods of starting your own plants. This chapter describes a few of the simpler methods of propagation.

STARTING FROM SEED:
There is nothing quite as gratifying to the gardener as a full healthy plant, producing either flowers, healthy foliage and/or tempting fruits or vegetables. Especially this is true when one has started it from a small seed and nourishing it with patience, water and a good sprinkling of tender, loving care.

There are many different and varied systems—each must evolve the system best suited to oneself and one's needs.

Using containers: The newest school in the art of plant propagation is cubism. From peat pots, the time-tested system, gardeners have graduated to cubes or "growing blocks" of inert or organic material, impregnated with fertilizers. Seeds or cuttings are simply set in a hole in the cube and grown until rooted. Then cube and all are planted. A sterile medium, great ease of handling and no transplanting shocks are distinct advantages.

Other recommended methods: Make rows in flats of soil. Place seeds in soil in individual plastic or peat pots, in egg cartons or halved, cardboard half-gallon milk cartons. Provide drainage holes.

Seeding soil mixture: The soil must hold moisture without becoming water logged. A good mixture is equal parts of peat moss, perlite and vermiculite. To this can be added small amounts of lime, composted manure, bonemeal and, if desired, a small amount of wood ashes. Sand may be included.

Light, heat and water: Many seeds are indifferent to light during germination, but, once sprouted, need bright natural or artificial light 16 to 18 hours a day. Heat and steady moisture are essential. Most seeds germinate between 65° to 75° F. It is best to water the soil before planting the seeds, then keep the medium moist with a plastic or glass covering until germination occurs.

Sprouting and growing: An excellent germination/growing arrangement is a simple flourescent light suspended over seed flats which are placed in a warm part of the house. If not grown in cubes or individual pots, the seedlings should be transplanted to individual containers when each plant develops two sets of true leaves, but trays should remain under lights until mild weather has arrived outdoors.

Outdoor seed sowing: All but the tiniest seeds, say commercial growers, germinate more quickly if presoaked in water 6 to 24 hours. Small seeds should not be covered by more than ⅛th inch of fine soil or peat moss. A tip for tiny seeds: either mix with fine sand or place single sheets of facial tissue in the furrow and sow the seeds on top so that they may be easily spaced with a toothpick. The tissue soon rots away.

PLANTING SEEDLINGS: To harden seedlings to be planted outside, gradually reduce temperature and watering and place flats outside for several days before transplanting into the ground. After setting in the ground, water with a weak mixture of fertilizer or fish emulsion and mist once a day for several days.

Tips To Prevent Loss Of Seedlings:

Avoid overwatering but keep evenly moist.

Avoid cold, wet soil which causes fungus disease.

Avoid hot sun immediately; shade or mist initially if deemed necessary.

ROOTING FROM CUTTINGS:

Rooting softwood cuttings from the stems of plants is simple, and ensures a new plant true to variety. The cuttings should be brittle, not stringy; when bent they should snap, not bend. It is not possible to give any definite month to root because each plant completes its growth at a different time. Generally lateral shoots are better than terminal shoots. Two or more nodes, or points of leaf origin, should be used for each cutting, but they should seldom be more than 3 to 5 inches long. Never allow flower buds to remain on the cutting; they will only exhaust its vitality. The ideal place to remove the cutting is one half inch below the eye or node.

Rooting medium: Coarse sand is a classic rooting medium, but mixtures of peat moss and sand, pure peat moss, peat and perlite or vermiculite may be used. The rooting medium should be kept moist, but not soggy.

Rooting hormone: Rooting hormone such as "Rootone" is very helpful to insure success, as it helps to promote development of roots and helps prevent "damping-off," or rotting of the stems. The cut stems are dipped in "Rootone" and then placed in the rooting medium.

Heat: Bottom heat from soil cables will induce root action and may be used.

Covering: Until roots form, the container should be covered with glass or plastic, unless a misting system is available. These coverings should be vented enough to prevent growth of fungi. After cuttings are rooted, the covering should be removed for increasing periods of time, until left off entirely.

The process of rooting: When a cutting starts to root, it gradually produces a layer of spongy tissue over the cut surface. This is a callus and usually precedes rooting.

Hardwood cuttings: hardwood cuttings are preferable for some plant material. They are cut and treated in a similar manner but take considerably longer to root. These cuttings are usually taken in the fall and are rooted by spring.

AFTER ROOTING:

When the roots of the cuttings are from ½ to 1 inch long, they can be transplanted to pots or directly to outside beds. Remove them carefully. Cover the roots, potted or in soil, and firm the soil gently around them. Water well and shade for 7 to 14 days. After this, your cuttings should be partially established, and you may increase the amount of light.

Cuttings placed directly in outdoor beds will need shading longer than those first grown in pots.

OTHER METHODS OF PROPAGATION:

Division of bulbs and tuberous-rooted plants: Dig and divide by cutting or pulling apart.

Root divisions (perennials): Same as above.

Layering, or burying in the ground, still attached branches of shrubs or perennials. When propagating by layering, the attached branch may be held down with a wooden clothespin, brick or other device. Keep the area moist until well rooted. Air layering is done when the stem or branch is not flexible enough to reach the ground. In this case, moist sphagnum moss is attached at a node to the plant to be rooted. The moss is kept moist by tying plastic around it. One inch of bark should be removed from woody stems at the point of attachment to the soil or sphagnum.

Grafting and budding are fascinating but complicated means of propagation. These methods need further research before they are attempted.

Propagation from **spores,** such as those from ferns, also requires further study.

TIPS: The substance released by willow cuttings increases the incidence of rooting in plants to be propagaged in water. Simply add a small cut branch of willow to the container holding the cuttings.

Many house plants are easily rooted in water.

The greatest danger in starting from seed and from cuttings is that of "damping off." This possibility is lessened if the amount of moisture in the soil is carefully watched and not allowed to be excessive.

PREPARING FOR WINTER AND WORSE

The temperatures in these zones are usually moderate. Average minimum temperatures are 15 to 25° F (-10 to -4° C). General measures, as outlined below, will protect even some of the more tender plants from freezing.

An early freeze, before plants have gone dormant, or a late freeze after early warm weather has encouraged bloom, may be particularly devastating. This is an uncontrollable variable.

The average date of the first frost is November 15, the last frost, March 15. Though frost may occur before or after these dates, one should be ready to take care between these dates.

PLANT SELECTION:

Perhaps the point is too obvious, but plants should be selected that are known to be hardy in your range of temperatures. Occasionally one wishes to try to grow something marvelous, but perhaps a bit too tender (brunfelsia, cassia). In those cases, extra attention should be paid to protective measures.

LOCATION:

Much of the damage in a freeze occurs because of the drying factors of sun and wind. For this reason, plants may do better if they are under shade or are on the north side of the house. A hedge or a fence may perform as a windbreak, or a temporary windbreak may be set up for a beloved specimen.

MOISTURE:

Cold weather is better tolerated if the plant has adequate moisture. Continue weekly watering (if no rain) of one inch through the winter.

After a frost, early morning sprinkling to wash the frost off the leaves will help to prevent the rapid drying and burning that may occur when the sun hits the leaves of tender plants.

The practice of sprinkling, while the temperature is still freezing, to coat the branches in ice is controversial. The ice does insulate from lower temperatures, but its weight may cause leaves and branches to break. Perhaps its greatest advantage is the delight provided children by the fairyland appearance of the draped icicles.

MULCH:

A 2 to 3 inch layer of mulch should be provided in the Fall to help insulate the root system against the fluctuations in temperature (see section on Mulches). If unusually low temperatures are forecast, a loose covering of Spanish moss, pine straw or pine branches (Christmas trees) should be placed over fall-planted annuals and other particularly tender plants. These mulches should be removed after the weather has warmed.

COVER:

Floating row covers, available at garden centers, are an ideal cover for winter protection of tender or young plants. Unlike plastics, used by many, these covers breathe and do not have to be removed as the day becomes warmer. They raise the temperature only 10 degrees, however, so more protection may be needed if the temperature drops below 20 degrees.

WRAP:

Trunks of newly planted trees may be wrapped with commercial tree wrap or with light colored burlap.

ASSESSING DAMAGE:

Occasionally, we have been known to have temperatures much lower than the anticipated average minimum. Plants that are usually hardy have succumbed to the cold under these conditions. When this happens, we are all impatient to know what has survived and what has not. A few clues will help in assessing damage.

1. Wait–First and foremost, one must be patient. Do not prune or dig and discard too soon. You may be surprised. The opposite may also be true. Plants that initially do well may die in the hot, dry summer months.

2. Foliage–Brown, slimy foliage should be carefully removed and discarded. Foliage that is bronzed or has brown edges may drop off to be replaced in the spring; bronze, crisp leaves are a less hopeful sign.

3. Flower Buds–Viability of flower buds may be determined by slicing through a bud. Internal browning indicates cold damage and loss of flower for that season.

4. Wood–Damage to wood may be detected by scraping the bark. If the underlying tissue is green, the outlook is good. Split bark is an ominous sign. If bark is split severely, the limb should be pruned back an inch below the split at the end of February. It is desirable to wait until May or even June, when new growth has appeared, to cut back the dead tissue on other plants.

5. Fertilization–The spring fertilization program should begin with a light application of fertilizer.

NOTES

28

Trees

TREES

with Thomas Perry, PhD
  Owner, Natural Systems Associates
  Raleigh, North Carolina

Trees are the largest and most permanent of all landscaping elements in your garden. **The Right Tree in the Right Place** is of utmost importance and should be the logical and aesthetic starting point for a well-planned homesite.

Each tree you plant should serve a purpose. Trees can give us many things. They are essential in providing a proper setting for a home—as a frame, border or background, thereby enhancing the beauty and value of your property. They provide protection from hot summer sun and become an important energy and economic factor. They can be planted as a windbreak, and used to prevent soil erosion. Trees reduce noise, screen out undesirable views, filter dust and pollutants, and maintain oxygen and carbon dioxide in proper atmospheric balance, giving a healthier micro-climate around your home.

Whether buying new trees or fitting existing ones into your landscape plan, you should give thought to their form, texture, and seasonal color. Characteristic growth patterns include rounded, oval spreading, pyramidal, weeping, columnar and vase. Texture is determined by leaves and greatly influences the degree of shade. Tree color should complement or offer an attractive contrast to the overall setting of your landscape.

Other points to keep in mind are:

Your site greatly affects what kind of trees you plant. Is it dry, wet, acid, alkaline, sandy or clay?

Try to visualize a tree at its ultimate height and breadth. A tree will reach its best natural beauty and shape if it has the proper room to grow. (Special consideration should be given to the live oak which will eventually require a very large area.)

Consider placement. This will affect open lawns, screening, location of flower beds and windbreaks, shade in summer and sun in winter. Large trees should not be planted too close to your house. Constant trimming and root damage to foundations can be an unwanted effect.

Keep in mind the mature height of the tree and any overhead wires.

Ascertain the location of any underground cables or lines, septic tanks or drain fields. Most tree roots respond to moisture and will invade drains.

Driveways, especially those paved with oyster or scallop shells, or crushed limestone, can be very damaging to tree root systems since they change the pH of the soil. Large tree roots may crack the driveway pavement.

A tree's ornamental value is especially significant if it is in a small garden.

Foliage, flowering and fruiting characteristics should be evaluated. Will your tree be shedding berries that stain a patio? (Crape Myrtle can be a problem.) Certain trees require more upkeep than others. (Magnolia leaves and fruit pods can be a problem.)

Where there is a choice, preference should be given to planting trees that are not weak-wooded and subject to disease. The removal of a large tree is expensive.

If it is practical to plant rapid-growing, but short lived trees (for shade, etc.), try to locate them where they will not interfere with the planting of slower growing, permanent trees.

Planting shrubs and especially seasonal flower beds under trees tears up tree roots and will produce a corresponding death of twigs and branches in the crown of the tree. These plantings also compete with the tree's roots for available moisture and minerals within the soil.

A tree in your garden is a long-term investment. To better care for this investment, it is important to understand how trees function. A tree contains a number of complex systems. All are interconnected and vital to its welfare. The root system has dual purposes—to anchor the tree to the ground and to take water and minerals from the earth. A major part of a tree's feeder root system lies within the top twelve inches of soil and often extends well beyond the dripline (point from the outermost branch tips to the ground). These feeder roots must receive moisture, oxygen and minerals for healthy tree growth. The trunk provides support for the crown, limbs and branches, and encases the pipeline system for transport of water and nutrients. The limbs branches and twigs support leaves, flowers and fruit and serve as conductors of water and nutrients to leaves. They take food manufactured by leaves back to other parts of the tree. The leaves, by a process called photosynthesis, manufacture the carbohydrates upon which a tree's life depends. The flowers and fruits produce the seeds from which new trees grow. Knowing a tree's growth and rest periods is essential for proper care. A year's cycle includes onset of growth, formation of leaves, formation of wood and inner bark, storage of energy and dormancy.

Most trees are monoecious, meaning that they have flowers of both sexes. However, there are dioecious trees with either male or female flowers, but not both on the same plant. Dioecious trees need to be planted in pairs, male and female, for pollination. (Di-Dioecious is noted in the key of the tree list.)

PURCHASING A NURSERY GROWN TREE:

Trees are sold in four different ways.

1. *Container grown:* Container grown trees come in a variety of sizes from 1 to 300 gallon containers. They are highly recommended because they are easy to handle and the root system is not disturbed during transplanting. Properly grown container plants should have a fully grown root system which extends to the outer limits of the container. When the plant is lifted from the container, the root growth should be sufficient to pull all of the soil from the container. However, one should check to see that the root system has not become seriously root bound

or is spiraling. Some circular root growth is normal and can be remedied when planting by loosening slightly. Unless you are having a large tree professionally planted, select a medium sized one as top and roots are in better balance.

2. *Containerized:* Often professional tree growers will place larger bare root trees in containers during the dormant season and will then hold the trees for a sufficient length of time to establish a new root system. When purchasing this type of tree, one should follow the same rules for container grown trees. The root system should be firmly established in the container.

3. *Balled and burlapped:* Known as "B & B" in the nursery industry, these trees are either deciduous or evergreen and have been field grown. These trees are dug by machine or by hand and should have a very firm ball of soil around the root system which is wrapped in burlap and often placed in a wire basket. If a "B&B" tree is purchased, one should insure that the root ball is not broken and that the tree is not loose in the root ball. "B&B" plants should always be lifted by the root ball and not by the trunk.

4. *Bare root:* These trees should be left to growers and land owners planting orchards or large stands of trees. Usually these are deciduous trees and have been field grown. They are dug only in the winter dormant season, kept in cold storage, and planted almost immediately after removal from storage. Few retail operations are equipped to handle bare root trees. Proper care of these trees includes keeping roots cool and moist at all times until planting. Professionally handled bare root trees can be either deciduous or evergreen seedlings; or, larger field grown deciduous trees. Evergreen trees should not be sold in a bare root condition in the lower south.

NATIVE TREES:

Trees that are indigenous to this area should be more widely used for shade and decorative purposes. They are best suited to our weather, moisture, soil and drainage conditions. They also require less maintenance. Since nursery grown native trees stand a better chance for survival than those grown in the woods, it is best to use the nursery grown ones for planting. Trees taken from the woods have extensive root systems that are easily damaged and, therefore, they often die after the first season. Furthermore, the natural habitat may be disturbed and other threatened flora and fauna may die. Reputable nurseries offer plants that have been grown from seed or from cuttings taken in the wild, or obtained from botanical gardens or from individuals. These plants have been regularly fed, watered and root pruned to develop a compact root system. Observe conservation laws and buy only nursery grown stock so that our valuable native trees will be preserved and perpetuated.

CHECK LIST FOR A HEALTHY TREE:

1. Buy from a reputable dealer.

2. There should be no broken branches or injured bark. This invites disease.

3. If the tree is balled and burlapped or container grown, there should be healthy green leaves.

4. When purchasing a dormant tree, be sure the twigs are green and not brittle.

5. Check the trunk of the tree. It should have a straight, tapered trunk. If wrapped, injuries may be hidden. Unwrap for inspection. Wrapping benefits the trunk only during transit to the planting site.

PLANTING:

Preparing the site: Remember the adage: "Don't put a $5.00 tree in a 50 cent hole." Preparing the planting site is of great importance to the healthy growth of your tree. Loosen the soil to at least twice the width and equal to the depth of the root ball. This will enable the roots to grow out into the surrounding ground. Plants have a tendency to settle after planting. To prevent this, firm some backfill soil at the bottom of the hole on which to set the tree. Plant it slightly above the original line. Use as much native soil as possible. Do not add amendments unless planting site has very poor soil. To extremely light, sandy or compacted soil, incorporate organic matter into the planting site (garden compost, peat moss, leaf mold, ground twigs or branches).

Do not put fertilizer in the hole at the time of planting.

Keep flowers, grass, weeds, or other landscaping away from the base of the tree (2' minimum).

A covering of well composted chips, or other mulch materials, may be placed around the base of the tree, but should not be piled around the trunk. Do not use fresh wood chips, aromatics (cedar, camphor) or black walnut wood chips for mulch.

To insure its growth and good health, your tree will need active maintenance for three to four years after planting.

1. Container grown planting: These may be planted at any time but are best planted in fall or spring. For best results avoid periods that will cause climate related stress to the tree. Have the nursery slit the container sides for you. Gently pull the container away from the tree and loosen any circular root growth. Put the tree into the hole at the same level as the soil in the can. Add backfill soil, gradually firming it toward the roots. Water well to settle soil and eliminate air pockets.

2. Balled and burlapped planting: The best time to plant is during the dormant season, generally October 15 to March 1. The planting pit should be approximately twice the diameter of the root ball. When placed in the prepared pit, the top of the root ball should be slightly higher than the surrounding soil. Use care to handle the weight of the tree by the root ball when placing and aligning the tree. Fill the hole with backfill soil, firming toward the ball while backfilling. Use water to settle the soil and remove air pockets. Do not remove burlap from the root ball since burlap will eventually rot away. A wire basket will

also decay. If wire or cord have been used across the top of the root ball, these should be removed to prevent girdling of the tree. Be cautious of trees wrapped in synthetic materials other than burlap. This material may not be biodegradable and may cause root rot and root girdling.

3. Bare root planting: If there is a delay in planting this type of tree, keep it moist and cool. It may be "heeled in" (roots covered with soil or mulch to keep them from drying out) in a shady spot for several weeks. Cut back any diseased, injured or twisted roots or broken branch tips. Set the tree in the hole so the soil line at the base of the trunk is at or slightly above the surrounding soil. Spread the roots out evenly. Fill in with soil between and around roots. Firm the soil in gently, making sure there are no air pockets. Do this by running water slowly over the root area.

STAKING:

A tree need not be staked unless it will not stand properly or is on a windy site. A young tree, standing alone, with its top free to move, usually becomes a stronger tree with a good supporting root system. If necessary, brace the tree in a way that allows the trunk to move slightly. Three stakes will reduce rubbing injury. Brace as low on the trunk as possible to provide stability for the tree. Do not use wire in a hose or put nails in the trunk. Use flat strapping that will not injure the bark.

WATERING:

Water is essential for growth and is especially important at the critical growing time when leaves are sprouting. Water often (weekly to twice a month during summer) and thoroughly the first three years after planting. Newly planted trees will need more frequent watering than established trees since the young roots will not have grown far from the planting pit. Signs of stress from lack of moisture include wilting, premature leaf fall, change in leaf color and leaf scorch. Watering early in the day is preferred. Foliage that does not dry out before evening is prone to fungal disease. Dogwoods are particularly susceptible.

FERTILIZING:

It is best not to fertilize a newly planted tree. Fertilizer can stimulate weed growth in competition with new tree roots as well as burn tender new root growth. New trees can be fertilized lightly after leaves have formed. Mature trees may need little or no fertilizer if leaf color is good and appearance healthy.

Most trees grow satisfactorily over a wide range of soil pH. A soil test will determine alkalinity or acidity. Your county extension agent or Forestry Commission Metro-forester can help with this and the type and amount of fertilizer needed. Light applications of a slow release fertilizer such as 12-4-8 in March, May and July may be used. A low nitrogen (5-10-10) fertilizer applied in September will aid root growth during the dormant season.

Fertilizer should be broadcast over the ground beneath the tree and slightly beyond the dripline. Do not fertilize close to the tree trunk. Remember the importance of watering after fertilizing.

PRUNING:

Proper pruning techniques are essential to the health of your tree. Correctly done, pruning can enhance the beauty, remove dead or drying branches, and correct improper or crossed branching. Incorrect pruning can kill your tree. Flush cuts damage a major tree defense system. Leaving stubs invites rot and cankers. Topping large trees and over pruning cause serious injury and often eventual death.

The necessity of pruning will be considerably reduced if you plan ahead. **The right tree for the right place** can not be over emphasized. Do not place a large-growing tree in a small area. Do not try to turn a tall tree into a short one. Do not plant large trees close to the house so that the limbs will eventually need to be removed. Know the natural growth habit of the tree before you prune, and do not try to trim to a completely different form. Trees grow in the particular shape that is most efficient for them.

Experts recommend a method of pruning called "natural target pruning." This method is based on years of research by Dr. Alex Shigo, plant pathologist and retired Chief Scientist for the U.S. Forest Service. See his diagram for instructions. "Tree Pruning—a Worldwide Photo Guide," published in 1989 by Dr. Shigo is an excellent source of information for anyone caring for trees.

Select pruning tools carefully and keep them sharp to lessen injury to the plant tissues. Do not force-cut a branch of a larger diameter than will fit into the blades of the half open tool. Clean tools and disinfect with alcohol after each use. Current research shows that use of pruning paints does more harm than good.

Major pruning requires the skill of a professionally trained tree surgeon. Protect yourself by hiring a tree service that carries workers' compensation and liability insurance. If necessary, ask the insurance company for proof of coverage. Protect your tree by requesting "natural target pruning." Do not underestimate the damage that can be done to trees by incorrect pruning.

NATURAL TARGET PRUNING

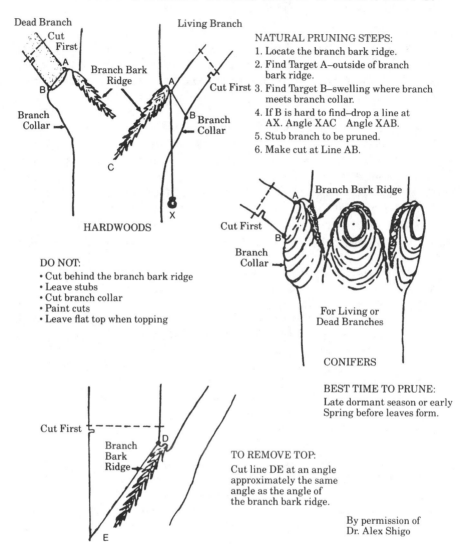

NATURAL PRUNING STEPS:

1. Locate the branch bark ridge.
2. Find Target A–outside of branch bark ridge.
3. Find Target B–swelling where branch meets branch collar.
4. If B is hard to find–drop a line at AX. Angle XAC   Angle XAB.
5. Stub branch to be pruned.
6. Make cut at Line AB.

Dead Branch
Cut First
Branch Bark Ridge
Branch Collar
Living Branch
Cut First
Branch Collar
HARDWOODS

DO NOT:

- Cut behind the branch bark ridge
- Leave stubs
- Cut branch collar
- Paint cuts
- Leave flat top when topping

Branch Bark Ridge
Cut First
Branch Collar
For Living or Dead Branches

CONIFERS

BEST TIME TO PRUNE:
Late dormant season or early Spring before leaves form.

Cut First
Branch Bark Ridge

TO REMOVE TOP:

Cut line DE at an angle approximately the same angle as the angle of the branch bark ridge.

By permission of Dr. Alex Shigo

36

DISEASES:

Anthracnose—A fungus that attacks trees, notably dogwoods. Flowers are small and poorly formed. Brown or maroon spots appear on leaves and flowers. Apply fungicides by spraying when the buds are first opening, again in two weeks and again in the fall. Raking up and burning leaves will help.

Cankers—Note die back starting at branch tip, and dead and diseased areas on branches or trunk. Prune and burn, or bury dead and infected branches. Hypoxylon canker is identified by the mottled grayish bark and the sloughing off of bark on the trunk and branches, exposing the patchy, grayish-black, crust-like fungus growth. Trees infested with this disease should not be stored for firewood as other trees may become infected. Hypoxylon can move quickly through a tree causing death in a short time.

Fireblight—Note sudden wilting of leaves which then turn dark and hang on. This may be prevented by a weakened bordeaux, copper or streptomycin spray during bloom. Prune out diseased wood, cutting several inches below infected parts. Sterilize tools between cuts. Some species of Bradford pear are especially susceptible.

Powdery mildew—Appears as grayish powdery coating on young shoots, leaves and flower buds. Use a fungicide labeled for this disease.

Mold—Sometimes leaves are blackened by mold. In winter use a dormant oil spray. In summer use a contact or systemic insecticide.

INSECTS:

Beetles—The leaves are skeletinized or completely eaten. Spray with an insecticide when first noticed and repeat as directed.

Borers—Any weakened tree will attract borers. Drought, sun, scald, frost, bark injury and pollution are major causes of stress. Tiny, to one inch, holes in the bark indicate their presence. Don't be misled by sapsucker holes which are usually in a row. Request current information on control from the extension agent or metro-forester.

Caterpillars—Entire leaves are eaten. Use contact insecticides or the microbial insecticide *Bacillus thuringiensis*.

Honeydew—Large numbers of ants, flies and honeybees appear on leaves which have a sticky, clear substance deposited on them. This is most often caused by aphids.

Scale insects—In summer tiny crawling insects can cause white scales on branches. These scales can be confused with other diseases. Consult your extension agent or metro-forester before treating.

Be sure to read all pesticide, insecticide or fungicide labels thoroughly, including the warnings regarding potential danger to pets and wildlife (including fish). Do not reuse the container and dispose of it properly.

PROTECTION OF TREES DURING CONSTRUCTION:

If you are going to build on a lot with existing trees, you have paid dearly for this advantage. Therefore, they are an investment and you should be concerned with protecting against the damages that occur during the building process.

Because home builders and developers are often lacking in information on how best to save YOUR trees, this will require diligence and knowledge on your part. There are no short cuts to proper protection. You cannot halfway protect a tree and expect it to survive as a healthy, attractive specimen.

First, decide which trees are worth saving. Consider their location, species, size, age and vigor. Small trees may survive the rigors of land disturbance better than large ones. Your extension service or Forestry Commission has good information on tree protection during construction. Also refer to points listed at the beginning of this chapter.

Any effort to save trees on a construction site should be well planned BEFORE the lot is cleared. You may want to consider including site protection specifications in your contract. Designate a place for the builder to keep paint cans, trash, etc. and for the cement truck to empty its residue. Consider putting black plastic on the ground in this area.

Trees to be saved should be prominently marked with tape or ribbon which does not injure bark. In order to prevent mechanical injury to trunks and roots, a wooden barricade should be built around each tree or group of trees to be saved. This barrier should be a minimum of 1 foot in diameter for each inch of tree diameter measured 4½ feet above ground level, or ideally, should enclose the whole dripline area inward to the trunk. Allowing heavy machinery to operate within the dripline may cause irreparable damage to the roots by cutting or by excessive soil compaction.

There may be grade changes and trees must be protected from either raising or lowering the level of soil. When the soil is removed from or added to the top of roots, the tree cannot obtain its necessary amount of air, water and minerals. Get professional help if this has to be done.

Trees must be protected when there is excavation for utilities. If a large portion of their root system is destroyed, a corresponding portion of the leaves and branches will die. Try to coordinate utilities (water, sewer, electrical, cable TV) beforehand for maximum consolidation and minimum trenching. Trenches should be routed as far as possible from the trunk, preferably outside the dripline. If this is not possible, the next best thing is to tunnel beneath the root system. Power-driven soil augers should be used for this. Tunneling should be offset to one side of the trunk. When trenching, if the tree has to lose half or more of its root system, it would be better to remove it. If trenching is absolutely necessary close to a tree:

1. Cut as few roots as possible.

2. Make all root cuttings as clean as possible.

3. Backfill the trench as soon as possible. Do not leave the roots exposed to the air. Avoid leaving air pockets. Water well for the next few weeks.

Other protective measures:

Do not allow the movement or storage of equipment, materials, debris or fill within the protective barrier.

Do not clean equipment or materials within the dripline.

There should be no attachments or wires to trees other than those of a protective nature.

Cleanup after construction can be a critical time for tree damage. Insist that fences and barricades remain around trees until after all debris is cleaned up and carried away. (Be sure to have debris removed; not burned or buried on your property.)

New home owners often unwittingly cause further damage to stressed trees by landscaping under them. Gardening under trees–lawns, daffodils, liriope, azaleas–tears up tree roots. Do not rototil root area for lawns or plantings. It is best not to plant near trees until they have gone through a growing season. One should plan on giving stressed trees at least two growing seasons of after-care following construction. "Gardeners should be aware of the biological compromises that need to be made in order to achieve the proper balance between trees and garden plants." (Dr. Thomas Perry). Your urban lot can support just so much plant growth for landscaping AND trees to be healthy.

Be aware of construction, trenching, spraying, etc. going on in your neighbor's yard; your trees growing near the property line can be badly damaged unless you are vigilant on their behalf.

OTHER INFORMATION:

When applying weed killers or other herbicides to lawns around trees, check with your nursery man or county extension agent to be sure they will not be injurious to tree roots which are close to the surface. Remember these roots are spread at least as far as the tree's dripline and, as in the case of live oaks, much farther. Improper use of herbicides is a common cause of tree death.

Planting ivy beneath a tree can be harmful. Be aware that it will be competing with the tree for nutrients. It also can become a problem when it climbs the tree and in time may take over with its long shoots.

Do not let Spanish moss get out of control. It should be pulled off periodically with a rake or by hand.

Children's swings can badly damage tree limbs. Chains or ropes wear through the bark allowing insect infestation and rot.

Driving and parking on tree roots causes soil compaction and injury.

Black plastic placed on top of soil to discourage weed growth can injure tree roots by prohibiting moisture, oxygen, and nutrients from reaching them. There are plastic weed barrier materials available which allow water and air exchange.

Keep grass away from tree trunks to prevent damage from mowing machines. Optimum distance is five feet.

Keep suckers and sprouts pruned from the base of the tree trunk.

As they decay, leaves beneath trees provide nutrients for the roots. Grinding them with a lawn mower saves raking. Excessive raking beneath trees often removes top soil, leaving roots exposed.

The importance of trees to our existence must not be underestimated. Since earliest times they have played an integral part in man's life—religiously, historically, economically, aesthetically and most importantly, environmentally. As our population expands, the scientific world is becoming increasingly alarmed over the global consequences of accelerated destruction of trees. We, as conscientious citizens and homeowners, should consider the planting of trees as a legacy for the future and their preservation an obligation to our heritage.

TREES

Key: C - Conifer; D - Deciduous; E - Evergreen; Di - Dioecious; F - Showy Flower; N - Native; bf - Bird Food; B - Berries

Botanical Name Common Name	Key	Height	Comments
Acer buergeranum Trident Maple	D	20-25'	Multi-trunk small patio tree; variable fall color; transplants readily; full sun; drought resistant; well drained acid soil.
Acer floridanum Florida Maple	D,N	40-50'	Medium growth; moist, well-drained soil; full sun; yellow in fall; excellent shade tree.
Acer palmatum Japanese Maple	D	20'	Slow growing; will take some sun, but prefers shade; foliage green in summer becoming yellow bronzed or purplish in fall; horizontal form, medium texture; small purple flowers May-June; many cultivars; excellent for specimen, accent plant or bonsai.
Acer palmatum 'Bloodgood'	D	15-25'	Cultivar; one of the best for holding red leaf color throughout the summer.
Acer palmatum 'Dissectum'	D	6-12'	Slow growing; likes *morning* sun; purple-red fern-like foliage fading to purple-green or green and then burnt orange in fall; wonderful twisted branching pattern; excellent in small gardens.
Acer rubrum Red Maple	D,N	40-50'	Medium to fast growth; slightly acid, moist soil; scarlet, orange or bright yellow in fall; red flowers in spring; does not tolerate heavily polluted areas; tolerates seashore conditions; long-lived; disease free; spreading symmetrical form, medium texture. 'October glory.'
Aesculus pavia Red Buckeye	D,N,F	10-20'	Moist, well-drained lime or sweet soil; full sun to part shade but will flower in rather dense shade; handsome small tree with showy red flowers in spring; seeds of fruit are poisonous.
Amelanchier canadensis Shadblow Serviceberry	D, F, N,bf	15-35'	Medium growing; moist, well-drained acid soil although seen in many types of soil; sun or partial shade; fruit-from red to green to black berries, ripen in June, edible; fall color varies from yellow to apricot-orange to dull red; very ornamental white flowers as leaves are emerging; subject to diseases and insects; oval shape, medium texture. 'Cumulus'-upright variety.
Anise (See *Illicium*) (See large shrubs)			
Apricot (See *Prunus*)			
Ash (See *Fraxinus*)			
Bay (See *Gordonia*)			

41

TREES

Key: C - Conifer; D - Deciduous; E - Evergreen; Di - Dioecious; F - Showy Flower; N - Native; bf - Bird Food; B - Berries

Botanical Name / Common Name	Key	Height	Comments
Beech (See *Fagus*)			
Betula nigra River Birch	D,N	50-60'	Fast growing; acid soil; yellow fall foliage; stream and river banks; tolerates poor drainage; roots tend to surface; messy; good choice for hot climates; tends to get leaf spot and defoliate in wet seasons; oval shape, fine to medium texture. Multi-trunk 'Heritage.'
Butia capitata Jelly Palm	E	15'	May be listed as *Cocos australis* in nurseries; fairly reliable in warmer areas; gracefully arching fronds; distinctive blue or gray-green color.
Carpinus caroliniana American Hornbeam	D,N, bf	20-30'	Slow growing; moist, rich soil; good understory tree; yellow to orange-red in fall; small, shrubby, one or more short angled trunks; pest free; fine texture. Screens, hedges.
Carya illinoinensis Pecan	D	30-60'	Slow growing; rich, moist, well-drained soil; grown for fruit; fragile branches, prone to caterpillars; seeds given by Jefferson to Washington - these pecans now the oldest trees at Mt. Vernon; many varieties.
Cedrus deodara Cedar	C	30-60'	Medium to fast growing; well-drained, dry, sunny location; protect from sweeping winds; light blue green needles, branches drooping to the ground; large accent or background tree; useful as screen. 'Kashmir'-hardier.
Cercis canadensis Eastern Redbud	D,F, N	25-30'	Medium to fast grower; adaptable to acid or alkaline soils; prefers dry area, sun or partial shade; purple spring flowers before leaves; flowers can be eaten as a salad or fried; form dense, round in sun; loose, open in shade; medium to coarse texture. 'Alba'-white.
Chionanthus virginicus White Fringetree	D,F, N,bf,Di	12-20'	Slow growing; moist, fertile, acid (pH 6.0-6.5) soil; full sun; good ornamental; pollution tolerant - no care; fragrant white feathery flower May-June; rounded form, coarse texture.
Cornus florida Flowering Dogwood	D,F, N,bf	15-25'	Slow to medium growing; cool, moist, well-drained soil; grows in wild in dry soil; prefers shade - good understory tree; red berries and scarlet leaves in fall; white bracts in spring before leaves; subject to borer and anthracnose; horizontal branching, medium texture; wonderful ornamental with four season character. 'Cherokee Princess'
Crape Myrtle (See *Lagerstroemia*)			
Cryptomeria japonica Japanese Cedar	C,E	30-100'	Medium growing; rich, light, acid soil; abundant moisture; full sun; protect from wind; conical shape; specimen tree. Smaller named varieties available.

TREES

Key: C - Conifer; D - Deciduous; E - Evergreen; Di - Dioecious; F - Showy Flower; N - Native; bf - Bird Food; B - Berries

Botanical Name Common Name	Key	Height	Comments
Cunninghamia lanceolata Common China-fir	C,E	40-50'	Slow to medium growing; moist, acid, well-drained soil; not very hardy; best in open spaces, shaded by trees and out of wind; becomes seedy with age; good for arrangements; pyramidal with slightly pendulous branches.
X *Cupressocyparis leylandii* Leyland Cypress	C,E	50-60'	Fast growing hybrid; adaptable to extremes of soil; withstands salt spray; makes good hedge or screen; difficult to transplant; columnar. Named varieties vary in size and color.
Cypress (See *Taxodium*)			
Diospyros kaki Japanese Persimmon	D,Di	20-30'	Moist, well-drained soil; full sun; orange, yellow, red leaves in fall; 3-4" yellow-orange edible fruit ripens October after leaves fall; white flowers May-June; dioecious - male and female flowers are on separate plants, therefore will not fruit without both; suggest planting another variety for good crop of fruit; low branched, wide spreading, medium texture. 'Tane Nashi' (not dioecious), 'Fuyugaki.'
Dogwood (See *Cornus*)			
Elm (See *Ulmus*)			
Eriobotrya japonica Loquat	E,F	20'	Medium growing; moist, well-drained, loamy soil; round form, coarse texture; edible fruit; fragrant white flowers in fall until January; subject to fireblight; good for espalier; may be damaged under 15 degrees F, but comes back from trunk; good accent tree.
Fagus grandifolia American Beech	D,N, bf	60-80'	Slow to medium growing; moist, well-drained, acid soil, not wet or compacted soils; fall color yellow; young trees retain leaves all winter; low branching, difficult to grow grass under; needs large area; nut is edible; broad rounded form, medium texture.
Ficus carica Sweet Fig	D,bf	30'	Moist, well drained soil preferred but adaptable to less than ideal conditions; full sun; comes up from roots if frozen; subject to nematodes; delicious fruit; round form, coarse texture. 'Brown Turkey,' 'Celeste'
Fig (See *Ficus*)			
Firmiana simplex Chinese Parasol Tree	D,F	30-45'	Large, rich green leaves; gray-green bark adds winter interest; yellow-green flowers in summer followed by interesting fruit.

TREES

Key: C - Conifer; D - Deciduous; E - Evergreen; Di - Dioecious; F - Showy Flower; N - Native; bf - Bird Food; B - Berries

Botanical Name Common Name	Key	Height	Comments
Franklinia altamaha Franklinia	D,F, N	10-20'	Moist, acid, well-drained soil which has been supplied with ample organic matter; full sun or light shade; orange and red in fall; white waxy flower in late summer and fall; most difficult to grow, one of the world's rarest trees; lost in wild; subject to wilt.
Fraxinus pennsylvanica Red Ash	D,N, Di	50-60'	Transplants readily; very tolerant, found in moist soil, but once established tolerates high pH, salt, drought, and sterile soil; requires full sun; prune in fall; dark green foliage, yellow in fall; brittle wood; round to oval head.
Fringe Tree (See *Chionanthus*)			
Ginkgo biloba Maidenhair Tree	D,Di	50-70'	Slow to medium growth; sandy, deep, moderately moist soil but grows in almost any site; full sun; yellow in fall; hardy, prehistoric; prune in spring; air pollution tolerant; one of world's oldest trees - fossils found of 200 million years; transplant when young; pyramidal form, medium texture; plant male only; fruit has bad odor; deer resistant. 'Autumn Gold'
Golden Rain Tree (See *Koelreuteria*)			
Gordonia lasianthus Loblolly Bay	E,F, N	40-50'	Moist soil; sun or light shade; showy white flower; excellent glossy evergreen foliage; kin to Franklinia; handsome but difficult to grow; prone to fungus.
Halesia carolina Carolina Silverbell	D,F, N	20-30'	Medium growing; well-drained acid soil; sun or semi-shade; yellow in fall; branches in early spring lined with snowdrop-like flowers, usually white, rarely pale pink; handsome lawn tree; low branched, variable form, medium texture.
Holly (See *Ilex*)			
Ilex Holly	Di		Hollies are dioecious; female plants produce fruit, most require pollination from a nearby male; much variation in leaf form, size, color, growth habits; tolerant of pruning; use nursery grown stock; deer resistant.
Ilex x attenuata 'Fosteri' Foster Holly	E,B, bf	10-20'	Hybrid; small, glossy leaf with spiny margin; deep red fruit persists through winter; most popular of Foster hollies; easy to root from cuttings; slender, conical shape; used as foundation plant, hedge, or specimen tree. 'East Palatka,' 'Humes #2,' 'Savannah'
Ilex cassine Dahoon Holly	E,B, bf,N	10-20'	Adaptable to most conditions of soil or exposure; native to moist woods; leathery, usually spineless leaves; small red to yellow berries; gray bark; narrow, pyramidal shape; fine texture.

TREES

Key: C - Conifer; D - Deciduous; E - Evergreen; Di - Dioecious; F - Showy Flower; N - Native; bf - Bird Food; B - Berries

Botanical Name Common Name	Key	Height	Comments
Ilex decidua Possumhaw	D,B, bf,N	25'	Easy to grow under most conditions of soil or exposure; red berries on female plant; light gray bark; attractive spreading tree, often several trunks; good for small gardens; ornamental.
Ilex opaca American Holly	E,B, bf,N	25-45'	Slow grower; use as a specimen in full sun; dull, green leaves; bright red berries; traditional Christmas holly; pyramidal, densely branched; new growth in spring; many cultivars; give space to develop; medium to coarse texture. 'Greenleaf'
Ilex opaca 'Savannah' Savannah Holly	E,B, bf,N	25-45'	Fast grower, better in full sun; light green leaf; profuse red berries; outstanding variety; fertilize regularly for good foliage color; loosely pyramidal shape; coarse texture.
Ilex vomitoria Yaupon Holly	E,N Di,B bf	20'	Handsome; salt tolerant; multi-trunk; pyramidal forms encouraged by cutting lower branches; red berries, gray bark; adapts to moist soils. 'Pendula' - weeping habit.
Juglans nigra Black walnut	D	50-75'	Prefers deep, rich moist soil for maximum growth; can grow to 150'; tolerant of dry soil; extensive taproot; difficult to transplant; open, rounded crown; medium texture.
Juniperus chinensis 'Torulosa' Hollywood Juniper	E	15-20'	Excellent screen; fast growth; tolerant of moist soil conditions; good for coast, salt tolerant; irregular growth habit; upright twisted appearance; dark green foliage.
Juniperus virginiana Eastern Red Cedar	E,bf, C,N	40-50'	Medium growth rate; tolerant of adverse soil conditions, salt spray; requires sunny location; blue, berry-like cones; aromatic wood; handsome red bark; many cultivars; pyramidal shape, medium texture. 'Canaertii' - compact form variety.
Koelreuteria elegans Flame Tree	D,F, B		Fall blooming; yellow leaves in fall with handsome pink flowers, showy fruit; endures poor dry soil, drought conditions; has weak wood.
Koelreuteria paniculata Golden Rain Tree	D,F	20-30'	Fast growth; tolerant of poor soil, drought, heat, wind; full sun; yellow flowers in June; very ornamental; excellent lawn tree; prune off old blossom heads; weak growth; dense, round shape, medium texture; may be trashy on patio.
Lagerstroemia indica Crape Myrtle	D,F	20-40'	Fast growth; moist, well-drained soil; prefers full sun; summer blooming - white, pink, red, lavender; handsome bark; clip old flower heads for repeat blooming; some fall color; multi-trunk; lovely ornamental; many cultivars ('Natchez'-white, 'Near East'-light pink); don't plant near patio - flower drop stains; fine texture.

TREES

Key: C - Conifer; D - Deciduous; E - Evergreen; Di - Dioecious; F - Showy Flower; N - Native; bf - Bird Food; B - Berries

Botanical Name Common Name	Key	Height	Comments
Laurel (See *Prunus*)			
Liriodendron tulipifera Tulip-tree, Yellow Poplar	D,E, N	80-100'	Rapid growth; does not tolerate drought well; full sun; unique shape; bright green leaves form lovely canopy; tulip-shape yellow flowers, yellow fall color; tallest of eastern hard-woods; needs room to grow; somewhat weak-wooded; specimen tree for open area; pyramidal to oval form; coarse to medium texture.
Loquat (See *Eriobotrya*)			
Magnolia grandiflora Southern Magnolia	E,F, bf,N	60-80'	Slow to medium growth; sun or part shade; large (8" +), fragrant, creamy white flowers, long blooming period, spring into summer; lustrous leaves (5-8") leaves; attractive fruit cone with red seeds; plant in open space with room for branches to ground level; beautiful tree; much litter from fruit and leaves. 'Braeken's Brown Beauty' - small brown backed leaves. Use named varieties.
Magnolia x loebneri Loebner Magnolia	D,F	20-30'	'Leonard Messel'-a beautiful hybrid; star-shape flowers, lilac-pink in spring before foliage. 'Dr. Merrill'-Large star-like white flower; preferable, faster grower than stellata.
Magnolia x soulangiana Saucer Magnolia	D,F	15-25'	Medium growth; prefers full sun; light pink to purple flowers in early spring; one of the first bloomers; lovely ornamental tree; often multi-trunk, wide spreading branches. Many varieties, newer ones from National Arboretum are late-blooming.
Magnolia stellata Star Magnolia	D,F	10-15'	Slow growth; sun, protect from wind; profuse star-shape, fragrant white flowers in early spring; may be hurt by late freeze; nice specimen or accent plant. 'Royal Star'
Magnolia virginiana Sweetbay Magnolia	E,F, N	25-60'	Medium to fast growth; prefers moist soil; tolerates shade; small white flowers, heavy lemon fragrance, long blooming period; handsome red fruit in fall; gray-green leaf, silver underside; often several trunks; open irregular branching.
Malus angustifolia Southern Crabapple	D,F, N	20'	Broad head; spring flowering with white to pink blooms.
Malus floribunda Japanese Crabapple	D,F	15-20'	Soil well-drained, moist; full sun; buds deep pink to red, flowers fading to white; small red-dish-yellow fruit; outstanding small ornamental for landscape planting; fruit stains paving; prune if necessary before bud - set in mid-June; broad-rounded, densely branched; there are many crabapple varieties available; new varieties are scale and fireblight resistant. 'Callaway'-white.

TREES

Key: C - Conifer; D - Deciduous; E - Evergreen; Di - Dioecious; F - Showy Flower; N - Native; bf - Bird Food; B - Berries

Botanical Name / Common Name	Key	Height	Comments
Maple (See *Acer*)			
Metasequoia glyptostroboides Dawn Redwood	C,D	80-100'	Fast growth; moist, well-drained, slightly acid soil; full sun; pyramidal, buttress-shape trunk, deeply fluted bark; horizontal pendulous branches; resembles bald cypress in foliage.
Myrica cerifera Southern Wax-myrtle	E,N	10-20'	Tolerates infertile soil, but responds well to good watering and fertilizer; full sun or part shade; new growth in spring gives bayberry candle scent; tolerant of salt spray; makes beautiful wispy broadleaf evergreen tree or shrub for excellent screen.
Oak (See *Quercus*)			
Osmanthus americanus Devilwood	E,N	15-20'	Handsome dark evergreen leaves; loose open habit; fragrant, white flowers March-April; moist soil; drought tolerant; use in screening or as specimen tree.
Ostyra virginiana American Hophornbeam	D,N	25-40'	Pyramidal tree with rounded top and drooping branches; moderate drought tolerance; full sun to part shade; dark green leaves turn yellow-red and purple in fall; fruit resembles hops; all season ornamental may be used as specimen, shade or even street tree.
Palmetto (See *Sabal*)			
Parkinsonia aculeata Jerusalem Thorn	D,F	30'	Rapid growth; prefers moist, sandy soil but tolerant of drought; sun or shade; resistant to salt spray and moderate wind; cluster of yellow, fragrant flowers, long blooming period beginning in spring; fruit pods 2-4"; green bark turning red-brown on older trees; leaves 7-12" like narrow ribbons; very picturesque tree; subject to freeze damage below 15 degrees F.
Pear (See *Prunus*)			
Pecan (See *Carya*)			
Persea borbonia Red Bay	N,E	20-40'	Evergreen with medium coarse texture; medium growth rate; moist soil in full sun; specimen tree; leaves aromatic when crushed may be used as a substitute for bay leaves in cooking.
Persimmon (See *Diospyros*)			
Pinckneya pubens Pinckneya	D,F, N	20-30'	Small tree; wet soil of swamps or streams; dark green leaves; lovely pink bracts in late June; usually several trunks; bark used in colonial days to treat malaria victims.

47

TREES

Key: C - Conifer; D - Deciduous; E - Evergreen; Di - Dioecious; F - Showy Flower; N - Native; bf - Bird Food; B - Berries

Botanical Name Common Name	Key	Height	Comments
Pinus Pine	E,C		One of this area's predominant trees; tolerant of adverse soil and climatic conditions; needle-like leaves, hard woody cones; plant balled and burlaped or container-grown stock; stake new plants.
Pinus elliottii Slash Pine	E,C, N	80-100'	Fastest growing of southern yellow pines; needles 7-10"; cones to 6'"; popular as shade tree; branching growth.
Pinus glabra Spruce Pine	E,C, N	100'	Grows naturally in damp coastal woods; cones 1½-2½"; low branching when young; smoother bark than most pines; attractive specimen tree.
Pinus palustris Longleaf Pine	E,C, N	80-100'	Sandy soil; largest of southern yellow pines; leaf to 18" long, cones to 10"; lovely tree; extensive tap root makes transplanting difficult.
Pinus taeda Loblolly Pine	E,C, N	80-100'	Fast growing; fragrant resinous foliage; extensive lateral root system.
Pinus thunbergiana Japanese Black Pine	C,E	20-40'	Dark green handsome leaves; pyramidal shape with pendulous branches; sun; sandy soil; salt tolerant; good accent plant.
Plum (See *Prunus*)			
Popcorn Tree (See *Sapium*)			
Privet (See *Ligustrum*)			
Prunus			Over 400 species and many hybrids; almond, peach, cherry, plum, apricot; lovely ornamentals, some have edible fruit; prone to insects and disease.
Prunus angustifolia Chickasaw Plum	D,F, N,bf	15-20'	Masses of small white flowers appearing before leaves in early spring; stems thorny forming dense thicket.
Prunus campanulata Taiwan Cherry	D,F	20-30'	Small graceful tree; handsome deep rose flowers bloom as early as February before foliage emerges; small red fruit; prefers sun; reseeds.
Prunus caroliniana Carolina Cherry-laurel	E,N, bf	20-30'	Fast growth; moist, well-drained soil; full sun, partial shade; fragrant small white flowers; black, berry fruit loved by birds; foliage dangerous to livestock; grows like a weed; can be used as hedge; subject to peach tree borer; deer resistant.

48

TREES

Key: C - Conifer; D - Deciduous; E - Evergreen; Di - Dioecious; F - Showy Flower; N - Native; bf - Bird Food; B - Berries

Botanical Name / Common Name	Key	Height	Comments
Prunus cerasifera 'Atropurpurea' Pissard Plum	D,F	15-20'	Full sun; commonest of purple leaved plums; small white to pink flowers in spring; purple foliage all season; red, edible fruit; twiggy, rounded form, medium texture.
Prunus mume Flowering Apricot	D,F	15-25'	Well suited to coastal plain climate; first to bloom in late winter - early spring; pink to white, double or single flowers.
Prunus persica Common Peach	D,F	15-25'	Double and single flowering forms as well as delicious fruit forms, but peaches are notoriously susceptible to insect and disease pests.
Punica granatum Pomegranate	D,F	12-20'	Small tree with rounded outline; handsome in flower - May-July; flowers red; sun or part shade; white, yellow, and double flowering as well as good fruiting varieties
Pyrus calleryana Callery Pear	D,F	35-40'	Adaptable to different soils; full sun; showy, white malodorous flowers in spring; variable fall foliage color; 'Bradford' not recommended as it has poor crotch development and, therefore, is self destructive; susceptible to fire blight and leaf spot; 'Aristocrat' better branching pattern; 'Capital' more upright, suitable for street use.
Pyrus communis Common Pear	D,F	40'	Full sun; pretty but malodorous white blossoms in early spring before foliage; hard fruit late summer; prune in January to keep branches sturdy enough to keep from breaking under weight of fruit; good edible and preserve varieties. 'Keiffer', 'Baldwin', 'Pineapple'-sand pear, grainy, malodorous, good for cooking; 'LeConte'-hybrid, good for eating.
Pyrus kawakamii	E or D	30'	White blossoms early spring; ovate shape; full sun; needs protection.
Quercus Oak			Some varieties subject to leaf gall, no known cure; valuable shade tree; deer resistant.
Quercus acutissima Sawtooth Oak	D	50-60'	Full sun; likes acid, well-drained soil; fast growing; acorns; brilliant yellow leaves in spring; green in summer, dull brown in fall; leaves last most of winter; pyramidal form; medium texture.
Quercus alba White Oak	D,N	60-80'	Slow grower; moist, well-drained soil; acorns; fall color varies green to red; pyramidal shape when young to rounded when mature; good shade tree; medium texture.
Quercus falcata Southern Red Oak	D,N	70-80'	Medium grower; tolerates poor, dry soil; acorns single and in pairs; leaves hold late in fall, dull red color; rounded form.

TREES

Key: C - Conifer; D - Deciduous; E - Evergreen; Di - Dioecious; F - Showy Flower; N - Native; bf - Bird Food; B - Berries

Botanical Name / Common Name	Key	Height	Comments
Quercus laurifolia / Laurel Oak	E,N	60-80'	Fast grower; no special soil requirements; green leaves persist until spring; acorns; weak, short lived tree; round topped; street tree; good shade; semi-evergreen; medium to fine texture.
Quercus myrsinifolia / Chinese Evergreen Oak	E	30'	Grown in collections; young leaves rich purplish red; acorns; true evergreen; round headed form, graceful.
Quercus phellus / Willow Oak	E,N D	40-60'	Medium growth rate; prefers moist, acid, fertile soil; tolerates adverse sites; shade, specimen or street tree.
Quercus prinus / Chestnut Oak	D	60-70'	Prefers well drained soil; has shown excellent drought tolerance; prefers full sun; fall color; good shade specimen or street tree.
Quercus virginiana / Live Oak	E,N	60-80'	Massive; adapts to any soil type; likes moisture; slow grower; great shade and specimen tree; acorns; long lived; drops leaves in March; rounded, spreading form; Georgia state tree.
Redbud (See *Cercis*)			
Redwood (See *Sequoia*)			
Sabal palmetto / Cabbage Palmetto	E,N	8-50'	Sun or shade; sandy soil; gives tropical look to landscape; hardy; palmate leaves 3-6'; white flowers and blackish fruit; grows about a foot a year; transplant by an experienced crew in spring or summer only; water well; salt tolerant; deer resistant.
Salix babylonica / Weeping Willow	D	20-30'	Full sun; heavy feeder; fast grower; likes water; yellow fall color; branchlets droop to ground; weak wood; makes good screen with wide spread; fine texture; do not plant near underground pipes.
Sapium sebiferum / Chinese Tallow Tree "Popcorn Tree"	D	30-40'	Terribly invasive in this area and should not be planted despite its historical significance and attractiveness; has popcorn like seeds in the fall; Benjamin Franklin sent the seeds to Noble Jones in 1772.
Sassafras albidum / Sassafras	D,N bf	30-50'	Moderate grower; irregular habit; full sun; good drainage; fragrant yellow flowers before leaves in spring on female tree; dark blue berries; roots made into tea; fabulous yellow-orange, red to purple fall color; hard to transplant; specimen tree; medium texture.

TREES

Key: C - Conifer; D - Deciduous; E - Evergreen; Di - Dioecious; F - Showy Flower; N - Native; bf - Bird Food; B - Berries

Botanical Name Common Name	Key	Height	Comments
Sequoia sempervirens Coast Redwood	E,C	50-90'	Fast grower; full sun; damp soil; small round cones; flat green narrow leaves; small flowers open in February, yellow for male, green for female; narrow pyramidal form; specimen tree, fine texture.
Silverbell (See *Halesia*)			
Snowbell (See *Styrax*)			
Sparkleberry (See *Vaccinium*)			
Stewartia malacodendron Silky Stewartia	N,D, F	10-15'	Difficult to grow; prefers moist well drained soil rich in leaf mold or peat moss; habit is that of a large shrub; large, white-petaled flowers with purple stamens appear in May; good understory tree.
Styrax americanus American Snowbell	D,F N	30'	Slow grower; rich, well-drained soil; needs protection; sprays of bell-like, fragrant, white flowers in early summer; flat-topped tree; horizontal branching form; great for small gardens.
Taxodium distichum Common Bald Cypress	D,N, C	70-80'	Fast grower; full sun; tolerates drought and poor drainage; bright yellow leaf in spring turning brown in fall; slender shape; produces light shade in spring and summer; pyramidal form; fine texture.
Trachycarpus Fortunei Fortune's Windmill Palm	E	40'	Very hardy; handsome in clusters.
Ulmus parvifolia Chinese Elm	D,N	40-50'	Handsome bark; dark green leaves changing to yellow and reddish purple in fall; easily transplanted; prefers moist, well drained, fertile soil, but tolerant of poor soil. 'Drake'
Vaccinium arboreum Farkleberry "Sparkleberry"	D,N	15-20'	Attractive understory plant with picturesque habit; dry soil; crimson fall color; white flower sprays in spring with inedible black fruits; found in wild.
Vitex agnus-castus Chaste Tree	D,F	9-15'	Fast grower; soil tolerant; medium to low moisture; any good soil; good drainage; small tree; lovely lavender flowers in late summer; handsome compound aromatic leaves and seeds; often multi-trunked; good shade tree; pest free; medium texture.
Wax-myrtle (See *Myrica*)			
Willow (See *Salix*)			

NOTES

Shrubs

SHRUBS

The beauty and importance of shrubs should not be underestimated. They are the basic framework for the garden. In the South we are fortunate to have a large variety available to us. There are fine evergreens with stately form and foliage; many have berries or flowers in their season. Deciduous shrubs are also valuable for berries, bloom and winter form. They may provide a background for annuals and perennials, or may provide a dramatic effect in themselves. They are an integral part of landscaping around a home. Try to imagine a house or garden without them!

The generally accepted definition of a shrub is that it is a woody plant with multiple stems or trunks that grows to less than fifteen feet in height. A woody plant is one which has stems and branches that survive from year to year, as opposed to herbaceous plants which die back to the ground each year. We all know that an occasional shrub will reach more than fifteen feet and that some are pruned or trained to one trunk called a standard. Likewise, some trees are multi-trunked, but these are exceptions.

Foundation planting softens the sharp break between the ground and the house or other building. It joins the house to the earth and seems to make it belong. Evergreen materials should be used to form the basis of the planting. There should be rhythm and continuity. Use groups of a few species rather than line up many species like soldiers. Interest may be provided with use of different shades of green and different textures. Deciduous and/or unusual plants should be used occasionally for accent or as a specimen. When landscaping a new home or rejuvenating an old home, have a plan. It is wise to use a professional who is trained to take into account seasonal interest, sun and soil needs and can identify any major problem, such as drainage, before you begin.

Hedges may be used to mark property lines or walks and to provide privacy or hide unsightly areas. They may be formal and carefully sheared or informal, allowing the plant to grow in its own form. We usually think of a hedge as an unbroken line of one type of plant, but several species of varying heights and textures may be used as effectively.

Shrubs are wonderful for year round interest in beds where bulbs, annuals and perennials are used. Thus, they are frequently used as background material. Shrubs may also be used as accent in such a bed displaying the bloom or form to full effect.

The effect in a garden is made by varying textures and shades of green in a shrub border. The small leaved hollies and boxwood have a fine texture; the darker green, larger leaved hollies a medium texture. Fatsia and loquat are larger leaved plants with a coarser texture. Vary these textures to provide depth and focus. Textures and colors used together appropriately make a dramatic statement.

PURCHASING:

Before buying your shrubs have a plan in mind. Your local nursery will carry many desirable landscape plants. The more unusual and hard to find shrubs may be ordered from a catalog. (See section on Sources.) Adding a treasure once in a while is a nice touch, while working within your basic plan. Maybe the plant blooms in January or perhaps it is a particularly spectacular form. These little additions are what will make the garden yours.

Most shrubs bought from the nursery will be container grown, some will be balled and burlapped. Those ordered from the mail order sources may be bare rooted. Examine the plants to make certain they are healthy.

Container grown shrubs should be neither too small nor too large for the container. Those that are too large will be rootbound or their roots will have grown into the soil beneath. Either way new growth upon transplanting will be delayed. Shrubs that appear too small for the container have probably been recently transplanted into the larger container. You pay for a five gallon size plant that is really a one gallon size. Check for this by tugging at the plant to see if the root ball is surrounded by loose soil.

It matters little whether you buy the one or the five gallon shrub. There is, of course, a difference in cost, and for a while there is the difference in size, but in two-and-a half to three years both shrubs will be the same size.

When purchasing balled and burlapped plants, be sure to look at the root ball. Make certain there are some small fibrous roots and that the-ball is moist and firm. Make certain also that there are no roots wrapping back around the trunk. These roots will girdle the trunk and prevent its growth.

Both balled and burlapped and container growth shrubs may be planted nearly anytime of the year in our climate, where the ground does not freeze. Fall planting gives the roots time to get established before spring growth. Summer planting may be difficult because of the amount of watering required, but planting in all seasons is possible.

Bare root shrubs, however, must be planted during winter dormancy before growth begins. They are, in general, a good buy and will become more quickly established than the others. Make certain the root system looks healthy with several good size unbroken brown roots growing in different directions. If you cannot plant immediately, cover the roots with damp earth (heal in) to keep the roots moist.

PLANTING:

Before planting, make sure you have the correct location for your plant's requirements. A shrub that requires shade will look pale and burned out in sun. Make the planting hole twice as wide and 12 inches deeper than the root ball. Add organic matter such as compost or peat to the soil, and return enough of the soil to the bottom of the hole, so that the plant will rest just above its original level. As the soil settles the plant will drop to the original level. The root ball of container grown shrubs must be pulled apart enough so the roots can grow outward. If you are planting a bare root shrub, make a cone of the soil and set the roots over it. Do not add high nitrogen fertilizer at this point as it may burn the tender roots. Lift the plant by the root ball, place it in the hole and return the soil, tamping it down as you go. If there is burlap, it need not be removed as it will rot, but it does need to be folded back from the top about one third of the way down the root ball. After the hole has been filled, water well so that all air holes will be filled. As the earth settles, fill depressions with more soil. Cut out broken branches and crowding or crossing branches. Mulch the plant with pine straw or leaves to conserve moisture. Water regularly until well established.

FERTILIZING:

Young shrubs need a regular program of fertilization. Mature shrubs need less fertilizer than young ones where accelerated growth is desired. To determine the optimum fertilizer analysis for your plants and your soil conditions, a soil sample should be taken to the county extension agent. The results of that analysis will tell you what type fertilizer to use, and will give you recommended amounts. It will also measure your soil pH, and tell you whether dolomitic lime should be added to sweeten the soil, or aluminum sulfate to acidify the soil.

Several small applications of fertilizer are recommended. For shrubs use one tablespoon per foot of plant height in March, May and July. Spread the fertilizer evenly throughout the estimated root zone. The estimated root zone may be beyond the branch spread, especially if the shrub crown is narrow.

MULCHING:

Mulch shrubs with pine straw, leaves or other organic material to a depth of 2 to 3 inches. This will conserve moisture and protect from extremes of temperature as well as add organic matter to the soil. (See section on Mulching.) Tender shrubs may be mulched more heavily to withstand winter temperatures, but the excess mulch should be removed as the temperature warms.

WATERING:

More mature shrubs may tolerate some drought, but newly planted shrubs require regular watering. It is much better to soak the ground to a depth of 12 inches about once a week. A hand held hose just does not do enough. A properly designed irrigation system is ideal, but it requires a sizable investment. Sprinklers on hoses that may be moved about are fine.

TRANSPLANTING:

With proper care your younger plants can be moved from place to place in your garden until you have achieved the effect you desire. Larger more mature plants do not tolerate such treatment. Always dig the plant with a proper root ball being careful that the dirt does not fall off the roots. Ideally, you will have root pruned for several seasons before transplanting to encourage new root growth. This is done by cutting into the earth with a shovel to eight or so inches all around the shrub, about twelve inches from the trunk. As with planting, dig a hole larger than the root ball, incorporate organic matter and set the plant just above its original soil level. Mulch and water well until established.

It is important to prune back the plant by about one third to achieve a balance between the roots and the branches they are supporting. prune selectively and carefully.

PESTS AND DISEASES:

Some shrubs are particularly susceptible to pests and diseases. Others, including plants native to the area, will be more resistant. The gardenia attracts whitefly and must be sprayed regularly. Euonymous is not recommended by some because of the problem with scale. On the other hand, such handome plants as cleyera and leucothoe are quite disease resistant. You may want to take this into account as you choose the plants for your landscape.

If problems do develop, take a portion of the affected plant to your extension agent or to your local garden center for advice on control. (See section on Pests and Diseases.) Recommendations are constantly being updated and new, sometimes safer, sprays are being developed.

PROPAGATION:

Most of you will want to use plants available in the nursery or in the catalogs. Certainly this will be true for the bulk of landscape plants. Occasionally, however, one may covet an especially unusual shrub in the neighbor's garden. Perhaps the bloom is a color not available in the trade. Or, perhaps, you have learned the satisfaction of starting your own plants after gardening with vegetables or perennials. Whatever the case, the techniques are not difficult. They require only a bit of patience.

Shrubs may be propagated from seed or from softwood or hardwood cuttings, or by layering. These methods are described in the section on Propagating. Hybrids will not be the same as the parent if started from seed. Certain shrubs, such as spirea and flowering quince, are easier than others.

PRUNING:

If planted in the appropriate location for size, most shrubs require only thinning and heading back to maintain shape and density. Even size can be controlled with careful removal of some old canes and heading back of others. Shearing is only appropriate for the very formal hedge or border. Most pruning cuts should be made well within the plant. A few shrubs, such as mahonia and spirea, must be pruned by cutting out old canes. Special pruning techniques are noted when appropriate in the plant list. See also the section on Pruning. One can prune and train a plant into almost any shape, form or size. To do this against the plant's natural inclination requires continuing work on your part. Except in special circumstances, as a topiary or espalier, it is best to appreciate the natural form of the plant.

For best bloom, most attention should be given to the pruning time of flowering shrubs. Shrubs that bloom in early spring bloom on old wood and should be pruned shortly after the flowers fade. Those that bloom in late spring or summer produce flowers on new growth, and should be pruned during February to encourage more new stem growth. Thus there will be more bloom.

SMALL SHRUBS (2-4 ft.)

Key: D - Deciduous; E - Evergreen; N - Native; DR - Deer Resistant

Botanical Name / Common Name	Key	Size Height/Spread	Exposure	Comments
Alexandrian-laurel (See *Danae*)				
Almond, Flowering (See *Prunus*)				
Ardisia japonica Coralberry	E	2-3'/1-2'	Shade	Autumn clusters of bright red berries; coarse textured, twisted leaf; loose upright form; seeds self readily, many cultivars.
Ardisia japonica Japanese Ardisia	E	1'/1-2'	Shade	Dark green, medium textured; may be used as a ground cover.
Aucuba japonica 'Nana' Dwarf Aucuba	E	4'/3-4'	Shade	Scarlet berries in fall on female plants; must have both male and female plants for bloom; coarse textured leaves easily burned by sun; growth upright and irregular; no pests; excellent in deep shade.
Azalea (See Azalea section)				
Berberis thunbergii Barberry	E,DR	1-1½'/3'	Sun, part shade	Fine textured; tolerant of many conditions; 'Atropurpurea'-foliage rose-pink maturing to reddish purple; 'Crimson Pygmy', 'Rose Glow.'
Brunfelsia australis Yesterday, Today and Tomorrow	E	3-5'/2-4'	Sun, shade	Bloom in spring opens violet, fades to white; prune after flowering; mulch well in November; may drop leaves after freeze, but will come back from crown; may be used in pot culture.
Buxux Harlandii Harland Boxwood	E	2-4'/2-3'	Sun, part shade	Fine texture; excellent as low hedge or for edging; requires regular pruning to maintain shape; very upright growth.
Buxus microphylla 'Japonica' Japanese Littleleaf Box	E	3-4'/2-3'	Sun, shade	Dark rich green color; fine to medium texture; open growth; mulch and water well in drought; cuttings root easily; susceptible to pests, especially scale, leaf miners and spider mites; prune regularly to retain compact shape; does better in lower south than the more classic *Buxus sempervirens*. Use as hedge, specimen.
Carissa grandiflora 'Nana' Dwarf Natal Plum	E	3-5'/3-4'	Sun	Fragrant, star-shaped white flowers; scarlet, plum-like fruit; glossy, leathery leaf; stands shearing; tolerant of salt spray; needs winter protection.

59

SMALL SHRUBS (2-4 ft.)

Key: D - Deciduous; E - Evergreen; N - Native; DR - Deer Resistant

Botanical Name Common Name	Key	Size Height/Spread	Exposure	Comments
Cassia corymbosa	D	4-8'/3-5'	Sun	Showy golden yellow flowers late summer-fall; rapid grower; pest free; endures heat and drought; specimen plant; severe winter may harm.
Cephalotaxus Harringtonia Plum Yew	E	2-4'/2-3'	Part shade, shade	Distinctly upright, multi-needled branches; dark green; used for hedges or foundation planting. 'Fastigiata'-leaves spirally arranged.
Cephalotaxus Harringtonia 'Drupacea'	E	1-3'/2-4'	Part shade, shade	Trailing bushes with dark green needle-like leaves; may be used as ground cover or in foundation planting.
Conradina canescens Dixie Rosemary	E	1½'/1'	Sun, part shade	Appreciated for blue-gray leaves, light texture; tolerates sandy soil; use in shrub border.
Danae racemosa Alexandrian-laurel	E	3'/2-3'	Shade	Unbranched stems arch gracefully; fine to medium texture; excellent for dark corners.
Daphne odora Winter Daphne	E	3-4'/2-3'	Shade, part shade	Fragrant February bloom, white or rosy on terminal clusters; medium texture; foliage dark green or variegated; growth slow to rounded form; needs good drainage, susceptible to root rot.
Deutzia gracilis Slender Deutzia	D	2-5'/3-4'	Sun, part shade	Spring bloom in white clusters along slender arching stem; medium texture; prune after flowering to keep shapely; pest resistant; growth slow.
Euonymus americanus Hearts-a-Burstin	D,N	3-4'/2-3'	Part shade	Upright irregular form; medium texture and growth rate; fruit attractive resembling strawberry.

SMALL SHRUBS (2-4 ft.)

Key: D - Deciduous; E - Evergreen; N - Native; DR - Deer Resistant

Botanical Name Common Name	Key	Size Height/Spread	Exposure	Comments
Euonymus fortunei Wintercreeper	E	1'/2-3'	Sun, part shade	Fine textured climbing shrub or groundcover; fast grower; avoid wet soil; watch for scale and fungal diseases; may be an aggressive grower.
Euonymus japonicus Dwarf Japanese Euonymus	E	2-3'/1-2'	Sun, shade	Fine textured, dense form with erect growth; adapts to various soil; withstands salt spray; watch for scale and fungal diseases; good bed edging. 'Microphyllus,' variegated forms 'Ovatus Aureus,' 'Aureus.'
Fothergilla gardenii Dwarf Bottlebrush	D,N	2-3'/2-3'	Sun, part shade	White fragrant flowers in April to early May; fall color brilliant yellow to orange to scarlet; slow growing; nice in mass plantings.
Gardenia jasminoides radicans Dwarf Gardenia	E,DR	1-2'/2-3'	Sun, part shade	Fragrant, small white flowers, June 'til summer; medium to fine textured, with interesting horizontal branching habits; white flies a definite problem.
Galphimia glauca (Thryallis glauca)	E	3-4'/2-3'	Sun	Semi-evergreen subtropical plant; prune in winter; blooms on new growth summer and fall; blooms are yellow and prolific; may be injured in severe winter.
Holly (See Ilex)				
Holly Fern (See under Ground Cover)				
Hypericum calycinum	E	3'/4'	Sun	Profuse yellow flowers, summer to fall; graceful pendulous branches; hardy; tolerate sandy soil.
Hypericum patulum St. John's Wort	E	3'/3'	Sun	Rich golden yellow flowers, June; spreading arching branches; medium texture; soil and drought tolerant; pest free; use in shrub borders and foundation planting.
Ilex cornuta 'Carissa' Carissa Holly	E,DR	3'/3-4'	Sun, shade	No fruit; dense dwarf form; leaves have single terminal spine.

SMALL SHRUBS (2-4 ft.)

Key: D - Deciduous; E - Evergreen; N - Native; DR - Deer Resistant

Botanical Name / Common Name	Key	Size Height/Spread	Exposure	Comments
Ilex cornuta 'Rotunda' Dwarf Chinese Holly	E,DR	3-5'/6-8'	Sun, shade	Occasionally produce red berries hidden in foliage; glossy spiny foliage; coarse in texture; compact rounded growth; tolerates hot, dry locations; no pruning necessary; watch for scale; tough, durable plant.
Ilex crenata 'Helleri' Heller Holly	E,DR	2-3'/3-5'	Sun, shade	Fine textured; compact low spreading growth habit; no pruning necessary; watch for scale and spider mites.
Ilex crenata 'Stokes' Stokes Holly	E,DR	1-3'/3-4'	Sun, shade	Fine textured; compact upright growth, densely twiggy; no pruning necessary; watch for scale and spider mites.
Ilex vomitoria Dwarf Yaupon Holly	E,DR	2-4'/3-5'	Sun, shade	Fine textured, small leaves, compact rounded shape; no pruning necessary; withstands drought. 'Schelling's Dwarf'-more compact than 'Nana,' 'Pendula.'
Jasminum nudiflorum Winter Jasmine	D	2-4'/6-10'	Sun, shade	Blooms January or early February, yellow blooms along branches; fine textured; grows in fountain-like formation; may be trained on wall or trellis to height of 8'; pest free.
Juniperus (See under Ground Cover)				
Leucothoe axillaris Coastal Leucothoe	E,N	3-4'/4-5'	Shade, part shade	White or pinkish-white flowers in April; foliage dark green - purple green in winter; form graceful and formal with arching branches; does well in masses; prefers acid conditions.
Lyonia lucida Fetterbush	E,N	3-5'/3-5'	Sun	fragrant, pink, bell-shaped flowers April-May; slow growth; upright habit; spreading branches; likes moist soil.
Nandina domestica 'Harbour Dwarf' Harbour Dwarf Nandina	E	2-3'/2-3'	Sun, part shade	Small white flowers, bright red berries; medium to fine texture; finest compact form of nandina, forms dense mound; requires little care and is tolerant of most conditions; pest free.
Nandina domestica 'Atropurpurea Nana' Dwarf Nandina	E	1-1½'/1-2'	Sun, part shade	Red fall color; mounded growth, leaves cupped.

SMALL SHRUBS (2-4 ft.)

Key: D - Deciduous; E - Evergreen; N - Native; DR - Deer Resistant

Botanical Name / Common Name	Key	Size Height/Spread	Exposure	Comments
Pittosporum tobira 'Wheelers Dwarf' Dwarf Pittosporum	E	3-4'/3-4'	Sun, part shade	Small fragrant white flowers in spring but grown as foliage plant; shiny dark green leaves; forms dense mound; may be damaged by severe cold (less than 10 degrees.) 'Laura'-variegated dwarf form.
Plum Yew (See *Cephalotaxus*)				
Plumbago capensis (*auriculata*)	D	3-4'/3-4'	Sun	Profuse pale blue (or variety 'Alba' with white) flowers summer into fall; drought tolerant.
Prunus glandulosa Flowering Almond	D	4'/3'	Sun	Pink or white pom-pom shaped or double flowers in spring; shapeless plant; prune severely after blooming; often damaged by borers; valuable for spring bloom.
Punica granatum 'Nana' Dwarf Pomegranate	D	2-4'/3'	Sun	Orange-scarlet bloom in summer, red fruit fall; soil well drained; tolerant of most soil types and tolerant of salt air; good for low hedges, flower border, or in pot culture.
Raphiolepis indica Indian Hawthorn	E	3-4'/3-5'	Sun, part shade	Covered with white or pink clusters of flowers in spring; broad, spreading; round, thick, dark green leaves; watch for scale, leafspot; avoid oil spray; use in shrub borders, foundation planting; several varieties-'Snow White.'
Rosemarinus officinalis Rosemary	E	2-4'/4-5'	Sun, part shade	Light blue flowers, grey-green leaf color; open sprawly growth habit; enjoys poor soil, tolerates drought, benefits from lime; stems root when they touch soil.
Ruscus aculeatus Butchersbroom	E	3-4'/3-5'	Sun, shade	Red berries effective but requires male and female and even then does not always set berries; dull olive sharp leaves, coarse texture; soil, drought and neglect tolerant; pest free.
St. John's Wort (See *Hypericum*)				
Santolina chamaecyparissus Lavender Cotton	E	1-2'/3-4'	Sun	Button like yellow flowers midsummer, but grown for fine textured silver-gray foliage; aromatic; clump like spreading growth; effective all year; needs well drained soil; good for herb or rock garden.

SMALL SHRUBS (2-4 ft.)

Key: D - Deciduous; E - Evergreen; N - Native; DR - Deer Resistant

Botanical Name Common Name	Key	Size Height/Spread	Exposure	Comments
Santolina virens Green Santolina	E	1-2'/2-3'	Sun	Fine textured, green leaves; useful in poor sandy soils; good in rock gardens or borders.
Serissa foetida Serissa	E,DR	3-4'/4-5'	Sun	Delicate white flower in spring and summer; fine texture; likes sandy soil; pest free; variegated form available.
Skimmia japonica Japanese Skimmia	E	3-4'/2-3'	Part shade, shade	Fragrant white flowers in spring, scarlet berries in fall; to bloom need male and female; loose rounded mound like growth; coarse textured; needs moist, rich, acidic soil; pest free; adapts well to small city gardens, use in foundation planting, shrub grouping.
Spirea x bumalda 'Anthony Waterer'	D	3-4'/4-5'	Sun, part shade	Deep pink blooms over a long period of time and even more if dead-headed; fall color.
Yucca filamentosa Adam's Needle	E,N,DR	1-2'/2-3'	Sun	Bell shaped white flower on 3-5' stalk in summer; leaves are stiff blades 2½ inches long; coarse texture; resistant to drought and adverse conditions; use as contrast, accent in landscape.

64

MEDIUM SHRUBS (4-8 ft.)

Key: D - Deciduous; E - Evergreen; N - Native; DR - Deer Resistant

Botanical Name / Common Name	Key	Size Height/Spread	Exposure	Comments
Abelia grandiflora Glossy Abelia	E	4-6'/3-6'	Sun, shade	Small pinkish white flowers in June, foliage bronze in winter; medium to fine texture; not spectacular but easy to grow; needs well drained soil; pest free; use as medium hedge, border or background planting; attracts butterflies. 'Edward Goucher'-abundant, showy flowers. 'Sherwoodii'-dwarf form.
Aucuba japonica Japanese Aucuba	E	4-6'/4-5'	Shade	Attractive foliage plant; coarse texture, grows well beneath trees, rapid grower; pest free. 'Variegata'-flecked with yellow.
Azalea (See Azalea section)				
Berberis julianae Wintergreen Barberry	E	4-8'/4-6'	Sun, part shade	Yellow bloom in spring followed by fruit; leaves bronze/wine red in winter; fine to medium texture; mound form, thorny; needs hand pruning; good barrier or hedges.
Boxwood (See *Buxus*)				
Buddleia davidii Butterfly bush	D	5-8'/4-6'	Sun	Flower clusters white, pink, red or purple all summer; coarse texture; dull green leaves on open arching branches; prune back to old wood late winter; use as accent plant or in large shrub border; attracts butterflies.
Callicarpa americana American Beautyberry	D,N	4-8'/4-6'	Sun, part shade	Large, medium green, coarse textured leaves; cluster of purple fruit in fall; difficult to incorporate into design except naturalistic; 'Lactea'-rare white berried form.
Calycanthus floridus Sweetshrub	D,N	6-8'/5-8'	Sun, shade	Fragrant purplish small flowers in spring, fruit brown; coarse texture; attractive but not showy; pest free; use in shrub border.
Chaenomeles speciosa Flowering Quince	D,DR	4-6'/5-6'	Sun, part shade	Red, white or pink flowers in early spring; fruits may be used for jelly; medium texture; pest free; prune old wood for better flowers; good for color in shrub borders, good in arrangements; 'Nivales'-white; 'Cameo'-peach, double flowers; 'Texas Scarlet'-bright red.

MEDIUM SHRUBS (4-8 ft.)

Key: D - Deciduous; E - Evergreen; N - Native; DR - Deer Resistant

Botanical Name / Common Name	Key	Size Height/Spread	Exposure	Comments
Clethra alnifolia / Sweet Pepperbush	D,N	3-8'/4-6'	Part shade, shade	Fragrant showy white flowers in summer; moist soil; pest free; good in shrub border; looks nice even in winter.
Cycas revoluta / Sago Palm	E	3-4'/3-4'	Sun, part shade	Coarse texture; tropical palm-like plant; slow growth; use as specimen plant or in large tub; may be damaged by severe cold (less than 10°).
Datura arborea / Datura	D	4-5'/4-5'	Sun	Large trumpet shaped white flowers in summer; likes rich loose soil; may be tender, showy specimen plant.
Euonymus japonicus / Evergreen Euonymus	E	6-7'/3-5'	Sun, shade	Medium textured shrub; green and variegated forms; much more compact in sun; pest problems; limited use.
Fatsia japonica / Japanese Fatsia	E	4-6'/4-6'	Shade	White flowers in fall; coarse texture; large dark green leaves; no pest problems; accent plant; tropical effect.
Gardenia jasminoides / Cape Jasmine	E,DR	4-6'/4-6'	Sun, part shade	Very fragrant waxy white flowers early summer; medium texture with dark green foliage; many pest problems, especially white fly; may be used for hedges, borders, specimen.
Hibiscus mutabilis / Confederate Rose	D	6-8'/5'	Sun	Flowers of varied colors with a dark brown center, may be 9" wide; blooms in fall, peony form; blooms open white, then pink, then red. 'Ruburm'-red.
Holly (See Ilex)				
Hydrangea macrophylla / Big Leaf Hydrangea	D	3-5'/3-5'	Shade, part shade	Large blooms, pink in alkaline soil, blue in acidic soil, or white in summer; coarse texture; bare, unattractive stalks in winter; 'Endless Summer' blooms until frost on old and new wood.
Hydrangea quercifolia / Oakleaf Hydrangea	D,N	6-8'/5-6'	Part shade	Large white flowers in summer; coarse oak-like leaves; spreading irregular shape. 'Snow Queen'-more upright.

MEDIUM SHRUBS (4-8 ft.)

Key: D - Deciduous; E - Evergreen; N - Native; DR - Deer Resistant

Botanical Name Common Name	Key	Size Height/Spread	Exposure	Comments
Ilex cornuta 'Burfordii Nana' Dwarf Burford Holly	E	5-8'/5-6'	Sun, part shade	Small red fruit; glossy foliage; rounded form, medium texture; good in foundation planting.
Ilex cornuta 'Needlepoint'	E	6-8'/5-6'	Sun	Long, narrow slightly twisted leaves; fast growing; dense.
Ilex crenata 'Compacta' Roundleaf Holly	E	4-6'/4-6'	Sun, shade	No fruit; dark green foliage; rounded irregular form; fine texture; plant in well drained soil; many pests including scale and spider mites; good in foundation planting in groups as a background.
Ilex glabra Inkberry	E,N	6-8'/4-6'	Sun, shade	Broad leaf with medium to fine texture and slow growth rate; upright oval form; black fruit not showy; excellent honey plant; good in naturalistic setting.
Itea virginica Virgina Sweetspire	D,N	4-6'/4-8'	Sun, part shade	White, fragrant spike-like flowers; moist soil; medium texture and growth rate; fall color can be spectacular crimson-red; attractive in mass plantings. 'Henry's Garnet'-good fall color.
Jasminum floridum Flowering Jasmine	E	4-6'/5-7'	Sun, part shade	Yellow flowers in May-June; fine textured; forms arching rambling mound; pest free; may be trained as vine.
Juniperus chinensis Chinese Juniper	E	4-6'/6-9'	Sun	Several varieties offer silvery blue color to gold tipped foliage; medium to fine texture; rapid growth rate; horizontal spreading habit; spider mites a problem; good in foundation planting; needs room. 'Armstrong,' 'Blue Vase,' 'Hetzii,' 'Glauca,' 'Hills Blue,' 'Mint Julep,' 'Old Gold,' 'Pfitzeriana.'
Kalmia latifolia Mountain Laurel	E,N	5-7'/3-5'	Shade, part shade	Handsome shrub with dark green leaves; blooms spring; moist, well drained acid soil.

MEDIUM SHRUBS (4-8 ft.)

Key: D - Deciduous; E - Evergreen; N - Native; DR - Deer Resistant

Botanical Name Common Name	Key	Size Height/Spread	Exposure	Comments
Kerria japonica Japanese Kerria	D,DR	4-6'/3-5'	Sun, part shade	Yellow flowers in spring; medium texture; moderate growth rate; few pest problems, specimen plant or borders; excellent contrast against fences or walls.
Lantana camara Lantana	E	2-8'/4-6'	Sun	Yellow and orange blooms all spring into fall; also pink, white and lavender varieties; rapid growth; dwarf and trailing forms also.
Ligustrum sinense Chinese privet	E	6-8'/5-7'	Sun, shade	Considered by many to be a weed, but variegated forms (creamy-yellowish and true white) are prized by arrangers; small leaves along stiff branches; white fly and scale are problems; growth rank.
Lonicera fragrantissima Winter honeysuckle	Semi-D	6-8'/6-10'	Sun	Small, very fragrant, cream colored bloom early spring; medium texture; no pests; specimen plant for fragrance.
Mahonia bealei; Leatherleaf Mahonia	E	5-6'/3-4'	Part shade, shade	Small yellow flowers in clusters in March, followed by blue grape-like clusters (good bird food); coarse texture; prune out old canes; pest resistant except for leaf spot; handsome specimen; good in foundation planting.
Mahonia fortunei Chinese Mahonia	E	3-4'/3-4'	Part shade, shade	Dark purple berries after unimportant spring bloom; medium texture; moderate growth rate; specimen plant.
Nandina domestica Heavenly Bamboo	E	4-6'/2-3'	Sun, part shade	Red berries in terminal clusters in fall; medium to fine texture; upright growth; prune out old canes; attractive foliage turns red in winter; no pest problems; foundation planting; hedge or specimen.
Pyracantha coccinea Scarlet Firethorn	E	5-6'/6-8'	Sun	Showy orange-yellow berries in fall; rank growth; medium texture; upright spreading habit; thorns toxic; has pest problems; excellent espalier, will grow to 18' against wall; varieties 'Kasan'-orange red berries, 'Lalandei'-orange berries.

Quince (See Chaenomeles)

MEDIUM SHRUBS (4-8 ft.)

Key: D - Deciduous; E - Evergreen; N - Native; DR - Deer Resistant

Botanical Name / Common Name	Key	Size Height/Spread	Exposure	Comments
Raphiolepis umbellata Indian Hawthorn 'Majestic Beauty'	E	6-8'/4-6'	Sun, part shade	Fragrant pink or white flowers in spring; medium to coarse texture; open upright; slow growth; drought resistant; withstands wind, salt spray; foundation planting.
Rhus aromatica Fragrant Sumac	D,N	4-6'/2-4'	Sun, part shade	A low spreading sumac with good fall color and red fruit on female plants; stems fragrant when crushed.
Rice Paper Plant (See *Tetrapanax*)				
Sago Palm (See *Cycas*)				
Spiraea prunifolia plena Bridalwreath Spiraea	D,DR	5-7'/6-8'	Sun, shade	Attractive sprays of white flowers in spring; medium texture; graceful and delicate in appearance; rapid growth; good in informal plantings; valuable for flowers as well as form.
Spiraea thunbergii Babysbreath Spiraea	D,DR	4-5'/3-5'	Sun, part shade	White flowers in January or February before leaves, earliest blooming spiraea; very fine texture; upright twiggy branches recurving to ground; thin and shape by cutting old canes to ground; use in informal plantings.
Spiraea vanhouttei Vanhoutte Spiraea	D,DR	5-7'/4-6'	Sun, shade	White flowers in April on long arching branches; medium texture; useful as a specimen or mass; as a natural hedge or in shrub borders.
Sweet Shrub (See *Calycanthus*)				
Tetrapanax papyriferus Rice Paper Plant	D,DR	4-6'/6-8'	Part shade	Greenish flowers in fall, spectacular foliage with large leaves; coarse texture; spreading habit; may winter kill; handsome specimen plant.
Vaccinium ashei Rabbiteye Blueberry	D	6-8'/6-8'	Sun	Very acid, organic well drained soil; white bell shaped bloom along stem in May; large edible fruit.
Yucca gloriosa Spanish Dagger	E,N	4-6'/3-4'	Sun	Greenish white flowers on spikes in September; coarse texture; long pointed dark blue-green foliage; resistant to salt spray, pests; sharp, stiff leaves may be dangerous; specimen or accent plant; use in groups.

LARGE SHRUBS (8-12 ft.)

Key: D - Deciduous; E - Evergreen; N - Native; DR - Deer Resistant

Botanical Name Common Name	Key	Size Height/Spread	Exposure	Comments
Aesculus parviflora Bottlebrush Buckeye	D,N	8-12'/8-15'	Sun, part shade	White flowers in summer; yellow color in fall; coarse texture; white spreading multi-stemmed shrub with many upright branches; prefers fertile moist soil; pest free; use for mass in shrub border.
Althea (See *Hibiscus*)				
Anise (See *Illicum*)				
Aralia spinosa Devils Walking Stick	D,N	10-20'/6-10'	Sun, part shade	Large bold plant; many white lacy blooms; pinkish-purple fruit, showy in fall; grows best in rich organic soil; best used as specimen.
Azalea (See Special Chapter)				
Baccharis halimifolia Groundsel Bush	E,N	8-12'/6-10'	Sun	Very showy in bloom; fruit appears to be covered with tiny white paint brushes; impressive at a distance; grows in salt marshes to dry upland sites.
Bambusa multiplex (*B. disticha*) Fern Leaf Bamboo	E	10-12'/4-6'	Sun, shade	Medium texture; massive clump but remains contained; fast growing; disease free; use as hedge or screen.
Banana Shrub (See *Michelia*)				
Beautybush (See *Kolkwitzia*)				
Callistemon lanceolatus Bottlebrush	E	6-12'/6-8'	Sun	Bloom is as a red spike in spring; fine texture; thorny; drought resistant; pest free; may be damaged by cold; use for background, hedge or screen.
Camellia (See Special Chapter)				
Cassia splendida Cassia	D	8-10'/4-5'	Sun	Impressive display of yellow flowers in fall; fine texture; tree-like form, may need to stake; pest free; prune back heavily after bloom.

LARGE SHRUBS (8-12 ft.)

Key: D - Deciduous; E - Evergreen; N - Native; DR - Deer Resistant

Botanical Name Common Name	Key	Size Height/Spread	Exposure	Comments
Cephalanthus occidentalis Button Bush	D,N	15-20'/10-15'	Sun	Likes moist soils; very adaptable; moderately drought tolerant; cut to ground every few years to rejuvenate; in bloom, covered with creamy white balls, reddish brown fruit.
Chimonanthus praecox Wintersweet	D	8-10'/8-10'	Sun, part shade	Fragrant yellow flowers in January; coarse, dark green foliage; rangy growth; valuable for fragrant winter bloom; use in large shrub borders.
Cliftonia monophylla Black Titi, Buckwheat Tree	E,N	15-20'/8-12'	Sun, part shade	Dark evergreen foliage; good backdrop for colorful plants; white flowers in terminal clusters in March; likes moist acid soils, high in organic matter; attracts bees.
Cleyera japonica Cleyera	E	8-10'/5-6'	Part shade, shade	Medium texture; upright growth; dark green leaves; pest free; use for screen accent or foundation planting.
Cyrilla racemiflora Red Titi	D,N	10-25'/10-20'	Full sun, light shade	Rich medium green foliage; white flowers in summer in 3-6" long spikes; can have beautiful red foliage; attracts bees; moist soil with good organic matter; moderately drought tolerant; found in wet coastal plains.
Deutzia scabra Fuzzy Deutzia	D	6-10'/4-8'	Sun, part shade	Small white flowers with purple tinge in May; coarse texture; tall and erect; showy in bloom; use in shrub border or as specimen; good background in flower bed.
Elaeagnus pungens Elaeagnus	E	6-20'/10-15'	Sun, shade	Fragrant small flowers in winter; spreading and dense with drooping branches; silvery back to foliage; no pests; drought resistant, tolerant of adverse conditions; needs aggressive pruning; rank growth; use in natural hedge or shrub border; excellent for espalier; attracts birds; edible small fruits; 'Fruitlandii'; E. umbellata is invasive.
Elliottia racemosa Georgia Plume	D,N	8-15'/5-12'	Full sun	Extremely rare; never dig from the wild—get nursery container grown plant; needs full sun in moist to dry, well drained soil; terminal-fragrant white flowers.

LARGE SHRUBS (8-12 ft.)

Key: D - Deciduous; E - Evergreen; N - Native; DR - Deer Resistant

Botanical Name / Common Name	Key	Size Height/Spread	Exposure	Comments
Eurya japonica Japanese Eurya	E	8-15'/10-12'	Sun, part shade	Dark foliage; medium texture; open irregular horizontal form; picturesque; foundation or specimen planting.
Exochorda racemosa Pearlbush	D	10-12'/8-10'	Sun, part shade	Panicles of white bloom in spring, loose irregular form; medium texture; mass or specimen for large area.
Feijoa sellowiana Pineapple Guava	E,DR	10-15'/10-15'	Sun	Flower white with red accent in spring followed by edible fruit; medium texture; gray-green leaf; well drained soil; pest free; excellent for foliage effect; good in screen or shrub border.
Forsythia x intermedia Border Forsythia	D,DR	8-10'/7-10'	Sun	Bell like yellow flowers before foliage in early spring; medium texture; rapid grower; needs pruning of old canes; no pest problems; good for specimen planting, bank planting.
Hibiscus syriacus Althea, Rose of Sharon	D	6-12'/6-10'	Sun	Flowers white, rose, lavender, pink, double or single in summer; rangy growth; no pests; cut back in spring for larger flowers; colorful in summer; use in shrub border. 'Diana'- white frilly flowers, long blooming. 'Helene'- off white.
Holly (See *Ilex*)				
Ilex aquifolium x I. cornuta Nellie R. Stevens Holly	E	10-20'/8-10'	Sun, part shade	Large red berries in fall; must have male and female plants for fruit; coarse texture, upright form; medium-fast growth rate; watch for scale; hedge and specimen planting.
Ilex cornuta Chinese Holly	E,DR	8-10'/5-7'	Sun, part shade	Red or yellow fruit in fall; dark green leaves; medium texture; dense rounded form; prune to control shape; watch for scale; specimen and foundation planting.
Ilex cornuta 'Burfordii' Burford Holly	E,DR	8-12'/6-8'	Sun, part shade	Orange-red berries in fall; heavily fruited; rich dark green foliage; medium texture; dense and bushy; needs little maintenance; occasionally scale a problem; rapid growth; use as specimen or in hedge.

LARGE SHRUBS (8-12 ft.)

Key: D - Deciduous; E - Evergreen; N - Native; DR - Deer Resistant

Botanical Name Common Name	Key	Size Height/Spread	Exposure	Comments
Ilex latifolia Lusterleaf Holly	E	8-12'/8-10'	Part shade	Dark green foliage; coarse texture; moderate growth rate; pest free; useful large evergreen as specimen or screen.
Illicium anisatum Japanese Anise Tree	E	8-12'/8-10'	Sun, part shade	Coarse, medium-green, aromatic leaves; upright growth; pest free; specimen or foundation planting.
Illicium floridanum Florida Anise Tree	E,N	8-10'/6-8'	Sun, part shade	Moist to wet soil; dark green aromatic foliage; deep red flowers in spring; interesting ornamental.
Illicium parviflorum Star Anise	E,N	8-15'/6-10'	Full sun, part shade	Rich, light green foliage with odor of anise (licorice); small yellow green flowers in June; pointed star shaped fruit; moist soil; use for screening or hedges; cold tolerant.
Kolkwitzia amabilis Beautybush	D	6-10'/8-9'	Sun	Pink flowers with yellow throat, bell-shaped in pairs in the spring; medium to fine texture; open irregular growth; needs pruning regularly to maintain shape; pest free; use in large shrub borders.
Leucothoe populifolia Florida Leucothoe	E,N	8-10'/4-6'	Shade, part shade	White to pink flowers on 2 to 3 year old wood; foliage dark green; irregular growth; after flowering, remove wood that flowered to stimulate new growth.
Ligustrum japonicum Japanese Privet 'Recurvifolium'	E,DR	6-10'/5-6'	Sun, part shade	Bloom in white panicles in spring; coarse texture; dense upright form; fast grower; keep pruned for site; use as hedge or screen. 'Variegatum'- creamy white margin.
Ligustrum japonicum 'Rotundifolium' (L. coriaceum) Curlyleaf Ligustrum	E	6-10'/5-6'	Sun, part shade	Dark glossy foliage, twisted effect, columnar form; slow grower; easily pruned for small space; good as specimen or in cramped city garden; wonderful for arranging.

73

LARGE SHRUBS (8-12 ft.)

Key: D - Deciduous; E - Evergreen; N - Native; DR - Deer Resistant

Botanical Name Common Name	Key	Size Height/Spread	Exposure	Comments
Ligustrum lucidum Glossy Privet	E	8-12'/5-10'	Sun, shade	Flowers in clusters 8-9 inches long in June; coarse texture; dense rounded form; fast grower; use for hedge or screen.
Lindera benzoin Spicebush	D,N	6-12'/6-12'	Sun, shade	Leaves light green in summer, yellow in fall; greenish yellow flowers in mid-April before leaves; in full sun gives excellent show in flower and in fall color; use in shrub border or in naturalistic setting.
Loropetalum chinense Evergreen Witchhazel	E	8-12'/8-10'	Sun, part shade	Flowers in feathery white petals in spring; medium texture; irregular form, fast grower; no pests; use for screen, shrub border or foundation planting.
Magnolia stellata Star Magnolia	D	10-12'/8-10'	Sun	Creamy white flowers before leaves in early spring; coarse texture; broad rounded mass; treelike with age; slow grower; look for scale; specimen. 'Royal Star'-best variety.
Michelia figo Banana Shrub	E	15-20'/8-10'	Sun, part shade	Banana-scented creamy-white flowers April, May; medium texture; dense and rounded; pest free; needs little care; use in large shrub borders.
Mock Orange (See *Philadelphus*)				
Myrica cerifera Wax Myrtle	E,N,DR	10-12'/10-12'	Sun, part shade	Fine texture; upright rounded form; care free; may be used in shrub borders or trimmed to tree form for accent.
Myrtus communis True Myrtle	E,DR	8-10'/4-7'	Sun	White bloom in spring; aromatic berries on female plant; fine texture; open upright form; may be difficult to establish; use as specimen or foundation planting. 'Glen St. Mary.'
Nerium oleander Oleander	E,DR	7-10'/6-9'	Sun	Red, pink, yellow or white flowers all summer; may be single or double; as flower matures pod develops; medium texture; upright rounded form; remove old wood when overgrown; pests include scale and mealybug; all parts of plant toxic; use as specimen, in shrub border, as hedge or screen.

LARGE SHRUBS (8-12 ft.)

Key: D - Deciduous; E - Evergreen; N - Native; DR - Deer Resistant

Botanical Name Common Name	Key	Size Height/Spread	Exposure	Comments
Oleander (See *Nerium*)				
Osmanthus fortunei Fortune Tea Olive	E	9-12'/5-7'	Sun	Small but fragrant white flowers in fall; medium texture; rounded compact form; no pest problems; use in border screen or hedge.
Osmanthus fragrans Fragrant Tea Olive	E	10-12'/10-14'	Sun, part shade	Small but fragrant white flowers October until January; medium texture; upright form; no pest problems; use as specimen where fragrance can be appreciated; will come back if damaged by severe cold.
Osmanthus heterophyllus False Holly	E	8-10'/6-8'	Sun, part shade	Luxurious dark green; medium texture; leaves spiny and holly like; blooms in fall are fragrant.
Pearlbush (See *Exochorda*)				
Philadelphus coronarius Mock Orange	E	10-12'/10-15'	Sun	Fragrant, snowy-white flowers in spring; coarse texture; rounded growth habit but may be straggly; requires little care; use in large shrub border for flower value.
Photinia x 'fraseri' Fraser Photinia	E	7-12'/8-10'	Sun	New leaves red; coarse texture; upright growth; no pests; use in foundation planting or as screen or hedge; often used as tree form.
Photinia glabra Redtip Photinia	E	6-10'/5-6'	Sun	New leaves red; flowers in summer form 4" flat cluster; red fruit in fall; medium texture; upright loose growth; pest free; rapid grower; use as hedge; beware of planting against red brick.
Photinia serrulata Chinese Photinia	E	7-12'/7-12'	Sun	New leaves coppery red; flowers in spring form 6" heads on terminal growth; red fruit in summer; coarse texture; rapid growth; specimen or accent plant for large area.
Pineappple Guava (See *Feijoa*)				

LARGE SHRUBS (8-12 ft.)

Key: D - Deciduous; E - Evergreen; N - Native; DR - Deer Resistant

Botanical Name Common Name	Key	Size Height/Spread	Exposure	Comments
Pittosporum tobira Pittosporum	E	8-12'/8-10'	Sun, part shade	Tiny fragrant flowers in spring; medium texture; mound form; interesting branching habit; watch for scale; use in foundation planting, borders and as a hedge; may be damaged in severe winters (less than 10 degrees F); variegated form available.
Podocarpus macrophyllus maki Southern Yew	E	8-10'/5-6'	Sun, shade	Dark green, ovate leaves; fine texture; upright growth; pest free; good contrasting foliage; easily pruned into interesting shapes, will espalier; used in hedge as specimen or screen; long lasting if cut for arrangements; may be damaged by extreme cold.
Podocarpus nagi Broadleaf Podocarpus	E	8-12'/5-6'	Sun, part shade	Long dark green needle like leaves; medium texture; columnar growth; use as specimen or in hedge.
Ptelea trifoliata Hoptree	D,N	15-20'/5-15'	Sun, shade	Moist well drained soil; performs well in dense shade; very adaptable; fruit resembles hops; fragrant inconspicuous flowers. 'Aurea,' 'Glauca.'
Pyracantha koidzumi Formosa Firethorn	E	6-10'/6-10'	Sun, part shade	Bright red fruit in fall, winter; medium texture; dense irregular spreading form; watch for scale; use as specimen, screen or in borders; needs aggressive pruning to maintain form; 'Victory'-showy, dark-red berries; 'San Jose'-widely spreading; 'Santa Cruz'-prostrate form; 'San Jose' and 'Santa Cruz' are scab resistant; 'Low Dense'-mounding habit.
Styrax americanus American Snowbell	D,N	6-15'/5-8'	Sun, part shade	White fragrant flowers in April; dark handsome bark; moist, acid sandy soil; naturalize along streams.
Viburnum macrophyllum	E	6-12'/6-8'	Sun, shade	Large dark green leaves; coarse texture; upright growth; good in shrub borders, hedge; may be damaged by extreme cold.
Viburnum nudum Possumhaw viburnum	D,N	6-15'/6-10'	Sun, part shade	Glossy foliage; colorful fruit and fall foliage.

LARGE SHRUBS (8-12 ft.)

Key: D - Deciduous; E - Evergreen; N - Native; DR - Deer Resistant

Botanical Name Common Name	Key	Size Height/Spread	Exposure	Comments
Viburnum prunifolium Blackhaw viburnum	D,N	12-20'/8-15'	Sun, part shade	Dark green summer foliage is red bronze in fall; flowers creamy white in clusters, May; fruit bluish-black in fall; adaptable; drought tolerant; fast grower.
Viburnum suspensum Sandankwa Viburnum	E	6-10'/4-6'	Part shade, shade	Dark green foliage; coarse texture; pest free; foundation planting or shrub border; may be damaged by extreme cold.
Viburnum tinus	E	10-12'/10-12'	Sun, part shade	White to pinkish flowers in spring; coarse texture; upright growth; use in border or for screen; may be damaged by extreme cold.
Yew (See Podocarpus)				
Yucca aloifolia Spanish Bayonet	E,N	8-10'/3-5'	Sun, part shade	White plumes in summer; coarse texture; mounded clumps; pest free; good contrast; use as specimen or clumped for screen.

NOTES

Azaleas

AZALEAS

The azalea is one of the most popular and easily grown shrubs in southern gardens. The variety of size, blooming period, and color make it an asset in any garden plan from the largest estate to the smallest walled courtyard. Azalea varieties range in size from a maximum of 10 to 12 feet for Southern Indicas to less than a foot for the Gumpo series. The colors vary from white, pink, lavender, violet, salmon, orange, to red. By choosing plants according to their blooming times (termed early, mid season, and late) one can enjoy azalea blooms in our area from late February through the end of May.

The large southern Indica azaleas can be used in hedges or the background; the medium size Kurumes are excellent for foundation groups or plantings in a confined space, and the dwarf Gumpos are perfect for very small gardens or borders.

Azaleas are divided into two groups: evergreen and deciduous. The evergreen azaleas originated in the Orient and were first introduced into this country around 1800. Our own deciduous native azaleas were first discovered in Virginia in 1690 and in Florida and the Carolinas in 1730.

PURCHASING:

When purchasing azaleas, one should rely on a well known nursery. Do not be tempted to buy where the quality of the plants may be inferior due to lack of care and mishandling. Look for plants with sturdy, well branched growth rather than weak and straggly growth, an indication of a poor root system. The ideal time to purchase azaleas is during blooming time, when one can be sure of nursery identifications and desired colors. Do not count on the blooming time of an azalea purchased from a nursery as the correct blooming time for our area. Most azaleas have been shipped from another climate zone and are blooming according to that zone. Don't choose old, heavily root-bound plants. Although more care must be given to smaller plants in the first two or three years of life, they eventually will be more vigorous growers and better plants than older, larger plants.

LOCATION:

Choosing the right planting site for azaleas means the difference between thriving and surviving. Azaleas will grow in sun or shade, but ideally they should be planted in filtered sunlight. If planted in a more open location full sun, either morning or late afternoon is desirable, but avoid a location where they will receive the full midday sun. The southern Indicas are the most tolerant of full sun. The ideal planting location is under the tall pines or high branched oak trees, not only because of the good shading provided, but also because decomposed pine needles and oak leaves make the kind of acid soil in which azaleas thrive. Also, in our area one should take particular care in planting late blooming varieties. They need shade from our late April and May sun, which can be very hot and will cause the blooms to wilt. A sprinkler system is desirable with these varieties. Azaleas do not bloom in dense shade. Although azaleas require a fair amount of moisture, they cannot tolerate wet roots for an extended period of time. Therefore, choose a planting site that drains well, not one that is low and swampy or floods during heavy rains. Although soil quality can be changed, it is best not to choose a planting area where the soil is heavy clay or pure sand.

Finally, do not make the mistake of mixing azaleas together in a disarray of spotty and clashing colors. In choosing a location for your azaleas, remember that they should be grouped together by color in compatible color zones and by similar blooming times. This kind of planting gives the most outstanding and showy effect.

PLANTING:

Evergreen azaleas are among the most easily planted and transplanted shrubs. They can be successfully planted or transplanted from early fall to late spring, and even during the summer months with a little extra care. It is best, however, to avoid transplanting when the azalea is in full lush growth around early June. The ideal time to transplant is during the winter when the plants have more time to become established. Deciduous azaleas definitely respond best to planting after the leaves have fallen during complete dormancy.

Unless you are fortunate enough to have a soil rich in humus, add 40 to 50% leaf mold, peat moss or other well rotted organic matter to your existing soil before planting. If planting a whole bed of azaleas, the bed should be thoroughly tilled, and 4 to 6 inches of humus should be applied to the surface, then thoroughly worked in to a depth of twelve inches. If you are planting individually, a wide shallow hole should be dug, approximately twice the width of the root ball and at least six inches deeper. The soil from the hole should be mixed thoroughly with 50% of humus. Fill the hole with the prepared soil, firming the soil beneath the plant with your foot to keep the plant from settling later. Be sure to plant at the same level or slightly above its former depth. Azaleas have a very shallow root system, and if planted too deeply their roots will suffocate, causing stunted growth or even death. After setting the plant in place, fill in around the roots with the remaining soil, firming as you go; then water thoroughly to continue to settle the soil and remove any air pockets. Avoid covering the uppermost roots with more than 1/4 inch of soil. Water newly planted azaleas thoroughly about every four or five days.

If you are planting container grown azaleas, your plant is probably going to be root bound. Before planting make four or five evenly spaced cuts from top to bottom of the root mass. This will promote root growth. If it is a transplant, care must be taken to thoroughly water several days before moving and to plant promptly after digging to keep the roots from drying.

Ideally, Indica azaleas should be spaced five feet apart, Kurume azaleas 3 to 4 feet apart, and dwarf Satsuki and Gumpos about 1½ feet apart. If an immediate effect is desired, azaleas can be spaced at half that distance and thinned out every few years as they grow.

MULCH:

Mulching is one of the most important aspects of azalea culture, since disintegrated mulch becomes the acid soil that azaleas love. Not only does mulch help maintain an acid soil, but it also helps conserve soil moisture and protects the plant from temperature extremes. A mulch of pine needles and oak leaves is ideal as we come by it so easily. A depth of about 2 or 3 inches should be maintained year round, adding more mulch as it decays.

FERTILIZING:

Although azaleas are light feeders, it should never be assumed that they can go without fertilization at all. Those planted under trees are particularly in need of fertilizer as they are competing with tree roots for their nutrition. All nurseries stock a complete, balanced plant food in the form of special azalea-camellia mix. Use this unless soil analysis suggests otherwise. Never use too much fertilizer. This could spell disaster. Three light applications are recommended; the first to be applied in March, and the second in May and a third in July. As a rule of thumb, a level tablespoon per foot of height is a safe amount per plant. Scatter the fertilizer evenly on top of the mulch, in and slightly beyond the drip line. Do not let the fertilizer touch the stem and never scratch the fertilizer into the soil as the surface roots will be burned and damaged. The use of organic fertilizers is more expensive but removes the danger of fertilizer burn. In any case, water the fertilizer in with a thorough soaking.

WATERING:

Although azaleas require good drainage, they are moisture loving plants. We are subject to long rainy periods and long dry periods. During dry periods it is necessary to water plants every four or five days. If you see that leaves have wilted, this is a serious warning and it may even be too late. Another important time to consider watering is in the dry fall. Plants are more likely to be weakened by the winter, if they go into winter suffering from drought. Another important time for watering is when the plants are in a period of lush growth in late spring and early summer.

PESTS AND DISEASES:

Azaleas are generally problem free. There are, however, several instances of leaf discoloration peculiar to azaleas, which are worth mentioning if only to make one aware of their causes and cures should they occur.

The insects that cause leaf discoloration are lace bug, red spider mite, and whitefly. The lace bug is the most common insect affecting azaleas. Adults are about ⅛″ long, have lacy wings, and brown and black markings. By sucking the sap from the underside of leaves they cause the upper surface to have a greyish appearance. Red spiders or spider mites also cause the leaves to turn to a grey-green or a bronze-green. The foliage will have a dusty appearance, and red spider can be detected by rubbing the underside of a leaf on white paper. Red streaks will be evident if the plant is plagued by red spider. Whitefly is the least threatening of the three insects as it only thrives in hot weather and only attacks certain varieties of azaleas. All three insects can be controlled by spraying. Consult your local nursery for the most effective spray. If spraying early blooming varieties, spray right after blooming. The late blooming varieties can be sprayed before flowering time. Subsequent spraying in June and July may be necessary if heavy infestation is evident.

Leaf discoloration can also be caused by soil inadequacies. A general yellowing is an indication of a lack of nitrogen in the soil. This general yellowing should not be confused with the condition known as "iron chlorosis." The latter condition causes only the area between the leaf veins to turn yellow rather than the whole leaf. Chlorosis is due to a deficiency of iron, which may result from poor drainage, improper pH, over fertilization or high phosphorus levels. The cause of discoloration is difficult to determine and requires professional help either from your county extension agent or a good nursery.

The most disastrous disease that can attack azaleas is petal blight or flower blight. It is a fungus, caused by high humidity and unseasonably warm weather. It starts with small water-soaked spots on the flower petals and rapidly increases to collapse the whole flower. Within a few days a whole yard of azalea blooms can be destroyed, leaving the leaves untouched. This disease mainly attacks the large flowering Indicas. Again, this is a problem to be faced with professional help.

Leaf gall is another fungus-related disease but is not considered as troublesome as the already-mentioned azalea problems. The galls appear as swollen leaf tips in the late spring, and the easiest way to deal with them is to pick off the deformed parts and destroy.

PRUNING:

Not only can pruning improve the quality of your azaleas as an evergreen shrub, it can also improve your plant's flowering ability. Pruning should be done to eliminate diseased or dead limbs, to expose healthy wood, and to eliminate long, straggly unbranched shoots that bloom sparsely. Cutting back shoots to a point below the general outline of the plant will result in the formation of as many as six new shoots on the cut branches. This should be done right after blooming. These new shoots, after 4 or 5 inches of growth, can be pinched back (or "tip pruned") before the first of July, producing more side branching. The end result is a thicker, healthier looking plant with an increased number of blooms. Each new shoot forms a flower bud. Old plants that have outgrown their space, extremely large plants that have been transplanted, and large sparsely-blooming plants can be severely pruned to within 12 inches of the ground. Generally, this refers to the rapidly growing southern Indicas. If this kind of pruning is done, it should be performed at least three to four weeks before bloom time to reduce the shock to the plant. The lush new growth should also be tip pruned during the early summer to produce more branching. Branching, compact growth, and increased flowering also can be stimulated in small varieties in the same way by tip pruning several times during the growing season. Any pruning done after the first of July will probably result in the loss of bloom for the next year, as azaleas start to set their bloom buds by then; however, you may find that after a summer of growth a few long unsightly shoots need to be pruned.

PROPAGATING:

The azalea is one of the easiest plants to propagate. The method called "layering" is the one that an amateur should use. To accomplish layering, choose a low hanging branch, bend it to the ground, notch with a knife, cover it with mulch, and leave it until it develops strong roots; then remove it as an independent plant. The branch should be pinned down securely so that it cannot move, and a method of bending the tip upward should be devised. The plant should be carefully watered during dry periods. Allow the branch to establish itself for a year before digging.

Another fairly simple method of propagation, but one that takes a little more care and patience, is the method of taking cuttings. Cuttings should be taken from semi- or well-hardened branches of the current year's growth. The cutting should be 3½ to 5 inches long depending on the growth rate of the variety. Four to six leaves should be left at the tip. The cutting should be dipped in rooting hormone then grown in a flat containing a rooting mixture of half peat moss and half sand. The flat should be elevated on boards for good drainage, placed in the shade, and kept moist at all times. A year's time is usually allowed for well-rooted plants, but sometimes it takes longer before plants are rooted well enough to set out. Other methods of propagating such as by seeds or grafting are more difficult.

NATIVE AZALEAS:

Although all evergreen azaleas in this country have been imported, gardeners in the southeastern United States are fortunate in having the deciduous azaleas as wild plants throughout their wooded and swampy areas. Because of the shape of their blossoms and their sweet smell, these beautiful shrubs are sometimes referred to as "Bush Honeysuckle" or "Wild Honeysuckle." They have a color range that varies from white to light pink, yellow, orange, scarlet and crimson, and they have a blooming period from March through August. They are most effectively used in mass plantings against an evergreen backdrop to show off their blooms, rather than as specimen or accent plants.

Although native azaleas are not readily available in local nurseries, some nurseries are beginning to sell a few, and specialty mail order nurseries are growing and selling many varieties. It is not advisable to dig them up in the woods unless the area is threatened by bulldozers.

Some native azaleas appropriate for use in our area are:

Rhododendron alabamense, Alabama Azalea, white, mid-season.

Rhododendron arborescens, Sweet Azalea, white, mid to late.

Rhododendron atlanticum, Coastal Azalea, white or white flecked with red, midseason.

Rhododendron austrinum, Florida Azalea, yellow, early

Rhododendron canescens, Piedmont or Florida Pinxter, pure white to light or deep pink, early.

Rhododendron prunifolium, Plumleaf Azalea, orange to deep red, late.

Rhododendron serrulatum, Hammock-sweet Azalea, white to creamy white, late.

Rhododendrom speciosum, Oconee Azalea, salmon to strong pink to yellow, early to mid-season.

Rhododendron viscosum, Swamp Azalea, white, mid-season.

EVERGREEN AZALEAS:

The various categories of evergreen azaleas are numerous and of complex origin. The following list includes the categories or groupings of azaleas that the amateur gardener should know. The varieties (cultivars) listed in each category are some of the more important ones. They are also the ones that are the most suitable to our climate and are most likely to be sold by local nurseries. The list includes approximate color description, bloom season, bloom size, and the form of the bloom.

FAVORITE EVERGREEN AZALEAS

Southern Indicas:

(These are larger azaleas, 6-12 feet.)

NAME	COLOR	BLOOM SEASON	SIZE	FORM
Duc de Rohan	orange/red	early/mid	2"	single
Duchess of Cyprus	salmon blush, reddish blotch	mid	2"	single
Fielder's White	white, chartreuse blotch	mid	3"	single
Formosa	magenta	mid	3½"	single
George Tabor	orchid lavender, magenta blotch	mid	3½"	single
Mrs. G.G Gerbing	white	mid	3½"	single
Iveryana	white, red flecks	late	3"	single
Judge Solomon	watermelon pink	mid	3½"	single
President Clay	cherry red, magenta blotch	mid	2"	single
Pride of Mobile	watermelon red	mid	3"	single
Pride of Summerville	salmon	mid	2"	single
Red Formosa	deep magenta	mid	3½"	single
Salmon Soloman	salmon pink	mid	3½"	single
Southern Charm	watermelon pink	mid	3½"	single

Kurume varieties:
(These are low, 2-4 feet.)

NAME	COLOR	SEASON	BLOOM SIZE	FORM
Christmas Cheer	brilliant red	early	1"	hose-in-hose*
Coral Bells	coral pink	early	1"	hose-in-hose
Flame	copper orange/red	early	1½"	single
Hino Crimson	brilliant red	early	1"	single
Hinode-giri	rose red	early	1½"	single
Salmon Beauty	salmon rose pink	early	1"	hose-in-hose
Snow	pure white	early	2"	hose-in-hose
Salmon Bells	peach pink	early	1"	hose-in-hose
Pink Pearl	salmon rose	early	2"	hose-in-hose

*hose-in-hose–appearing as if one flower grew in another.

Satsuki varieties:
(These are low, 2-4 feet.)

NAME	COLOR	SEASON	BLOOM SIZE	FORM
Goshu	white to rose	late	2"	double
Kow Ko-Ku	white, salmon red flecks and stripes	late	2½"	single
Wakebisu	rich shrimp pink	late	2"	single

Glenn dale varieties:
(These are of medium height, 4-6 feet.)

NAME	COLOR	SEASON	BLOOM SIZE	FORM
Fashion	salmon/rose pink	mid	2½"	hose-in-hose
Glacier	white	mid	2½"	single
Treasure	white, pale pink blotch	early/mid	3"	single

Pericat varieties:
(These are of medium height, 4-6 feet.*)

NAME	COLOR	SEASON	BLOOM SIZE	FORM
Dawn	phlox pink, white center	mid	2½"	hose-in-hose
Flanders Field	rich orange/red	mid	2"	single/semi-double
Glory	peach pink	early	2"	semi-double hose-in-hose
Willie Bell Mayo	rich deep pink	mid	2"	hose-in-hose
Sweetheart Supreme	rose pink	mid	2"	semi-double hose-in-hose

Outstanding hybrids:

(All listed are of medium height except the Gumpos and Pink Cascade which are low.)

NAME	COLOR	SEASON	BLOOM SIZE	FORM
Delaware Valley White	pure white	mid	2″	single
Gumpo, Pink	light pink	late	3″	single
Gumpo, White	white, occ. red specks	late	3″	single
Hershey's Red	deep bright red	early	2″	hose-in-hose
H.H. Hume	white, yellow throat	early	2″	hose-in-hose
Laura	rich pink	early	2″	hose-in-hose
Macrantha Pink	rich pink	late	2″	single/double
Macrantha Red	orange red	late	3″	single/double
Mary Corcoran	white flushed pink	early	2″	single
Massasoit	bright red	early	2″	single
Pink Cascade	salmon pink, red blotch	late	2″	single
Pink Ruffles	rich rose pink	early	3″	hose-in-hose
Red Ruffles	bright red	early	3″	hose-in-hose
Rosea	violet pink	mid	2″	double, hose-in-hose
Rosebud	light rosy pink	mid	1¾″	double, hose-in-hose

Encore azaleas:

Repeat bloomers of mid size; more than 20 different cultivars of varying color, growth habit and size.

NOTES

Camellias

CAMELLIAS

Camellia! What a beautiful word! We have been blessed with these exquisite flowers in colors of brilliant ruby red, snow white and pale pink to deep dusty rose. Delicate white blossoms may be fringed with ribbons of pink or touched with streaks of red. There is nothing comparable to a magnificent camellia in all its glory. As the empress of flowers it reigns supreme in its beauty.

Camellias are native to Japan, China, Indochina and the off-shore islands of Asia neighboring those countries. They were introduced into this country over 200 years ago.

In our warmer climate camellias are valuable landscape plants with their luxuriant dark green foliage and fall and winter blooms. Camellias are slow growers, but ultimately may grow to 10 to 20 feet or more. They may be used as a hedge or accent, or may be espaliered against a wall.

The culture of camellias is a fascinating and rewarding hobby with many facets. Some enjoy hybrid development, others use gibberellic acid to obtain specimen blooms for show.

This chapter is intended to give the amateur gardeners a non-technical insight into the culture of camellias in the garden. There are 45 different species within the camellia family. By far the most popular is the *Camellia japonica* which has over 3000 named varieties. This camellia is known for its showy flowers which vary from white to pink to red, and blooms from late fall into spring. Blooms may be of one color or may be variegated. They are as desirable for flower arranging as they are in the garden.

The second species used frequently is the *Camellia sasanqua*. It blooms early in the fall, but the flowers are not as spectacular as those of *Camellia japonica* and they do not last as well when cut. The plants are valued for their landscape effect. What appears in the following pages regarding the culture of camellias applies equally to *Camellia japonica* and *Camellia sasanqua* as well as other less popular species.

PURCHASING:

As the bloom is of the most importance, one should buy camellia plants from a reliable source or when in bloom.

PLANTING:

First consider the correct location. All plants grow more succesfully in a location that is as similar to their natural environment as possible. For the camellia it is in the forest, subordinate to trees which shade, protect, and provide for it through decaying vegetation. Camellias, therefore, will thrive in semi-shade under pine trees where they are protected from the wind and other elements. The shade must not be too dense as that will reduce flowering.

Camellias require moisture and good drainage. Do not plant them in low places as the roots will tend to stay too wet and will rot.

When ready to plant make a hole larger than the root ball. Mix in organic matter. Plant the camellias with the surface of the ball slightly higher than the surrounding ground. This will produce a dome effect to help with drainage. Firm the soil around the plant and fill the hole with water to remove air bubbles. Keep well watered until established.

FERTILIZE:

Camellias prefer slightly acid soil with a pH from about 5 to 6. The soil must contain large amounts of humus and have good drainage. Since the plant's first growth appears about the first of April, you should fertilize around March first for growth. Fertilize again in May and June for production of good blooms. Apply fertilizer around the plant starting about 6 inches from the trunk. Spread the fertilizer outward to reach the feeder roots. Use a balanced fertilizer or the one recommended from your soil analysis. Use 1 tablespoon per foot of plant height. Well fertilized plants are more disease resistant.

MULCHING:

Mulching is very important as the camellia is a surface rooted plant. The roots are not protected from extreme heat, cold or dryness, so mulch will provide this protection. Oak leaves and pine straw are excellent mulches.

WATERING:

Camellias do not like to have their "feet" wet. Water should not collect under a plant as may happen in clay like soil. It is better to soak a plant once a week than to sprinkle it often. Do not over water as the roots will rot.

The camellia is a subtropical, evergreen plant and, therefore, thrives in a mild, humid climate. Great damage results from sudden extreme changes in temperature. In either freezing weather or extreme heat keep the plants adequately watered to lessen damage.

TRANSPLANTING:

The older the plant the more difficult it is for the plant to adapt to transplanting. Camellias may be planted nearly any time of the year, but for best results they should be transplanted from the end of November until March. It may be best to root prune 6 to 12 months in advance of moving the plant. Do this by taking a shovel and cutting into the ground the depth of the shovel. Do this all the way around the plant 12″ out for every 1″ diameter of trunk. When ready to plant cut back the volume of top-growth by at least one third, carefully wrap the root ball in burlap, and plant as above. Take care to avoid soil loss. The burlap need not be removed as it will rot.

PESTS:

Tea scale is the major pest on camellias. It is recognized by the presence of a cotton-like matter on the underside of the leaves. The following are some of the methods used for control.

An oil spray (Volck) is relatively safe. It is sometimes mixed with other chemicals. Follow all directions carefully. When spraying be sure to cover the underside of the leaves. Be very careful not to spray if the temperature is over 85° or under 40° F. Extremes of temperature may result in leaf burn. Tea scale usually becomes more apparent in the fall. The oil spray may be used preventatively in fall and early spring for control.

Systemic insecticides may also be used. These are applied during the time when temperatures are excessive. They may be applied as a spray or as a drench. Use the safest chemical currently recommended by the county extension agent or nurseryman.

PRUNING:

The ideal pruning season is after the bush has finished blooming. You may prune at any time of the year, but you will lose blooms if you prune before the buds are set. Camellias set their buds in June.

Pruning is desirable to keep a plant healthy. It will induce new growth and improve the quality of bloom. See the section on pruning for tips on how to prune.

HANDLING THE BLOOMS:

The blooms of *Camellia japonica* are beautiful and long lasting. There are several techniques which will give you larger blooms.

Disbudding–When several flower buds are growing together remove all buds but one. Do this in September and October. Do not confuse flower buds with leaf buds.

Gibbing–Gibbing produces larger, more spectacular blooms at an earlier time. This is done in early fall with gibberellic acid, a plant growth regulator, which speeds up the blooming process. It should be applied in several sessions in no more than 20% of the plant. To gibb twist off the pointed leaf bud which is found adjacent to the bloom bud. This leaves a tiny "cup" which can now be filled with one drop of acid squeezed from an eyedropper.

VARIETIES:

Upon asking a camellia enthusiast to confide his favorite variety he quickly answered, "Why, it's the one I happen to be admiring at the moment." It is difficult to choose but the following list includes favorites that do well.

Camellia japonica Favorites:

PINK

Debutante	Fashionata	High Hat
Pink Perfection	Elegans Supreme	Wildwood
Dr. Tinsley	Betty Sheffield Pink	Mrs. Lyman Clark
Rosea Superba	China Doll	Magnoliaflora
Blonde Betty	Hariett Bisby	

WHITE

Mary Alice Cox	Elegans Champagne	White Empress
Gus Menard	Mathotiana Alba	Joshua Youtz
Snow Man	Imura	Alba Plena
Allie Habel		

RED

Mathotiana	Don Mac	Kramer's Supreme
Woodville Red	Blood of China	Empress

VARIEGATED

Carter's Sunburst	Tomorrow Park Hill	Guillio Nuccio
Tomorrow Variegated	Tomorrow Crown Jewel	Latifolia
Campari	Helen Bower Variegated	Daikagura
Morris Moughan	Miss Charleston	Herme
Betty Sheffield	Lady Kay	Tiffany
Ville de Nantes		

Camellia sasanqua Favorites:

WHITE	PINK	
Frosty	Cleopatra	Elfin
Mine-No-Yuki	Dwarf Rose	Pink Snow
	Sparkling Burgundy	

NOTES

Roses

ROSES

William Shakespeare wrote, "Of all the flowers me thinks a rose is best." From the early days of civilization, roses have been cherished as a symbol of love and beauty. Today, people all over the world still derive the same pleasure from roses as did the ancients. Roses have touched and inspired artists and poets, and they will inspire you, too, as you work with, or just gaze upon blooming roses. You will find it impossible to walk through your garden without pausing to cup a bloom in your hand and appreciate its fragrance and delicacy. No other plant will give you as much pleasure or as many blooms as will a rose. Their long blooming season and the baskets full of fragrant flowers are a two-fold reward for your hours spent caring for them. Roses are not complicated to grow if you begin with top quality plants, place them in a sunny spot, and follow a program of regular care.

TYPES:

Hybrid Tea–These are the classic long stemmed roses. Flowers are double or single and are often fragrant. Blooms are long lasting and good for cutting. A separate bed is recommended. Plants are usually 3 to 5 feet tall.

Floribunda–Blooms are smaller than the hybrid tea and are often borne in clusters. Flowers may be single, semi-double or double. The plants are 2 to 4 feet tall.

Grandiflora–These are prolific bloomers from spring until frost. Flowers are usually clustered or may be single. Abundance of blooms are like the floribunda, but their size and shape similar to the hybrid tea. Plants may grow 8 to 10 feet tall.

Old Fashioned–Old garden roses are hardy and often very fragrant. Most bloom once a year in early summer. These plants have a great diversity of flower shapes as well as a wide range of growing habits. There are runners, ramblers, vines, and compact shrubs.

Climbers–There are climbing varieties of all the above types (hybrid tea, floribunda, etc.) The plants range from 10 to 50 feet, and the type of bloom depends on the variety. These are excellent as covers for fences, trellis, arbors, and banks.

PURCHASING:

It is important to purchase plants from reputable sources, either well known nurseries or mail orders houses, and always purchase top quality roses. Rose plants are graded according to the size and the number of canes. Plants of top quality (#1 Grade) should have at least three heavy canes approximately 18″ long and ⅝″ in diameter. Beware of plants that appear dry or discolored, that have waxed canes, or ones that have abnormal swelling on the canes.

Bare root plants grow as well as container grown, but should be ordered from catalog sources early in the fall in order to get the best selections. Specify an early February delivery date. Container grown plants are usually offered in nurseries by the first of February.

CHOOSING THE SITE:

Sunlight, fertile soil, and good air circulation are the three essential ingredients needed to begin a successful rose garden. Prepare your site well before planting time, preferably in the fall.

Roses are happiest when they receive both morning and afternoon sun, but if that is not possible, morning sun is best. They require a minimum of six hours of sunlight.

The soil must be well-drained, fertile, and slightly acid, with pH 6.0 to 6.5. The pH condition may be determined by a soil test done through the county extension agent.

Place roses in an area with good air circulation, as leaf disease and mildew are encouraged by moisture and lack of air movement. Roses, except for climbers, grow best in open beds, with a wall or a fence for a background. Planting too close to trees or other shrubs creates competition for water and nutrients.

PREPARING THE SOIL AND PLANTING:

Dormant, bare root plants should be planted late in January or early in February. Earlier plantings may cause the plants to leaf out only to suffer later damage from a delayed winter freeze.

Container grown plants may be planted from February until the onset of hot weather. Take care when transferring leafed-out specimens from pot to garden. Be extremely careful not to break the ball of soil.

Dig your planting hole to measure two feet deep and two feet wide. Remove the soil from the hole and mix one third of it with peat moss and sharp sand, or mix it with compost. Add to this mixture, one cup of peletized limestone and one cup of steamed bone meal. Mix these ingredients well and put them into the planting hole in the form of a cone. Bare root plants should be soaked overnight in water containing a root stimulator. When ready to plant, place the bare root plant on the top of the cone with the roots slanting downward. Open up roots before covering with soil and prune any that are broken.

Fill the hole two-thirds full with the soil mixture and press down lightly with your fingers to eliminate air pockets. Fill the hole with water and let it soak in. Add the remainder of soil and soak again. Plant just deep enough to leave the graft or crown of the rose bush at least one or two inches above the level of the soil. Almost any rose can be killed by being set too deeply.

Plant Hybrid Tea, Grandiflora and Floribunda roses 4 to 6 feet apart on center. Mulch the newly planted roses. After planting, keep well watered.

WATERING:

Roses are very thirsty plants and take a great deal of water. If there has been no rain for 5 to 7 days, water thoroughly. Apply enough water to soak the soil down to a depth of at least 12 inches at least two times a week. Allow time for the water to soak in, then check the soil for moisture. After several times, you will be able to gauge how long you must water your roses to adequately soak the soil. A good method of watering is to use either a soil-soaker hose or a flat hose sprinkler turned upside down. If overhead sprinklers are used, water in the morning so the foliage will dry out. Moisture promotes the development of black spot disease.

FERTILIZING:

Do not use any commercial fertilizer at planting time. When plants start to grow, you can begin sparingly at first, to apply a commercial fertilizer. Use a fertilizer that contains ample content of a slow-releasing form of organic nitrogen. Once a month, during the blooming season, apply ⅓ cup around the drip line of each plant. Be sure your plants are thoroughly watered before, as well as after, fertilizing. It is not necessary to remove the mulch to fertilize.

If the fertilizer does not contain the trace elements, add 2 tablespoons each of chelated iron, minor elements and magnesium sulfate (Epsom salts) for each bush.

Beginning in the second year, after the rose bushes are established, two tablespoons ammonium nitrate may be used once each year to give the plants a good start. Use no other fertilizer at that time. Two weeks later begin a regular fertilization program.

MULCHING:

Mulch heavily with pine straw or oak leaves. A 5 inch mulch will settle down to 2 inches. While some rosarians continue to remove the old mulch at the end of the blooming season, others feel that the rotted mulch is good for the soil, and that one may spray the mulch for possible over-wintering diseases. If you choose to remove the mulch be careful not to disturb any tiny roots that have grown into the bottom layer of mulch.

PRUNING:

Valentine's Day is the favorite day to prune hybrid teas, grandifloras, floribundas and old fashioned roses, but monthly grooming is necessary throughout the growing season. The purpose of pruning is to rid the plant of old wood every year, thereby encouraging the regular development of strong and healthy stems. Never allow shoots from below a graft to develop.

Begin pruning by removing all of the dead wood. Next, cut out all of the small thin canes and any that have been injured. Leave 4 to 6 of the healthiest canes. Cut canes 2 inches below any diseased area, into healthy wood. The cut should be just above a growth bud which points away from the center of the bush. Slant your cut in the direction of the growth bud. Any large cut may be sealed with Elmer's glue, hot candle wax or pruning paint.

The culture for CLIMBING AND OLD FASHIONED ROSES is the same as for other roses. Only the time and method of pruning is different. The main season for pruning climbers and old roses is after they have bloomed. Do not prune them in February, except for cutting out dead wood and shaping lightly, as you will destroy their potential bloom.

Climbers with one time blooming period, such as the white Cherokee *(Rosa laevigata)*, require very little pruning until they are 3 to 4 years old. Never cut off their canes at the base until they have been well established (about 5 years). They should only be pruned when they have finished blooming.

The repeat blooming climbers should be pruned lightly when their first big burst of bloom is past. Do not prune too heavily or the next crop of blooms will be lost. Remove blooms as they fade, leaving a group of at least 3 leaves on the stem. This will stimulate more bloom. Strong new canes coming up from the base may be cut back ⅓ at the end of the first blooming period. This makes for more lateral shoots. Repeat blooming climbers flower constantly all summer with a final burst of bloom in the fall.

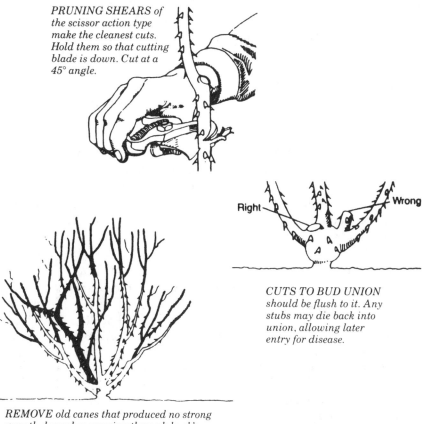

PRUNING SHEARS of the scissor action type make the cleanest cuts. Hold them so that cutting blade is down. Cut at a 45° angle.

Right — Wrong

CUTS TO BUD UNION should be flush to it. Any stubs may die back into union, allowing later entry for disease.

REMOVE old canes that produced no strong growth, branches crossing through bush's center, weak stems. Shorten remaining canes. Healthy growth may be reduced by ⅓.

PESTS AND DISEASE:

Although a regular system of spraying and dusting is commonly practiced, it is safer to identify specific problems and then treat accordingly. In February use lime sulphur, a safe dormant spray, to eradicate over-wintering pests and diseases. Spray both the ground and the mulch.

If a regular program of spraying is used, begin as soon as new leaves are formed in early spring. Spray every two weeks with a mixture of an insecticide and a fungicide. It is important to spray the undersides of the leaves as well as the tops.

PROBLEM	SYMPTOM	REMEDY
Black spot	Black spot with yellow margins causing loss of leaves.	Spray weekly with a fungicide.
Powdery mildew	White deposit on tender new growth causing browning.	Remove affected leaves and stems or spray with a fungicide.
Thrips	Tiny sap sucking insects on bloom and buds causing browning.	Spray with insecticide. This may be added to the fungicide.
Aphids	Small green sucking insects on stems and foliage.	Add insecticide to spray mixture.
Spider mites	Almost microscopic crawlers on underside of leaves causing them to bronze and defoliate.	Spray with miticide every two weeks. A hard spray of water helps.

Use a 3 gallon plastic tank, pump-up sprayer. Add a few drops of dishwashing detergent as a sticker to the mix. Read directions carefully and apply at the rate recommended.

CUTTING ROSES:

It is best to cut roses in the early morning or late afternoon. Food stored in the plant at this time lengthens the cut life of the flower. Put the stems in very hot water as soon as possible, and put the flowers in a cool dark place for several hours before arranging. Cut the blooms just above 5 leaves on the stem. The leaf bud just below your cut should slant outward, just as in pruning. You will have better bushes and more flowers if you leave 50% of flowers and growth stems on each bush.

Roses are unable to tolerate full blooming the first year. Do not allow the first crop of flowers to bloom. Instead, pinch off the bud and first five leaflets as soon as the bud is showing. Don't let blooms form until the second or third cycle.

Whenever you cut roses from your garden, take a few extra minutes to pick off the yellow leaves and cut out dead wood. Always remove all faded flowers to the first five leaflets to prevent rose hips from forming and drawing on the plant food supply.

A FEW FAVORITES:
HYBRID TEAS

First Prize–deep rose pink
Garden Party–white, pink trim
Sweet Surrender–silvery pink
Louisiana–creamy white
Frau Karl Druschki–white
White Masterpiece–double white
Peace–soft yellow edged with pink
Oregold–lemon yellow
Double Delight–white with deep red trim
Georgia–peach-apricot
Fragrant Cloud–dark red buds, orange red blooms
Savannah–soft apricot

Tiffany–deep pink, yellow at base
Pink Radiance–silvery pink, disease resistant
Pascali–white
Shasta–white
Eclipse–yellow
Talisman–yellow and orange
Chrysler Imperial–dark red
Mr. Lincoln–dark red
Tropicana–brilliant orange red, small blooms
Sea Shell–peach and salmon pink on yellow base

FLORIBUNDAS AND GRANDIFLORAS

Summer Snow–white, prolific
Europeana–red, good for borders
Pink Parfait–delicate pink blend, small, single
Queen Elizabeth–light pink, carmine, bushy, upright, everblooming

The Fairy–delicate pink blooms on compact bush
China Doll–bright rose pink small plant, everblooming

OLD FASHIONED ROSES

Jacques Cartier–medium pink
Nuits de Young–dark red
Rosa alba–white
Konigin von Danemark–pink cottage rose
Rosa des peintres–rose pink stripe

Fairy Rose–blush pink, small, compact
Four Seasons–rose, blooms spring and fall, fragrant
Rosa mundi–pink, candy

CLIMBERS
Repeat blooming climbers:

New Dawn–pink, cut spent blooms
Golden Showers–daffodil yellow
Handel–creamy white, rose edge

High Noon Climber–yellow
Summer Snow–white clusters
Fred Edmunds–burnt orange
Cl. Tiffany–rose to pink, yellow at base

Cl. Queen Elizabeth–blend of carmine rose and dawn pink

Cl. Peace–yellow flushed with pink

Blaze–red clusters

Dr. J. H. Nicolas–double rose pink

Don Juan–deep red, hybrid tea like bloom

Once blooming climbers:

Cherokee *(Rosa laevigata* 'Lutea')–white yellow center, Georgia state flower

Lady Banks Rose *(Rosa Banksiae* 'Alba Plena')–Yellow and white varieties

Sweetheart–pink

Silver Moon–blush white with yellow center, large

X Fortuniana *(R. Banksiae* x *R. laevigata)*–2" fragrant white flowers; disease resistant, soil tolerant.

SHRUB ROSES

Rosa chinensis mutabilis–grows 3-6 feet, upright habit; single crimson to pink to white flowers 2" across.

Rosa rugosa–many varieties available; very hardy, good for seashore planting as it can withstand salt spray and sandy soil; grows to 6 feet.

Meidiland (group of everblooming, hardy, disease resistant and low care hybrid roses from the House of Meilland, rose breeders) range of colors; may be used in the landscape as specimen, hedge or groundcover.

MINIATURE ROSES

Little Jackie–orange, pink, yellow

Rise 'N' Shine–bright yellow

Toy Clown–white, edged with red

Beauty Secret–red, blooms in abundance

Snow Bride–white, hybrid tea form

Peaches 'N' Cream–pink and cream

Winsome–lavender

Green Ice–double white, fades to green; spreading

Red Cascade–red, spreading

RECENT INTRODUCTIONS

David Austin Roses - New breed of roses blending the beauty of the old roses with the disease resistance and repeat flowering of the modern rose; bloom size, shape and color vary; many are fragrant.

Knockout Roses - Compact shrub rose to 4-6' which is more resistant to black spot and other diseases; blooms from early spring until frost; no deadheading required, but blooms more profusely with heavy pruning; several shades of pinks and reds.

Annuals

ANNUALS

Annuals are plants that naturally complete their entire life cycle from seed to flowering within one growing season. Thus, annuals are temporary plants in your garden, but their glorious, long-lasting display make them well worthwhile.

In the landscape, annuals are used for their brilliant color. They are indispensable where a fast, prolonged summer display is needed. They may be used creatively in "annual redecorating." They may be used to fill in bare spots. This is especially important in a young garden where the shrubs have not matured. They also tie together the other permanent elements and will cover unsightly remnants such as the yellowing foliage of daffodils. Annuals in pots provide special, or impromptu, color during lulls of bloom.

Annuals are invaluable for providing cut flowers. The plants tend to like being cut as it stimulates new growth and keeps the plant growing and blooming rather than producing seed.

SELECTING AND BUYING:

Annual plants may be bought in the spring from any nursery and from many retail stores. Look for new breeding advances that have improved annuals, made them more colorful, and often more compact. In the fall, nurseries will have hardy annuals, such as stock, snapdragons and larkspur. The price you will pay will be low relative to the amount of pleasure derived. Make certain that the plants are in good condition and without pests or disease. Look carefully at the color of the leaves and at the undersides of the leaves. If there is any mottling or evidence of webs or of leaf drop, the plants should be rejected. Avoid leggy, yellow or root bound plants.

For variety, low cost, and the greatest sense of accomplishment, one should try seeds of a few annuals each year. Try new ones that are not in the stores, and try the All-American selections. Be adventurous! Catalogs are irresistible. Many show color photographs of the bloom. (See the section on Sources.)

Virtually, any annual may be grown in warm climates if given the proper conditions. Hardy annuals such as sweet pea, poppy and larkspur tolerate moderately cold weather without being killed. Seed should be sown where the plants are to grow in the fall (October-December), or plants may be put out in the fall or early spring. Occasionally, very cold (less than 10° F) weather will kill the plants, but most years they will survive. Nurseries often carry a few varieties for planting in the fall. Bloom time is in the spring. Plants die out in the hot weather. Pansies, though biennials, are treated in the same way. Usually plants are bought and planted in the fall for spring bloom. Certain perennials, notably *Delphinium cultorum* and *Bellis perennis* (English daisy), may also be treated and grown in this way as annuals since they die out in the hot weather. Half-hardy annuals and tender annuals are sown or planted in the spring. Many may be started indoors and planted outside after danger of frost.

Whether you buy plants from nurseries or start seed, be careful to note ultimate height of the plant and select compatible colors.

LOCATION:

Most annuals require full sun and well-drained soil. Impatiens, begonias and coleus enjoy shade.

STARTING FROM SEED:

There are advantages to starting plants from seed. First of all, one is not limited to what someone else has been willing to grow for planting. The variety is endless. Just as important is the sheer miracle of a sprouting seed that ultimately produces a colorful flower.

The variety of annuals that we can grow is endless. Choose a few new or unusual ones to grow from seed each year. (See section on Propagating for instructions on how to start from seed.)

PLANTING:

Plants may be grown individually or in flats. If in a flat, the plants must be cut carefully one from another. In either case, the plants should not be so potbound that one cannot preserve the roots in transplanting. It is best to put out young plants on a cloudy day or in the late afternoon, so they are protected for awhile from the sun. If hot and sunny, shade the small plant with leafy branches, or a plastic flower pot. To prepare beds for planting, dig the beds 8 to 12 inches deep, add organic matter and incorporate. In most cases, one is planting the annuals among permanent plants. Space the plants as you wish. At each spot, dig a hole larger than the plant's root ball. Loosen the root ball around the small plant. Place in the hole. Press the earth in around the plant leaving a small depression to catch the water. Water well after the area has been planted. You will ultimately have bushier, stronger plants if you will pinch out the growing tip, including any flower buds, after planting.

CARE:

Fertilize lightly 2 weeks after planting and every month thereafter, or use a pelleted slow release fertilizer. Water in well.

Keep the plants weeded. As they grow larger it will be more difficult for the weeds to become established.

If rain is not plentiful, water deeply once a week. In the hot summer months, more frequent watering may be necessary. Mulching will help conserve moisture as well as inhibit weed growth.

PESTS:

Annuals are particularly susceptible to slugs, snails, thrips and aphids. Watch for signs of these problems and respond appropriately (see section on Pests and Diseases). Slugs and snails may completely strip young plants of their foliage. Thrips and aphids are seen on new growth especially.

PROPAGATING:

Most annuals are best grown from seed. Collecting seed from plants that you particularly like is not difficult, but remember seed will not come true from hybrids. Allow a few of the flowers to remain on the plant until after they are spent. The seed will form and then begin to dry. Pick the seeds before they are dispersed, complete the drying, store in a dry place, and plant the next season.

A few annuals, such as impatiens, begonias, and geraniums, may be easily propagated from cuttings. The plants may be kept from year to year in this way. Make a 3 to 4 inch cutting, dip in rooting hormone, and place carefully in a hole (made with a pencil) in loose earth, peat, and/or sand. Cuttings will also take root in plain water but the roots tend to be weaker.

PRUNING:

When annuals reach 4 to 5 inches, the first inch or so (the growing tip) should be cut back to just above a leaf. This will promote a bushier, stronger plant. Spent blooms should be removed so that energy will not be put into seed production.

ANNUALS

*native Botanical Name Common Name	Height	Color	Space Apart	Exposure	Planting Time	Bloom Time	Comments
Ageratum houstonianum Ageratum	6-18"	Blue, white, pink	6-12"	Sun	Seed or plant early spring	Spring to frost	Good cut flowers; dwarf variety good for edging; hardy; drought resistant; excellent cut fresh or dried; reseeds itself.
Alyssum (See *Lobularia*)							
Amaranth, Globe (See *Gomphrena*)							
Angelonia angustifolia Summer Snapdragon	18-24"	Varied	2'	Sun	Spring	Spring to fall	White, lavender, pink, and blue orchid-like flowers on tall spiky stems; little care; dead head for repeat bloom.
Antirrhinum majus Snapdragon	12-36"	Varied	15"	Sun	Fall best, or spring	Spring	Good for border, best for mass planting and cut flowers; taller varieties must be staked.
Aster (See *Callistephus*)							
Bachelor's Button (See *Centaurea*)							
Balsam (See *Impatiens*)							
Basil (See Herb List)							
Begonia semperflorens Wax Begonia	8-18"	Varied	12"	Part shade, shade	Any time after frost	Until frost	Use for bedding, hanging baskets, containers; cuttings may be rooted for the following year, or the plant may be potted and kept inside.
Bellis perennis English Daisy	6"	White, pink	8"	Sun, part shade	Fall	Spring	In colder climates is a perennial, treat as hardy annual.
Blanket-Flower (See *Gaillardia*)							

ANNUALS

*native Botanical Name Common Name	Height	Color	Space Apart	Exposure	Planting Time	Bloom Time	Comments
Brassica oleracea Ornamental Cabbage	12"	Varied	12"	Sun	Fall	Winter	Good for winter color; freeze resistant; also ornamental kale.
Calendula officinalis Pot Marigold	12-15"	Yellow, orange	12"	Sun	Fall	Spring and fall	Better growth if planted in fall; cut flowers; bedding.
Calibrachoa Million Bells	6-10"	Varied	18"	Sun	Spring	Spring to frost	Little care; good in containers or hanging baskets; mounding or cascading forms.
Callistephus chinensis China Aster	10-36"	Pink, red, purple, white, lavender	12"	Sun, shade	Spring	Fall	Good bedding plant; cut flowers.
Carnation (See Dianthus)							
Celosia cristata Cockscomb	10-36"	Red, yellow, orange, magenta	24"	Sun	Spring	Spring to frost	Good bedding plant; cut or dried flowers; plumed and crested varieties.
Centaurea cyanus Cornflower (Bachelor's Button)	24-30"	Pink, blue, purple, white	24"	Sun, shade	Spring	Summer to fall	Bedding plant; cut or dried flowers.
Chrysanthemum coccineum Painted Daisy	12"	Varied	12"	Partial shade	Fall or spring	Spring	Good for cutting; bed or border plants.
Cleome spinosa Spiderflower	36-48"	Orchid, pink, white	15"	Sun	Spring or summer	Summer to early fall	Self-sows; good cut flowers.
Coleus blumei Coleus	8-16"	Variegated foliage	12"	Sun, shade	Spring	Color to frost	Grown for foliage; incredible new colors variations!
Cornflower (See Centaurea)							
*Coreopsis tinctoria Calliopsis	2-4'	Yellow, orange, maroon	6-15"	Sun to part shade	Early spring	Early summer	Feathery foliage; reseeds itself.

ANNUALS

*native

Botanical Name Common Name	Height	Color	Space Apart	Exposure	Planting Time	Bloom Time	Comments
Cosmos bipannatus Mexican Aster	11-21"	Varied	6-8"	Sun, part shade	Seeds in spring	Spring summer fall	Colorful; reseeds itself 3 times during growing season; hardy; good cut flower.
Cosmos sulphureus	18"-2'	Golden, red, yellow	18"	Sun	Spring	Spring summer fall	Vigorous; self-reseeding annual as above; heat resistant.
Daisy, Dahlberg (See *Thymophylla*)							
Daisy, English (See *Bellis*)							
Daisy, Painted (See *Chrysanthemum*)							
Daucus carota Queen Anne's Lace	36-48"	White	12"	Sun	Plant or sow seeds in fall	Spring and early summer	A biennial; will reseed; such a wonderful display in a larger garden that it is worthwhile cultivating; good for cutting.
Delphinium ajacis (*Consolida spp.*) Rocket Larkspur	24-36"	White, blue, pink, lilac	6"	Sun	Sow seeds in fall	Spring	Good for bedding and cut flowers; will reseed; fertilize frequently.
Delphinium spp. Belladonna	12-24"	White, pink, deep blue	12"	Sun, part shade	Fall	Spring	Perennial in colder climate, but we treat this classic as an annual; beautiful cut flowers.
Dianthus caryophyllus Carnation	18-24"	Varied	12"	Sun	Spring	Early summer	Good cut flowers; needs staking; dwarf varieties available.
Dianthus chinensis Chinese Pinks	12-30"	Scarlet, pink, white	18"	Sun	Fall or spring	Spring to frost	Good for bedding and cutting; fragrant.
Digitalis purpurea Foxglove	1-2'	Varied	12"	Part shade	Fall	Spring	Colorful; hardy biennial; reseeds.

ANNUALS

*native

Botanical Name Common Name	Height	Color	Space Apart	Exposure	Planting Time	Bloom Time	Comments
Eschscholtzia californica California Poppy	12"	Orange, yellow, pink, red	8"	Sun	Sow seeds in fall	Spring	Colorful spring show; transplants poorly.
Euphorbia marginata Snow-on-the-Mountain	3-4'	White	18"	Sun	Sow seeds in spring	Late summer	Hardy; self-seeding; drought resistant.
Eustoma grandiflorum Lisianthus	12"	Pink, white, purple, blue	12"	Sun	Sow seeds in fall or plant in spring	Summer to frost	May be perennial in Zone 9; tolerates drought and heat; pinch regularly; sandy soil; long-lasting cut flowers; good bedding; recently available again; mulch.
Four O'Clock (See *Mirabilis*)							
Foxglove (See *Digitalis*)							
Gaillardia pulchella Blanket-Flower	12-18"	Cream, orange, yellow	12"	Sun	Early spring	Spring to frost	Colorful cut flowers; good at seashore; many varieties. 'Sundance'-new bicolor.
Geranium (See *Pelargonium*)							
Gomphrena globosa Globe Amaranth	10-18"	Varied	6-10"	Sun	Early spring (seeds)	All summer	Hardy; drought tolerant; excellent cut flower, fresh or dried; reseeds itself.
Helianthus annuus Sunflower	3-7'	Yellow, gold	12"	Sun	Seeds in spring	Summer	Hardy; colorful new hybrids.
Impatiens balsamina Balsam	12-18"	Varied	6-8"	Sun, part shade	Anytime after frost	Until frost	Use for bedding; hanging baskets, containers.

ANNUALS

*native *Botanical Name* Common Name	Height	Color	Space Apart	Exposure	Planting Time	Bloom Time	Comments
Impatiens wallerana Impatiens	12-18"	White, pink, magenta, salmon, red	18"	Shade	After frost	Until frost	Shade-loving; forms masses of color; good in pots and hanging baskets; cuttings may be rooted for the following year.
New Guinea hybrids				Sun			Heat resistant; full sun; plants often with variegated leaves. 'Tango'-bright orange.
Ipomoea batatas Ornamental Sweet Potato Vine	8-10'	Varied Magenta		Sun	Spring	Fall	Striking ground cover or cascading container plant; many new cultivars with foliage of bronze, bright green, plum.
Johnny Jump-Up (See *Viola*)							
Larkspur (See *Delphinium*)							
Lathyrus odoratus Sweet Pea	8-36"	Varied	12"	Sun	Sow seeds in fall	Spring	Bush or vine varieties; good cut flowers.
Lunaria annua Dollar Plant	2'	Purple	3'	Sun, part shade	Spring	Spring, summer	Flowers followed by flat, round silvery pods.
Lisianthus (See *Eustoma*)							
Lobelia erinus Lobelia	4-10"	Blue	4-6"	Sun, shade	Early spring	Spring	Good for bedding, edging; likes sandy soil.
Lobularia maritima Alyssum	2-6"	White, lilac	6"	Partial sun	Sow seed in fall or plant in spring	Spring to frost	Keep spent flowers removed by shearing for succession of bloom; border plant; hanging baskets.
Marigold (See *Tagetes*)							
Matthiola incana Stock	15-30"	Varied	15"	Sun	Fall best or spring	Spring	Good either as cutting or bedding plants.
Melampodium	1½-2'	Yellow	1½'	Sun	After frost	July to October	Heat and drought resistant; self reseeding; mounded form; vigorous.

ANNUALS

*native

Botanical Name Common Name	Height	Color	Space Apart	Exposure	Planting Time	Bloom Time	Comments
Million Bells (*See Calibrachoa*)							
Mirabilis jalapa Four O'Clock	24-36"	Varied	18-24"	Sun	Sow seeds in spring	Spring to frost	Profuse bloomer, brightly colored flowers open at 4 p.m.; reseed or may remain as a perennial in warm climate.
Nasturtium (See *Tropaeolum*)							
Nemophila menziesii Baby Blue Eyes	6"	Sky blue with white eye	6"	Sun, part shade	Sow seed in fall or plant in early spring	Spring	Lovely for border; will bloom only once.
Nicotiana alata Flowering Tobacco	12-18"	White to scarlet	18-24"	Sun, part shade	Fall, early spring	Spring	Fragrant, night-blooming.
Oxypetalum caeruleum Southern Star	18"	Blue	10-12"	Sun	Set out seedlings in spring	Early summer	Dainty, blue, star-shaped flowers.
Pansy (See *Viola*)							
Papaver nudicaule Iceland Poppy	8-12"	Yellow, white, red	8"	Sun	Sow seeds in fall	Spring	Colorful dainty blossoms; good in border.
Papaver rhoeas Shirley Poppy	36"	White, red	8"	Sun	Sow seeds in fall	Spring	Good in border and for cutting.
Papaver somniferum Opium Poppy	3-4'	Pink, white, red	1'	Sun	Fall	Spring	Wonderful double and single flowers.
Pelargonium Geranium	12-15"	White, pink, red	12"	Sun, part shade	After frost	Spring and fall	Good container plant; tolerates our winter better than our summer; cover when temperature goes below 30°.

ANNUALS

*native Botanical Name Common Name	Height	Color	Space Apart	Exposure	Planting Time	Bloom Time	Comments
Pentas lanceolata Star Cluster Egyptian Star	2'	Pink, red, purple, white	1-2'	Sun	After frost	Spring until fall	Showy, compact, domed cluster of flowers on knee-high bush; may survive a mild winter.
Periwinkle (See *Vinca*)							
Petunia hybrida Petunia	12-18"	Varied	12"	Sun, part shade	Fall	Spring and fall	Feed and pinch regularly; dislike heat of summer; good for bedding and mass planting.
Phlox drummondii Annual Phlox	10-20"	Varied	12"	Sun	Winter	Spring to summer	Good for bedding and cutting. Self sowing.
Pinks (See *Dianthus*)							
Portulaca grandiflora Portulaca	4-6"	Multi except blue	4-6"	Sun	Spring to summer	Spring to frost	Good in sandy soil; likes drought; colorful display.
Queen Anne's Lace (See *Daucus*)							
Salvia spendens Salvia	10-24"	Red	14-21"	Sun, shade	Spring or summer	Spring to frost	Good bedding; other colors now available.
Sanvitalia procumbens Creeping Zinnia	8"	Yellow or orange	18"	Sun	Spring	Spring to frost	Deep green foliage with yellow or orange blooms with dark eyes; trailing form; heat, drought and humidity resistant.
Scaveola aemula Fan Flower	24"	Blue White	12"	Sun	Spring	Summer	Blooms through summer heat; excellent for the border or container.
Snapdragon (See *Antirrhinum*)							
Stock (See *Mathiola*)							
Strobilanthes dyerianus Persian Sheild	3'	Plum	24"	Sun, part shade	Summer		Grown for the leaves which are bronze green overlaid with purplish-pink and frosted silver; great in containers or bed.
Sweet Pea (See *Lathyrus*)							
Tagetes Marigold	6-36"	Orange, yellow, brown, many shades	12"	Sun	Spring or summer	Summer until frost	Good bedding, edging, cut flowers; used in companion planting to dissuade pests; many varieties and sizes.

ANNUALS

*native Botanical Name Common Name	Height	Color	Space Apart	Exposure	Planting Time	Bloom Time	Comments
Thymophylla tenuiloba Dahlberg Daisy	6-8"	Golden yellow	6"	Sun	Spring	Spring to frost	Edging; feathery foliage.
Tithonia speciosa Mexican Sunflower	2-3'	Scarlet, orange	12"	Sun	Spring	Spring to frost	Compact; freely blooming; heat resistant.
Torenia fournieri Wishbone Flower	12"	Violet, yellow, white	8-10"	Sun, part shade	Late spring	Summer to fall	Blooms through heat of summer.
Trachymene coerulea Blue Laceflower	30"	Blue	12"	Sun	Seed or plant after frost	Spring to frost	Lacy blue clusters, reminiscent of Queen Anne's Lace.
Tropaeolum majus Nasturtium	12"	Shades of yellow to mahogany	15"	Sun	Sow seeds in fall	Spring	Prefers poor soil, poor flowering in rich soil; pinch regularly; good bedding, pot culture.
Verbena x hybrida Garden Verbena	8-18'	Pink, red, blue, lilac	18"	Sun	Spring	Spring to frost	Good drainage; heat tolerant; likes rich soil.
Vinca catharanthus roseus Vinca	6-18"	Varied	10"	Sun to part shade	Plants in spring	Spring to fall	Excellent; hardy; drought resistant; reseeds itself.
Viola tricolor Johnny Jump-Up	4-6"	Purple with white, yellow	6"	Sun, part shade	Plants in late winter or seeds in fall	Spring	Hardy, heavy bloomers; reseeds itself.
Viola tricolor hortensis Pansy	6"	Varied	6-8"	Sun, part shade	Plants in fall	Fall to spring	Biennial grown as annual; plants available in early fall; feed every two weeks; pick frequently.
Zinnia angustifolia Zinnia	8'	Orange	12'	Sun	Spring	Summer	Mounded or trailing form; very heat, drought, humidity resistant; not affected by mildew.
Zinnia elegans Zinnia	12-36"	Varied	12"	Sun	Seeds or plants in spring into summer	Spring to frost	Seeds sown every 2 weeks will give bloom until frost; may need staking; does not fail in heat of summer; feed frequently; colorful, good cut flowers; new creeping or trailing varieties. 'Rose Pinwheel'-deep pink, compact, mildew resistant.

Perennials

PERENNIALS

A most desirable attribute of perennials is that they need not be re-planted each year. Some need dividing every three or four years, while some prefer to remain undisturbed for years.

In gardening we refer to perennials as blooming herbaceous plants, ones with fleshy, soft, non-woody stems, the top growth of which usually dies back in winter. The crown remains alive and sends up new growth in spring.

Long hot humid summers and the short period of cold weather limit the number of perennials that can be grown successfully. However there are many varieties whose color, form, and time of blooming create a very important part of our landscape.

Perennials can be used effectively in borders or beds and in a combination with annuals and shrubs. They usually show up better against a background of shrubs, a wall or fence. The low growing ones are lovely in borders and in front of evergreen foundation and boundary plantings. There are perennials for dry, sunny sites, for low-lying damp areas, and for deepest shade. They are also at home in a low maintenance landscape.

PURCHASING:

Recent increased interest in perennials has assured their availability in the nurseries. The greatest selection of color and variety will be found in garden catalogs. These are listed in a separate chapter, "Sources."

PLANTING:

Since perennials will remain in one location for years, soil preparation before planting is of great importance. Basic needs are good drainage and a friable, fertile soil. Prior to working soil apply 2 inches of peat moss, 2 inches of compost, a complete fertilizer and lime. Work soil to a depth of 8 to 12 inches. Perennials are tolerant of variations in pH, but most do better under slightly acid conditions. Before preparation of the soil have your soil analyzed through the county extension agent for precise pH and nutrient recommendations.

FERTILIZING:

Perennials need regular fertilization for good bloom. Use a general purpose fertilizer at a rate of ¼ cup per 10 square feet every month during the growing season. Alternatively, you may use a slow release fertilizer.

MULCHING:

Use a 2 inch layer of mulch around each plant to conserve moisture and cut down on weeds.

WATERING:

Water weekly to a depth of 12 inches if there is no rain.

PROPAGATING AND TRANSPLANTING:

Propagation of perennials is best accomplished by division. Lift clumps in spring or fall with a spading fork. Carefully pull, cut or pry the clump into a number of divisions. In some plants such as chrysanthemums a hard woody center will appear. Discard this, resetting only the young outer sections.

You may also make stem cuttings. These will be true reproductions. Cuttings may be rooted in sand, peat or vermiculite. Review the chapter on "Propagation" for more specific instructions.

Seeds may vary from the parent plant because of cross-pollination, and because many of the plants are hybrids. When planting seeds of perennials, propagate at approximately the same time they would sow themselves. Usually they will not bloom until the second year.

PRUNING:

To promote continuous bloom spent flower heads should always be removed. Pinch out the growing tips for bushier plants. Clean up perennial beds during winter before new growth comes along.

PESTS AND DISEASES:

Perennials are among the healthiest of garden plants. Some are susceptible to disease and damage by various pests. Good hygiene practices in your flower bed will prevent much damage. Removing accumulated weeds and dead flower stalks removes the breeding ground for pests. Planning well drained beds eliminates the moist conditions favored by fungi. Avoid late afternoon sprinkling and over watering. Cut away, remove and destroy diseased portions. Pull weeds before they spread or go to seed. Practice a thorough clean-up before winter. Remove any debris and other likely homes for overwintering insects and diseases.

When the above fails and pests appear be ready to take appropriate measures. Aphids and spider mites can usually be removed with a strong stream of water from the garden hose. These and beetles, white fly, leaf hoppers, thrips and leaf miners can also be controlled, if necessary, by spraying with an insecticide. Follow package directions carefully.

PERENNIALS

*native *Botanical Name* Common Name	Height	Color	Space Apart	Exposure	Bloom Time	Comments
Acanthus mollis Bear's Breeches	1½-3'	Creamy	2'	Shade	Late Summer	Handsome; moist sites.
Achillea millefolium Yarrow	3'	Yellow, cerise, red, pink, white	12"	Sun	Summer	Pungent, long lasting, good for drying; native species invasive; many hybrids and cultivars.
Agapanthus africanus Lily of the Nile	3-4'	Blue, White	12"	Sun	Early spring- late fall	Tender bulb; heavy feeder; good container plant; not evergreen.
Agastache foeniculum Anise hyssop	2-3'	Varied	12-18"	Sun	Summer	Licorice scented leaves; attracts pollinators; drought tolerant; many new cultivars being introduced.
Ageratum (See *Eupatorium*)						
Amsonia *tabernaemontana* Blue Star	2-3'	Blue	1½'	Sun, part shade	Spring	Star-like flowers in clusters; moist, fertile soil.
Aquilegia spp. Columbine	18"	Various	8-12"	Part shade	May	Well drained but moist soil; blooms 2 weeks a year; morning sun only.
Artemisia ludoviciana Artemisia	2-3½"	Silver gray foliage	12-18"	Sun, part shade	Summer	Needs moisture, but good drainage; any soil; feathery, aromatic foliage. 'Huntingdon Gardens'; do not prune until late winter.
Asclepias incarnata Swamp Milkweed	2-4'	Pink, white	2'	Part shade	Late spring, Summer	Tolerates moist areas.
Asclepias tuberosa Butterfly Weed	1½-3'	Orange	1-2'	Sun	Summer	Native milkweed; dry, sandy soil; good for cutting; transplants poorly, dig deeply, do not separate; easily grown from seed.

PERENNIALS

*native Botanical Name Common Name	Height	Color	Space Apart	Exposure	Bloom Time	Comments
Aspidistra elatior Cast Iron Plant	1½"	Green foliage	8"	Shade, part shade	NA	Will withstand much heat and poor soil; variegated form available.
Aster spp. Michaelmas Daisy	½-6'	Lavender, blue	12-18"	Sun	Late summer	Best from divisions; good for cutting; average soil, not too rich.
Athyrium Goeringianum 'Pictum' Japanese Painted Fern	1'	Green-gray	1'	Shade, part shade	NA	Gray silver central stripe on green fronds, wine red stems; weeping habit.
*Baptisia alba Wild Indigo	2-3'	White	2'	Sun part shade	Late spring	Drought and soil tolerant; pea like flowers on erect stems.
Baptisia australis Wild Blue Indigo	3-4'	Blue	3'	Sun part shade	Spring	May be longer lived.
Bee Balm (See Monarda)						
*Belamcanda chinensis Blackberry Lilly	2-4'	Orange, yellow with black spots	12"	Sun	Summer	Grown from roots, seed, division; any soil; dried seed clusters good in arrangements; flowers close at night.
Blackberry Lily (See Belamcanda)						
Black-eyed Susan (See Rudbeckia)						
Bletilla striata Chinese Ground Orchid	1'	Lavender	10"	Part shade	Spring	Blooms on spikes; looks like miniature orchid. 'Alba'-white.

119

PERENNIALS

*native

Botanical Name Common Name	Height	Color	Space Apart	Exposure	Bloom Time	Comments
Bulbine frutescens	8-12"	Orange yellow	12"	Sun	Spring	Bright green succulent foliage with airy spires of orange yellow flowers.
Butterfly Weed (See *Asclepias*)						
Calopogon barbatus Grass-pink	1½-2'	Rose-pink	6"	Sun, part shade	Spring	Orchid, native to pinelands and grassy swamps; difficult to cultivate.
Candytuft (See *Iberis*)						
Cardinal Flower (See *Lobelia*)						
Ceratostigma plumbaginoides (*C. larpentiae*) Blue Plumbago	6-10"	Blue		Sun, part shade	Late summer	Tolerates drought; long-lived, vigorous grower; spread by underground runners; well drained soil, not too rich; deciduous.
Chrysanthemum leucanthemum Oxeye Daisy	1-2'	White	12"	Sun	Late spring, early summer	Blooms before shasta.
Chrysanthemum x morifolium Garden Chrysanthemum	2-5'	White, maroon, pink, lavender, bronze, yellow	12"	Sun	Fall	Best grown from cuttings and division; numerous varieties and forms; rich soil; fertilize.
Chrysanthemum nipponicum Nippon Daisy	18"	White	12"	Sun	Spring	Tolerant of seaside; pinch back to promote compact growth.

PERENNIALS

*native Botanical Name Common Name	Height	Color	Space Apart	Exposure	Bloom Time	Comments
Chrysanthemum parthenium Feverfew	8-24"	White with yellow centers	12"	Sun	Early summer	Hardy, long lasting; holds up well in arrangements.
Chrysanthemum x superbum (C. maximum) Shasta Daisy	1-2'	White	12"	Sun	Spring	Good for cutting; best propagated from clump divisions; many varieties.
Columbine (See *Aquilegia*)						
Coral Bells (See *Heuchera*)						
Coreopsis auriculata 'Nana'	8-10"	Yellow	6-8"	Sun	Early summer	Grown from division or seed easily.
Coreopsis lanceolata	1-4'	Yellow	12-18"	Sun	Summer	Grown from division.
Coreopsis verticillata Thread-Leaf Coreopsis	1-2'	Yellow	1½'	Sun	Summer-Fall	Erect bushy plant; drought resistant. 'Moonbeam' pale yellow.
Cuphea hyssopifolia Mexican Heather	1-2'	Varied	4'	Sun part shade	Spring summer	Tiny linear, leathery leaves with small flowers; use in boarders, several cultivars.
Daisy, Michaelmas (See *Aster*)						
Daisy, Shasta (See *Chrysanthemum*)						
Daylily (See *Hemerocallis*)						
Dianthus caryophyllus var. Border Carnations Pinks, many varieties	10-12"	White, rose, pink, maroon	10"	Sun	Spring	Forms mats of narrow leaves, blue green; attractive all year; do not mulch clumps.
	4-6"	Same				
Dicentra spectabilis Bleeding Heart	1-2'	Pink	1½'	Shade	Spring	Moist shade
Dryopteris erythrosora Autumn Fern	18"	Olive-green foliage	1'	Shade	NA	Evergreen though foliage becomes burned; well drained moist soil.

PERENNIALS

*native Botanical Name Common Name	Height	Color	Space Apart	Exposure	Bloom Time	Comments
Dusty Miller (See *Senecio*)						
Echinacea purpurea Purple Coneflower	2-3'	Varied	18"	Sun	Many weeks in summer	Divide every fourth year; good for cutting; many new cultivars available.
Eupatorium coelestinum Hardy Ageratum	2-3'	Lavender, blue	12"	Sun	Late summer	Delicate, fluffy flower heads; garden soil; good for cutting; invasive.
Eupatorium purpureum Joe-Pye Weed	4-7'	Purple	18"	Sun	All summer	Adapts well to average conditions; compact form good for wet areas.
Euphorbia corollata Redneck Baby's Breath	2'	White	12"	Sun	June to September	Wild Baby's Breath; leaves red in fall; cushion of small white flowers.
Feverfew (See *Chrysanthemum*)						
Four-O'Clock (See *Mirabilis jalapa*)						
Gaura lindheimeri	3-4'	White	1'	Sun, part shade	Late spring to fall	Rich well drained soil; remove spent flower spikes for continuous bloom; tolerates drought, heat.
Gazania rigens	6"-1'	White, yellow, orange	12"	Sun	May-July	Daisy-like flowers close at night; propagate by division and cuttings.
Gerbera jamesonii Gerbera Daisy	1½'	White, cream, yellow, orange, pink, red	12-15"	Sun	Spring-fall	Deep soil, rich in humus; excellent drainage; plant with crown above soil level; feed and lime often; protect from freeze; good for cutting; divide in early spring; heavy mulch.

PERENNIALS

*native Botanical Name Common Name	Height	Color	Space Apart	Exposure	Bloom Time	Comments
Geum Quellyon	12"	Scarlet	1'	Sun	Spring	Stunning; may be short lived; well drained moist area protected from afternoon sun.
Golden Rod (See Solidago)						
Hamelia patens Mexican Firebush	3-5'	Scarlet	3'	Sun	Spring until frost	Grey green foliage covered by clusters of scarlet flowers; drought tolerant; attracts pollinators.
*Hedyotis crassifolia Bluets	5"	Violet	4"	Sun	Spring	Diminutive wildflower found in open fields, dry places.
Helianthus angustifolia Swamp Sunflower	6-8'	Yellow	3'	Sun	Late summer	Large flowers for 4-6 weeks into fall; water and fertilize; many named cultivars.
Helleborus orientalis Lenton Rose	12-15"	Varied	2'	Shade	Winter	Pale green, pink or creamy white flowers in January lasting for months; handsome dark green evergreen foliage; needs rich soil.
Hemerocallis Daylily	2-3'	Shades of orange, pink, red, yellow	18"	Sun, part shade	Spring-fall	Grow from roots and divisions; any soil; hardy; outstanding; divide after 6 or 7 years.
Heuchera sanguinea Coralbells	6-8"	Red, pink, white	18"	Shade	Spring	Prized for its evergreen foliage; many new cultivars with colorful foliage; dainty flowers in spring.
*Hibiscus moscheutos Rose Mallow	4-6'	White, pink, red	30-36"	Sun, part shade	Summer	Moist soil; ample space; regular fertilizer; beautiful large flowers.
Hosta spp. Plantain Lily	16-24"	White, blue, lavender	1-2'	Shade	Summer	Grown mainly for foliage; some variegated; propagate by division; moist, rich soil.
Justicia brandegeana (Beloperone guttata) Shrimp Plant	2-3'	Red to brown bracts; also green and yellow	24"	Part shade	April-Nov.	Rich soil, moist but well drained; pinch to shape; good for cutting and in pots; protect in winter, red hardier than yellow; good for pot culture.

123

PERENNIALS

*native

Botanical Name Common Name	Height	Color	Space Apart	Exposure	Bloom Time	Comments
Lamb's Ears (See *Stachys*)						
Lantana camara Lantana	2-4'	Bi-color mixtures of yellow, red, pink, white, orange	2'	Sun, part shade	Summer to frost	Drought, sand and salt tolerant though hybrids less tolerant; tip pruning promotes more flowers; attracts butterflies.
Lantana montevidensis Trailing Lantana	1-2'	Lavender	2'	Sun	Summer to frost	Trailing form.
Liatris elegans Blazing Star	3-4'	White, purple	12"	Sun	July-Aug.	Native wild flower; grow from woody corms, rhizomes or seeds in deep soil; soil sandy, not too rich; good for cutting and drying.
Ligularia stenocephala Farfugium	2-3'	Yellow		Part shade	Summer	'The Rocket'-a superior cultivar; finer texture than most others.
Ligularia tussilaginea Ragwort Farfugium	2-4'	Yellow, orange		Part shade	Early fall	Humus-rich soil; abundant moisture; propagate by division; grown for foliage; dark green and variegated; many cultivars.
Lily-of-the-Nile (See *Agapanthus*)						
Lobelia cardinalis Cardinal Flower	2-3'	Red	12"	Part shade	Late summer	Attracts hummingbirds; must have moist soil; self sows; divide and replant each year after flowering.
Mirabilis jalapa Four-O'Clock	3'	White, red, yellow	18-24"	Sun	Summer	Fast spreading; free blooming; fragrant; well drained soil.
Monarda didyma Bee balm	30-40"	White, pink, lavender, red	12"	Part shade full sun	Summer	Moist soil; mint family; rampant growth; attracts hummingbirds.

PERENNIALS

*native

Botanical Name Common Name	Height	Color	Space Apart	Exposure	Bloom Time	Comments
Neomarica gracilis Walking Iris	2½'	Bluish-white	24"	Part shade	Early summer	Small, orchid-like flowers; mulch and protect in winter; also other species.
Nepeta x faasenii 'Walkers Low' Catmint	18-24"	Bluish purple	3'	Sun	April to October	Prolific bloomer; suggest shearing during season to remove spent blooms; not attractive to cats though catnip family; other cultivars.
Nierembergia scoparia	12-18"	White	10-12"	Sun	All summer	Best in mass; dainty but showy white flowers.
Odontonema strictum Firespike	3-6'	Red	3'	Sun	Summer	Glossy green, wavy-edged leaves; spikes of bright red tubular flowers; attracts hummingbirds.
Penstemon Beardtongue	1½-3'	Varied	18"	Sun	Spring	Bell shaped flowers on erect stems similar to foxglove; dead head to encourage reblooming; many hybrids.
Perovskia atriplicifolia Russian Sage	2-3'	Lavender-blue	12"	Sun	Late summer	Attractive cut-leaf gray foliage; flowers in spikes; cut back in winter.
Persicaria 'Red Dragon"	2-3'	White	4'	Sun part shade	Summer	Arching red stems; grown for foliage which is patterned and purple/burgundy with mint green and silver; forms large mounds; tiny white flowers.
Phlox divaricata	6-8"	Blue	6"	Part shade	Spring	Moist, rich soil. Easily propagated by seeds, cutting or division; well-drained soil.
Phlox maculata Wild Sweet William	2'	Mauve, pink	12"	Sun, part shade	June to September	Moist site; thin woods or in open; disease resistant.
Phlox paniculata	2-4'	White, pink, red	12"	Sun, part shade	Summer	Well-drained soil; best from division or roots.
Pinks (See *Dianthus*)						
Plumbago auriculata Blue Plumbago	3-4'	Light blue to white	2'	Sun, part shade	Spring to frost	Drought and heat tolerant; continuous bloom with masses of flowers.
Plumbago (See *Ceratostigma*)						

PERENNIALS

*native Botanical Name Common Name	Height	Color	Space Apart	Exposure	Bloom Time	Comments
Rudbeckia Black-eyed Susan Coneflower, Gloriosa Daisy	2-3'	Yellow, gold, mahogany	14"	Sun	Summer-fall	Well-drained soil; cut to encourage bloom; dwarf sizes available.
Ruellia Brittoniana Mexican Petunia	3'	Lavender	2'	Sun, part shade	Spring, summer, fall	Drought resistant plant that blooms for long period; requires no maintenance; tolerant of most conditions.
Salvia 'Anthony Parker'	3'	Purple	3'	Sun	Summer to fall	Dark purple flower spikes; compact, clump forming.
Salvia coccinea Texas Sage	1-2'	Red	1'	Sun	Spring-summer	Flowers on 2-7" spikes similar to the annual Salvia.
Salvia elegans Pineapple Sage	3-4'	Red	3'	Sun	Fall	Pineapple scented leaves; attracts hummingbirds in fall.
Salvia farinacea Mealy Cup Sage	2-3'	Blue	3'	Sun, part shade	Spring to fall	Slender spikes above foliage. 'Blue Bedder'-medium blue; 'Victoria'-dark blue-purple; 'White Porcelaine'-gray-white.
Salvia Greggii Autumn Sage	2-3'	Rich red, white, pink	2'	Sun	Spring to frost	Heat and drought tolerant; shrublike.
Salvia guarantica	3'	Blue	2'	Sun, part shade	Summer to fall	Rich dark blue to violet-blue flowers with long bloom period; several cultivars
Salvia 'Indigo Spires'	3-5'	Blue	3'	Sun	Summer until frost	Attractive to pollinators; twisting columns of furry blue flowers; do not cut to ground until spring.
Salvia leucantha Mexican Bush Sage	3-4'	Blue-white	3'	Sun	Fall	Drought tolerant; forms mound; deer resistant.
Salvia madrensis Forsythia Sage	6-7'	Yellow	6"	Sun	Fall	Butter yellow flower spikes until heavy frost.
Sedum acre	3-6"	Yellow	6"	Sun	April	Hardy; sun-loving; drought resistant ground cover; propagates easily.
Sedum spectabile	18"	Pink, red	8"	Sun	Sept.-Oct.	Easy to propagate; drought resistant; very hardy. Reliable classic-'Autumn Joy'.

PERENNIALS

*native

Botanical Name Common Name	Height	Color	Space Apart	Exposure	Bloom Time	Comments
Senecio cineraria Dusty Miller	1'	Silver gray foliage	10"	Sun	Spring-fall	Foliage plant; good for borders.
Shrimp Plant (See *Justicia*)						
Sisyrinchium atlanticum Blue-eyed Grass	1'	Blue	10"	Sun, part shade	Spring	Grass like leaves and starry blue flowers; moist areas; new cultivars.
Snow-on-the-mountain (See *Euphorbia*)						
Solidago spp. Goldenrod hybrids	18-36"	Light to deep yellow	12"	Full sun	Late summer-fall	Hardy, drought resistant; fine, new-named varieties.
Spiderwort (See *Tradescantia*)						
Spiranthes gracilis Slender Ladies'-tresses	1-3'	White	1'	Sun, part shade	Spring, summer	Native orchid found in thin woods, meadows and dunes; small flowers on a spike.
Stachys byzantina Lamb's-ears	12-18"	Lavender	12"	Sun	Summer	Handsome large, gray, wooly leaves; needs good drainage; afternoon shade.
Stokesia leavis Stokes' Aster	1-2'	Blue	1'	Sun, part shade	Early summer	Light sandy soil; grown from division; good for cutting but closes at night; native S.C. to Fla. and La.; outstanding perennial in this area; good border plant. 'Alba' white variety.
Strawberry Geranium (See *Saxifraga*)						

PERENNIALS

*native

Botanical Name Common Name	Height	Color	Space Apart	Exposure	Bloom Time	Comments
Tagetes lucida Mexican Marsh Marigold	2½'	Yellow to orange-yellow	12"	Sun	Spring to fall	Clusters of bloom fall to frost; mite resistant, drought resistant. (See Herbs)
Tiarella cordifolia Foam Flower	1'	White	9"	Part shade	Spring	Excellent, low maintenance perennial for shady garden, rich woods.
Tradescantia virginiana Spiderwort	2'	Blue	9"	Sun	Spring	Any soil; closes at night; related to wandering jew; divide by slicing into clumps; hybrids available.
Trillium cuneatum Sessile Trillium	10"	Deep red	12"	Shade	Early spring	Most common of trilliums; grows in deep woods.
Verbena canadensis Rose Verbena	8-18"	Red, pink	12"	Sun	Summer	Requires good drainage.
Verbena tenuisecta Moss Verbena	1'	Blue, purple	8"	Sun	Spring to fall	Long blooming, low growing. 'Alba'-white.
Veronica spicata Speedwell	2'	Blue, pink, white	1'	Sun	June to October	Well drained soil; flowers on spikes.
Viola Violet	6"	Purple, white	6"	Part shade	Early spring	Rich loamy soil; fertilize with bone meal; many species; native.

Yarrow (See *Achillea*)

Bulbs

BULBS

Bulbs are for every season and can be planted with ease in almost every conceivable garden condition. They can be planted indoors or outdoors, in beds or as borders. They can be massed alone or in combination with other blooming plants. They can be used for color, form, texture, and scent in the garden or cut and used indoors for flower arrangements. Bulbs can give a garden a very formal, planned appearance or, if naturalized, bulbs can make an area seem a carefree garden tended by Mother Nature herself.

Although each bulb has its own characteristics, they all share one that makes them different from other plants. They have a self contained food storage mechanism that gathers food from the leaves of the plant during the growth cycle and stores it to provide nutrients for future plants. These bulbous plants are divided into five different categories.

Bulbs: A true bulb is a miniature plant encased in leaves called scales, which contain a reserve of food. These scales are thin and paperlike and are tightly wrapped around the bulb. A disk, called a basal plate, holds the food-storing scales together at the base of the bulb, where the new roots emerge when the growth cycle begins. (Examples: tulips and daffodils)

Corms: A corm is the base of the stem that becomes solid with nutrients. It is covered by one or two dry leaves. Like the bulb, it has a basal plate from which new roots grow. A corm uses its food reserve during the growth cycle and perpetuates itself by developing new corms from buds that appear on top of or on the side of the old one (Examples: crocus and gladiolus)

Tubers: The tuber is unlike the bulb or corm because it has no dry leaves or basal plate. It does have a tough skin that generates roots from areas on its surface. It is usually fat and round with no particular shape. New growth shoots from buds or eyes. (Examples: caladium and ranunculus)

Tuberous Roots: This bulb is the only one that is a real root because its food supply is kept in the root tissue, not in the stem or leaf as in the other bulbs. These bulbs grow roots and through this fiber system they take in moisture and nutrients from the soil. They produce budlike tubers from which the new plant forms (Examples: dahlias)

Rhizomes: The rhizome grows horizontally below the surface of the ground and has stems that grow at intervals from the top and sides of the rhizome. (Examples: canna and some iris)

PURCHASING YOUR BULBS:

Bulbous plants are among the easiest to grow, but for real success one must select bulbs of high quality. Always buy from a reliable source, whether shopping at a local nursery or ordering from a catalog. Remember, it is better to pay for quality bulbs rather than to buy for quantity. Choose bulbs that are heavy, firm and free from soft spots and blemishes. It is important that the basal plate be solid. While considering your purchase, think of color, height and blooming time as well as where you wish to plant the bulbs. Have a general plan in mind and select accordingly. Plant your bulbs as soon after purchase as possible to prevent them from drying out. If storing is necessary, put the bulbs in a cool place, such as a refrigerator (except caladiums). Do not store in plastic bags because moisture can collect in the bag and cause damage to the bulb. Instead, transfer to a paper bag for proper storage.

PLANTING YOUR BULBS:

When ready to plant, choose a sunny location. Only a few bulbs will bloom in the shade. Bulbous plants can adapt to many types of soil, but most prefer a loose well-drained garden soil prepared with coarse builder's sand, bone meal and peat moss. Prepare the soil by digging approximately 12″ deep, thus loosening the earth so that the bulbs can be planted, and the roots will have room to grow. Consider the growth pattern of your bulb, so that it won't be crowded when it reaches the peak of its growth cycle. Dig your hole to the required depth. A bulb planter will make the chore easier. Place the bulb in the hole and cover. Water thoroughly. Fertilize with a balanced fertilizer at planting and again as the leaves begin to sprout. Use at the rate of 1 ounce per 2 square feet.

WATERING:

Watering becomes more and more important as the plant begins to grow and then bloom. The growing period is short and very quick, so the soil should be kept evenly moist during this period and until the leaves turn yellow.

MULCHING:

Mulching will help hold moisture in the soil and is recommended.

FERTILIZING:

Current studies show that bulbs do best when fertilized when the leaves begin to break through the ground, and again after blooming has ceased. Use a balanced fertilizer at the rate of ½ ounce or 1 tablespoon per square foot.

PRUNING:

Having now prepared for the growth of your bulb, you can enjoy the bloom. Remove the spent bloom with clippers or scissors, so that there will be no seed production. The bulb will then use its energy in storing food for next year's bloom. The leaves should be left to yellow because they are providing nutrients for the bulb. Once the leaves turn yellow they can be carefully cut off because the bulb is now dormant.

PESTS AND DISEASES:

Bulbs are relatively free of pests. Should rodents become a problem, mix red pepper or tobacco in the soil, or scatter a few moth balls around the bulbs.

LIFTING:

When bulbs are dormant they may be lifted or removed from the soil, but do so very carefully. Either divide or replant immediately, or shake off loose soil and dry for 7 to 10 days in the shade. Destroy the bulbs with soft spots. Dust those remaining with a fungicide to help control rot and disease. Store the bulbs in a dry mixture of peat moss and sand to prevent their becoming dry. This can be done in a porous bag or shallow tray. Place the bulbs in a cool, dry place where they won't freeze, and label them. Replant as you did the previous year.

FORCING:

To cause bulbs to flower under other than natural climatic conditions is called forcing. Crocuses, daffodils, hyacinths and tulips need an extended period of low temperatures for best flowering. Place in the refrigerator for 8 to 12 weeks. Mild climate bulbs as amaryllis *(Hippeastrum)*, paper whites and clivia do not require low temperatures. The key to success is good timing and a strong root system. Allow 6 to 10 weeks until bloom.

Tulips, daffodils, and ixias as well as those listed above may be forced in soil. Place rich potting soil in a pot with a hole for drainage or the bulbs will rot. Then put the bulbs in the pot almost touching each other. The flat side of the tulip bulb should face front as the lower leaf will appear at that point. They should be placed so that the bulb tip is even with the rim of the pot. Fill in soil around the bulbs, leaving just the tips showing, and then water to settle the soil. Add more soil if necessary. The bulb contains enough nutrients to support the growth cycle so do not fertilize. During early stages keep moist, but not wet, because the roots are forming. Place the pots in a cool, dark place where there is no threat of freezing. To force, bring the pots gradually into a warm, lighted (not in sunlight) environment. It will require approximately three to four weeks for the bloom to appear. If planted in October for January bloom, force the bulbs beginning in December. For continuous bloom, stagger bringing the pots into the light. Keep moist. If growth is occurring too quickly, delay the bloom by moving the pots out of the light. Narcissus can be transplanted outdoors in the spring, although their blooming cycle will be weakened for a few years. Discard all other bulbs.

CUT FLOWERS:

Many bulbs produce blooms that may be cut and used indoors for flower arrangements. Blooms that are just beginning to open should be selected for cutting. Cut the bloom, leaving behind as much foliage as possible. The remaining foliage will provide the nutrients for next year's bloom. Use a sharp pair of scissors to make a clean cut. Place the bloom stem in a bucket of water immediately after cutting. Do not mix tulips and daffodils in the same water because the sap from the daffodils injures the tulips. Let the blooms sit separately in water for a few hours before arranging together.

Because low foliage will foul the water, remove it as you arrange. Cut the stems at an angle under water and then arrange. To keep blooms from moving to the light, place a few copper pennies in the water. Flowers from bulbs are heavy drinkers so add water to the vase frequently.

HINT: In warmer climates, bulbs such as tulips, anemones, and hyacinths must be treated as annuals since they will not bloom as well after the first year. Nevertheless, the bulbs are fun for the gorgeous show they produce.

BULBS, RHIZOMES AND TUBERS

Key: R - Rhizome; B - Bulb; T - Tuber; TR - Tuberous Root; C - Corm; N - Native

Botanical Name Common Name	Key	Height	Color	Planting Directions Season Deep/Apart	Bloom Time	Comments
Achimenes	R	12-18"	Blue, red, purple, pink	Fall 1"/3"	Summer	Morning sun or light shade; loose soil; fertilize lightly.
Agapanthus orientalis Lily-of-the-Nile	R	24-30"	Blue, white	Fall, spring 2" deep 24" apart	Early summer	Sun or part shade; plant high; incorporate organic matter into soil; fertilize after blooming and again early spring; likes to be crowded or pot bound; dwarf form exists. 'Alba'-white.
Allium spp. Flowering Onion	B	8-18"	Pink, white, yellow	Fall, spring 2-3" deep 6-15" apart	Spring-summer	Sun; use for borders, small gardens, naturalizing and potting. *A. giganteum* (violet) grows to 5'.
Alstroemeria spp. Peruvian Lily	TR	2½-4'	Colorful blends	Fall, spring plant horizontally 6-9" deep 12" apart	Spring-summer	Light shade; protect from wind; mulch for winter, divide every other year; excellent for cutting; *A. pulchella* may be invasive.
Amaryllis (See *Hippeastrum*)						
Amaryllis belladonna Belladonna Lily	B,N	1½-2½'	Pink, white	Fall plant with necks just below soil level, 12" apart	Early fall	Sun; leaves appear spring and die back before flowering.
Anemone coronaria	B	10-14"	White, violet, rose, red	Fall soak overnight before planting; plant stem up, 2" deep, 6-8" apart	Spring	Sun; likes sandy soil and not too much water; 'De Caen' variety has single blooms, 'St. Bridget' double blooms; excellent for cutting; replant each year.

BULBS, RHIZOMES AND TUBERS

Key: R - Rhizome; B - Bulb; T - Tuber; TR - Tuberous Root; C - Corm; N - Native

Botanical Name Common Name	Key	Height	Color	Planting Directions Season Deep / Apart	Bloom Time	Comments
Belamcanda chinensis Blackberry Lily	TR, N	30-36"	Orange, yellow, red-spotted	Spring 1" deep 6" apart	Summer	Sun; leave undisturbed until crowded; easily grown from seed; black seeds follow bloom, these are good in dried arrangements.
Caladium bicolor	T	12-24"	Variegated foliage: red, white, pink, green	Late spring 2" deep 12" apart	Until frost	Semishade; mass in one color more effective; likes hot humid climate; dig and store in winter; can also be used in pots inside and out.
Canna X generalis	R	2½-6'	Pink, red, white, orange, yellow	Spring 1-2" deep 15-24" apart	Summer until fall	Full sun; plant in groups of 12 or more and divide every 3rd year; use for beds, pots and cutting; interesting large foliage; new dwarf varieties especially attractive.
Chionodoxa luciliae Glory-of-the-snow	B	6-8"	Blue	Fall 2" deep 3" apart	Early spring	Sun - part shade; plant in masses of 12 or more; replant every 3 years; needs little care; naturalizes.
Clivia Kaffir Lily	B	24"	Salmon	Fall	Spring 1" deep	Not cold hardy, therefore, plant in a pot; bring in and give a dry period in the winter; likes part shade and damp soil; prefers to be pot bound.
Crinum spp. Crinum Lily	B	1-5'	White, pink, crimson	Fall or spring 6" deep 12-18" apart	Spring 'til frost	Sun - part shade; plant bulb high and don't disturb; water well during growing season; fertilize in spring; mulch in winter.
Crocosmia spp. (Montbretia)	C	18-24"	Yellow, orange, red	Early spring 3" deep 2-3" apart	July-September	Sun; divide every third year; naturalizes well but may be invasive; excellent for cutting.
Crocus spp.	C	2-6"	White, yellow, purple	Fall 2-3" deep 2-3" apart	Early spring	Sun; best in mass planting; naturalizes; small gardens.

Daffodil (See *Narcissus*)

BULBS, RHIZOMES AND TUBERS

Key: R - Rhizome; B - Bulb; T - Tuber; TR - Tuberous Root; C - Corm; N - Native

Botanical Name Common Name	Key	Height	Color	Planting Directions Season Deep/Apart	Bloom Time	Comments
Dahlia	T	1-5'	All colors, except blue	Late spring 6-8" deep 3-4" apart	Summer to frost	Sun; pinch early for bushier, stronger plant; feed heavily; larger varieties may need staking; smaller varieties good for bedding, plant close together.
Daylily (See Perennials)						
Ginger Lily (See *Zingiberaceae*)						
Gladiolus spp.	C	To 3'	All colors except blue, bicolor blends	Spring 3-6" deep 6-8" apart at 10 day intervals to extend blooming	Summer to frost	Sun-part shade; water freely and fertilize regularly; stake as necessary-more deeply planted corms require less staking; use for cutting, leave four to five leaves on plant so corm may mature; lift and store after foliage dies. (Flowering diminishes each year if left in ground.)
(dwarf type)	C		Yellow, white, pink, salmon	Spring 1" deep 3' apart	Summer to frost	As above; may leave in ground.
Gloriosa rothschildiana Gloriosa Lily	T	6-10'	Crimson-margined with yellow	Spring, lay tubers on side 2-3" deep	Summer	Sun-at least half day; vine with tendrils forming at the ends of the leaves, give stout shrub, trellis or wire fence to climb on; exotic blooms (see cover graphic); excellent for cutting; tubers may remain in ground permanently but they tend to move around. To move, dig 2 weeks after the vine has died.
Gloriosa superba			Smaller bloom		Fall	
Haemanthus katharinae	B	12"	Hot pink	Early spring 4" deep 10" apart	Spring	Part shade; impressive flower balls, 6" diameter; plant bulb half out of soil; good in pot or in garden; allow a dormant period.

BULBS, RHIZOMES AND TUBERS

Key: R - Rhizome; B - Bulb; T - Tuber; TR - Tuberous Root; C - Corm; N - Native

Botanical Name Common Name	Key	Height	Color	Planting Directions Season Deep/Apart	Bloom Time	Comments
Hippeastrum spp. Amaryllis	B	1-2'	Red, salmon, white	Fall 2-3" deep 12-15" apart	Late spring early summer	Sun or part shade; plant with ½ of bulb out of soil; feed after blooming and again in fall. May force indoors.
Hyacinthus orientalis Dutch Hyacinth	B	8-15"	White, blue, pink, purple	Fall 4-6" deep 6-8" apart	Spring	Sun; fragrant blooms; use in small gardens and borders; refrigerate 6-8 weeks before planting; best treated as annual as subsequent bloom smaller (but more graceful).
Roman Hyacinth		6-8"	Blue, white, pink	As above	Early spring	Blooms less formal and bloom earlier.
Hymenocallis calathina Peruvian Daffodil	B	18-24"	White with green	Spring 4" deep 8-12" apart	Late summer	Sun or shade; water heavily in growing season; divide when blooming deteriorates.
Hymenocallis caroliniana Spider Lily	B,N	3-9"	Greenish white	Fall	Spring to summer	Found on riverbanks in semi-shade; rich moist soil.
Ipheion uniflorum (Brodiaea) Spring Starflower	B	6-9"	Blue	Fall 3" deep 3" apart	Spring	Sun; divide when bloom diminishes; naturalizes; may be invasive.
Iris						Vast genus with many species and hybrids; broad range of colors, bi-colors and blends. Divided into two main root classifications: rhizomes and bulbs.
THOSE WITH RHIZOMES:						
Bearded Iris (many hybrids)	R	4-10" 15;18" and 32-42"	Many	Fall-Winter 1" deep 12" apart	Spring	Bloom-prominent gold beard at top inside of falls; sun; alkaline, well drained soil; divide every 3-4 years; cut seed pods as they form. Some may resent heat but others will thrive; plant high.
Iris cristata Crested Iris	R,N	4-6"	Blue, white	Spring just cover 4" apart	Spring	Bloom-small crest in the middle of each fall; semi-shade; prefer alkaline soil, but will tolerate acid soil.

137

BULBS, RHIZOMES AND TUBERS

Key: R - Rhizome; B - Bulb; T - Tuber; TR - Tuberous Root; C - Corm; N - Native

Botanical Name Common Name	Key	Height	Color	Planting Directions Season Deep/Apart	Bloom Time	Comments
Iris japonica		16"	Lilac, white	16" apart	Spring	Mulch for freeze protection.
Iris laevigata	R,N	24"	Blue, white		Spring	Good bog plant.
Iris tectorum (Roof Iris)		8-10"	White, blue	Same	Spring	As above for bearded iris.
Beardless Iris	R			Fall		
Iris hexagona Flag Iris	N	2-3'	White, purple	1" deep 18" apart	Mid spring	Bloom-smooth stiff falls; sun or shade; moist soil.
Iris kaempferi Japanese Iris		2'	White	1" deep 12" apart	Late spring	Sun or shade; moist acid soil.
Louisiana Iris (several species)		2-3'	White, pink, red, purple, yellow	1-2" deep 8" apart	Late spring	Sun; moist soil, acid tolerant; keep mulched.
Iris pseudacorus Yellow Flag		3-4'	Yellow	1" deep 15" apart	Mid spring	Sun or part shade; fertilize; moist soil.
Iris siberian Siberian Iris		1½-2'	White, blue, purple	1" deep 12" apart	Early spring	Sun; moist soil; leave clumps undisturbed.
Iris spuria Spuria Iris		2'	White, yellow, bronze, blue, purple, bicolors	1-2" deep 12" apart	Late spring	Sun; acid soil; leave clumps undisturbed for years.
Iris unguicularis		1'	White, lavender, purple	1" deep 12" apart	Winter	Sun; good drainage.
Iris virginica	R,N	3'	Blue		Spring	Semi-shade; wet places, shallow water; thin damp woods.

THOSE WITH BULBS

Botanical Name Common Name	Key	Height	Color	Planting Directions Season Deep/Apart	Bloom Time	Comments
Dutch Iris (many hybrids)	B	1½-2'	Blue, yellow, white, wine red	Fall 5" deep 5" apart	Spring	Sun; well drained soil; good for cutting; most effective when planted in clumps. Of all iris, do best in Zone 9.

BULBS, RHIZOMES AND TUBERS

Key: R - Rhizome; B - Bulb; T - Tuber; TR - Tuberous Root; C - Corm; N - Native

Botanical Name Common Name	Key	Height	Color	Planting Directions Season Deep/Apart	Bloom Time	Comments
Iris reticulata	B	4"	Violet, purple	Fall 4" deep 4" apart	Early spring	Sun, alkaline soil; good drainage; blooms fragrant.
Ixia spp. Corn Lily	B	1-3'	Various	Fall 1" deep 4" apart	Early spring	Sun; sandy soil; rare but quite beautiful.
Leucojum vernum Snowflake	B	6-10"	Greentip white flowers	Fall 3" deep 4" apart	Early spring	Sun or part shade; naturalizes.
Lilium Hybrids Lily Hybrids	B	3-4'	All except blue	Fall 6-8" deep 8-12" apart	Spring and summer	Numerous varieties, sizes, shapes; plant in loose rich, well drained soil with deep penetration. Full sun to light shade with some needing protection from hot summer afternoon sun. When planting spread roots out placing bulb on a mound of dirt. Cover with soil, water and mulch. Divide in fall only when bulbs become overcrowded. Excellent long-lasting cut flowers. Most are fragrant.
Lilium auratum		4-6'	White with gold band		Late spring June	
Lilium candidum Madonna Lily		3-4'	White			
Lilium regale		3-4'	Ivory, white, shaded pink		Mid spring	
Lilium speciosum 'Rubrum'		4-6'	Pale pink with crimson spots		Summer	
Lilium tigrinum 'Album'		3-4'	White, orange-brown spotted		Early summer	
Lycoris radiata Red Spider Lily	B	15-18"	Rose red	As above	As above	As above
Lycoris squamigera Spider Lily	B	15-18"	Rose pink	Fall 4" deep 6-9" apart	Late summer early fall	Light shade; foliage in early spring dies early summer; best when crowded.

BULBS, RHIZOMES AND TUBERS

Key: R - Rhizome; B - Bulb; T - Tuber; TR - Tuberous Root; C - Corm; N - Native

Botanical Name Common Name	Key	Height	Color	Planting Directions Season Deep/Apart	Bloom Time	Comments
Montbretia (See *Crocosmia*)						
Muscari botryoides Grape Hyacinth	B	6-12"	Blue, white	Fall 3" deep 3" apart	Spring	Sun, part shade; naturalizes; does well if un-disturbed.
Narcissus Daffodil, Narcissus Jonquil	B	8-20"	Yellow, orange, white or combination of the three	Fall 3-6" deep 3-6" apart	Early through late spring	Loves sun, but tolerates light shade; naturalize well; excellent for cutting or forcing; hundreds of varieties and forms.
CLASSIFICATION						
Trumpet Narcissus						1 large flower to a stem; trumpet (cup) as long or longer than petals.
Large-cupped Narcissus						1 large flower to a stem; cup large (more than ⅓ the length of the petals) but relatively flat.
Small-cupped Narcissus						1 flower per stem, cup less than ⅓ the length of the petals.
Double Narcissus						More than one layer of petals; one or more flowers per stem.
Triandrus Narcissus						One to six dainty flowers per stem.
Cyclamineus Narcissus						One nodding flower with a tiny tubelike cup per stem; petals curved back from wavy-edged cup.
Jonquilla Narcissus						2-6 sweetly scented flowers on long stem; cup ⅓-⅔ length of petal.
Tazetta Narcissus						Clusters of 4-8 sweetly scented flowers; cups shorter than length of petals. 'Paper-white.' May bloom in December; fragrant.
Poeticus Narcissus						1 flower to a stem; white petals; small flat crown, edged with red.

BULBS, RHIZOMES AND TUBERS

Key: R - Rhizome; B - Bulb; T - Tuber; TR - Tuberous Root; C - Corm; N - Native

Botanical Name Common Name	Key	Height	Color	Planting Directions Season Deep/Apart	Bloom Time	Comments
Ornithogalum umbellatum Star of Bethlehem	B	12"	White	Fall 2-3" deep 3-4" apart	Spring	Sun; naturalizes well; excellent under trees.
Polainthes tuberosa Tuberose	T	to 3'	White	Spring 2" deep 8" apart	Summer, fall	Sun or shade; profusion of bloom; plant in groups; treat as annual; very fragrant.
Ranunculus asiaticus	T	12-15"	Orange, pink, red, white, yellow	Fall 1½" deep 6-8" apart	Spring	Part shade; well drained soil; soak tuber overnight and plant claws down; excellent for cutting.
Scilla siberica Squill	B	4-6"	Dark blue	Fall 3-4" deep 6" apart	Spring	Part shade; plant in masses; naturalizes well; mulch in fall; divide when crowded.
Tigridia pavonia Tiger Flower	C	1½'	Red, orange, yellow, rose, white	Spring 3" deep 6" apart	Summer until frost	Sun; water well in growing season; bloom lasts one day.
Tulbaghia violacea	B	12"	Violet	Fall just cover 6" apart	Summer	Sun or shade; continuous bloomer; plant in groups.
Tulipa Tulip	B	6-30"	Various	January after refrigeration 6" deep 6" apart	March-April	Sun, part shade; protect from wind; refrigerate for 6-8 weeks after purchase; best when planted in mass; lift and discard most varieties after bloom; excellent for cutting.

Tulips are grouped according to bloom time:

Early Blooming
   Fosteriana
   Mendel   Good for forcing.
Mid-season blooming
   Darwin Hybrid   Good for forcing; best in garden.
   Triumph   Good for forcing.

BULBS, RHIZOMES AND TUBERS

Key: R - Rhizome; B - Bulb; T - Tuber; TR - Tuberous Root; C - Corm; N - Native

Botanical Name Common Name	Key	Height	Color	Planting Directions Season Deep/Apart	Bloom Time	Comments
Late Blooming Darwin Cottage Lily-flowered Parrot						Good for forcing; good in garden. Good in garden. Flowers resemble lilies; good for forcing. Twisted ruffled petals.
Species tulips *Tulipa clusiana* Candystick Tulip		8"	Rose, white			May be left to naturalize.
Zantedeschia Calla Lily	R	2-3'	White, yellow, pink	Spring 3-4" deep 12-24" apart	Spring-summer	Good container plant; part shade, rich, moist, soil, good drainage; not easy to grow, needs right spot and conditions.
Zephyranthes atamasco Rain Lily	B,N	6-10"	White	Fall 2" deep 4-6" apart	Summer-fall	Sun or shade; good in small gardens; naturalizes well; leave undisturbed; bloom follows rain; leaves and bulb poisonous if eaten.

Herbs

HERBS

Herbs, long neglected in the United States, have experienced a recent revival. With the growing emphasis on the freshness and quality of the food that is consumed has come an awakened interest in the traditional culinary herbs for seasoning. Grown and cherished in Europe, the Far East, and the Mediterranean countries, herbs are a welcome addition to the American culinary scene.

There are also a number of herbs for landscape or decorative use. Some overlap with the culinary herbs, and with herbs for medicinal purposes. Many of these plants are beautiful and add unusual texture and color to a landscape plan with little additional cost. They have been used for this purpose for many centuries in Europe, in both formal and informal settings.

USES:

The uses of the culinary herbs are many. The flavor of many foods is enhanced by the addition of herbs, preferably fresh. When fresh herbs are not available, dried herbs are acceptable, but only one-third (1/3) of the volume is needed as the dried products have a far stronger flavor.

As mentioned, there are medicinal herbs, but this field should be researched thoroughly as many have potent side effects and should be used with caution.

The landscaping properties of the decorative herbs are well worth investigation and are encouraged as a long-neglected plant material, with a relatively low cost. A distinct advantage is the fact that the large majority are heat and drought resistant and even thrive on neglect. The decorative herbs have long been used to form the intricate patterns in knot gardens, a fascinating landscape tool as yet largely unappreciated in this country. The small, formal gardens in the restored areas of our southern cities would be enhanced by these traditional and beautiful designs.

A number of herbs may also be used for dyes and several have insecticidal properties. Three herbs, namely southernwood, tansy and wormwood, are effective as a flea repellent in a dog's bed, as a gnat repellent around a sunny pool or terrace, or, combined with mint and dried, as an effective moth repellent when placed in cheese-cloth bags and stored with woolens.

PREPARATION OF THE BED:

To determine whether lime and/or other additives are necessary, a soil sample, analyzed through your local county agent's office, is recommended. The soil of the southeastern U.S. is generally quite acid and, as the majority of herbs like a "sweet" soil, with a pH of 6 to 7, lime is usually a necessity, as is organic material such as well-rotted compost or weed-free manure. A mulch is seldom required as most herbs prefer a well-drained soil.

A bed raised with bricks, railroad ties, etc., is worth consideration. Where moisture and humidity are high, a number of herbs, namely thyme, rosemary and sage, would benefit from the added drainage of a raised bed. It is quite possible to lose these herbs during the humid heat and soggy, cool winters, if care is not taken to provide extra drainage. Sand may be introduced to the soil to aid in drainage. It becomes easier to remember the reason for this if one considers their native habitat— the dry, Mediterranean countries.

BUYING:

An increasing number of local nurseries and farm supply stores carry herb plants and seeds. It is important to choose plant material that is vigorous and not overly pot-bound or leggy. Alternatively the plants may be mail ordered. (See section on Sources.)

PLANTING:

Most herbs like as much sun as possible, but would find welcome relief in the summer if some shade were provided from the late afternoon sun. A cloudy day should be chosen for planting small plants if the weather is hot, or even warm. Hose watering is recommended immediately, with light misting for several days afterward. But take care not to overwater herbs. It is easy to rot the plants with too much moisture.

There are several good times to plant herbs. Hardy perennials should be planted in February and March, or in October and November. Cool weather annuals are planted also in February and March and in September and October. Hot weather annuals will not thrive unless planted after the soil is warm in the spring; April is the ideal time. Cool weather annuals include dill, chervil, parsley (biennial, but treat as an annual), upland cress, mache, arugala, borage, coriander, and fennel (Florence). Hot weather annuals include all kinds of basil, summer savory, and anise.

After seeds are planted, care should be taken to keep the soil fairly moist until germination occurs, and until the plants become well established. Thin as necessary.

CARE:

Herbs require relatively little care. Weed competition should be eliminated. After the plants are established, weekly watering should be sufficient, except during the summer heat.

Light applications of fertilizer, monthly during the growing season, will keep your herbs in good condition. A balanced fertilizer is recommended unless a supply of well-rotted compost is available.

Rosemary is the main herb that benefits from mulch. Hay or most leaves (not pecan), make a good mulch. Pine straw is not recommended as it produces acid conditions as it decays.

PESTS AND DISEASE:

Herbs are notoriously resistant to both pests and disease and are often used as repellents when interplanted with vegetables. Watch for holes in the leaves caused by insects, or defoliation of dill and fennel by caterpillars. On occasion, it may be necessary to spray or dust with a non-toxic insecticide.

PROPAGATION:

Both hot and cool weather annuals are propagated readily from seed. Care should be taken to soak parsley seeds overnight in warm water to hasten germination. Other seeds may be put directly in the ground.

Hardy perennials are difficult to start from seed, so it is recommended that plants be purchased, or cuttings rooted. Thyme, marjoram, tarragon, sage and rosemary root in moist soil in the spring, summer and fall. The mint family, including lemon balm, sweet basil, oregano, and any kind of mint, can be rooted at any time in water or damp soil. All of the above mentioned herbs may also be rooted by layering.

PRUNING:

Blooms should be pruned off all annuals regularly to keep the plant in the business of the production of leaves. In addition, other pruning need be done only for aesthetic purposes, e.g. to maintain a nicely shaped plant or hedge, or to retain the desired shape and design of a formal garden. It is unwise to prune perennials after October 1st, as this could encourage tender, young growth that would be susceptible to winter kill.

HERBS

Key: C - Culinary; D - Decorative; I - Insecticidal; A - Annual; P - Perennial; B - Biennial

Common Name / Botanical Name	Key	Spacing / Height	Planting Time Spring	Planting Time Fall	Varieties and/or Comments
Anise / *Pimpinella anisum*	C,A	Thin to 9"	April	X	Does not transplant well; seeds and leaves used for licorice flavor.
Artemisia	D,I,P	8-18" mound	Feb.-Mar.	Oct. Nov.	'Silver Queen,' 'Silver King,' 'Silver Mound'; heat and drought resistant; an addition to any landscape; do not prune in fall.
(Sweet) Basil / *Ocimum basilicum*	C,A,D (Opal)	Thin to 5-6"	Apr.	X	"The taste of summer"; 'Sweet,' 'Opal,' 'French Bush' and 'Cinnamon Basil'; harvest before flowering.
(Sweet) Bay / *Laurus nobilis*	C,D,P (tender)	Small tree in protected location, or put in pot and bring indoors in winter	Early spring in the ground, or anytime in a pot		Will probably be killed at less than 20 degrees F; well worth treasuring and protecting; a useful and decorative plant; adds delicious flavor to long cooked foods such as stews or soups.
Bee-balm / *Monarda didyma*	D,P	Invasive habit, mint family, keep contained/2-3' tall.	Feb., Mar.	Oct., Nov.	Pink, red, lavender blooms most of summer; takes some shade; leaves may be used for tea.
Borage / *Borago officinalis*	C,D,A	6-8" apart 12-18" tall	Feb., Mar.	X	Reseeds readily; cucumber-flavored leaves for salad and star-shaped blue flowers for garnish; not heat tolerant.
Caraway / *Carum carvi*	C,B	Thin to 6-8" 2' tall	Feb., Mar.	X	White or pink flowers; sow seeds where plants can remain for 2 seasons; seeds produce 2nd summer.
Chervil / *Anthriscus cerefolium*	C,A	No need to thin 6-12" tall	Jan., Feb.	Oct., Nov.	Cool weather, shade-loving annual; delicate, lacy leaves have mild flavor; one of the French "fine herbs"; sow seeds on top of soil; keep moist.
Chives / *Allium schoenoprasum*	C,D,P	Plant clumps 6" apart; thin every 2 years/10" tall	Feb.-Mar.	Oct., Nov.	Sun, rich soil; delicious mild, onion seasoning and charming border plant with lavender flowers; needs shade in hot weather.
Coriander / *Coriandrum sativum*	C,A	Thin to 4-5" 3' tall	Mar.	Sept.	Cover seeds well, they germinate in darkness; used extensively in Eastern and Mid-Eastern cuisine; not heat tolerant.
Dill / *Anethum graveolens*	C,A	Thin to 3-4" 3' tall	Mar.	Sept.	Dies out in heat and freezing weather; replant in fall; likes full sun, moderately rich, loose soil.

147

HERBS

Key: C - Culinary; D - Decorative; I - Insecticidal; A - Annual; P - Perennial; B - Biennial

Common Name / Botanical Name	Key	Spacing/Height	Planting Time Spring	Fall	Varieties and/or Comments
Dixie Rosemary / *Conradina canescens*	D,P	8-10" apart 12-18" tall	Feb., Mar.	Oct., Nov.	Small, silvery leaves, lavender flowers; very decorative year 'round; heat and drought resistant; dries well; full sun.
Fennel (Florence) / *Foeniculum vulgare*	C,B	10-12" apart 18-24" tall	Feb., Mar.	Oct., Nov.	Sweet, fertile soil; leaves and seeds used particularly with seafood; base of plant used as steamed or sauteed vegetable by Italians.
Garlic / *Allium sativum*	C,P D (flowers)	8-10" apart 2' tall	Feb.-Mar.	Oct., Nov.	Sun, sweet soil.
Garlic or Chinese Chives / *Allium tuberosum*	C,P,D (flowers)	6-8" apart 8-10" tall	Feb.-Mar.	Oct., Nov.	Hardy, heat and freeze resistant; mild garlic flavor used as chives; forms clump; divide every 2 years.
Horseradish / *Armoracia rusticana*	C,P	12" apart 2' tall	Feb., Mar.	Oct., Nov.	Plant 4 in. deep: may be harvested any time; rich, moist soil; regular nitrogen; may be divided in several years; part shade.
Lemon Balm / *Melissa officinalis*	C,P	6-8" apart 2'tall	Feb., Mar.	Oct., Nov.	Lemon scented and flavored; used where lemon flavor is desired or as dessert garnish, or to garnish ice tea, or gin and tonic; shade.
Lemon Grass / *Cymbopogon citratus*	C,P,D	12" apart 2' tall	Feb., Mar.	Oct., Nov.	Forms spreading clump of graceful grass; lemon flavor excellent for tea, marinade and in Oriental cuisine.
Lemon Verbena / *Lippia citriodora* (*Aloysia triphylla*)	C,P (tender)	10" apart 2' tall	Anytime		Sun to partial shade, moist soil; regular fertilizer; graceful plant useful for tea or wherever a lemon flavor is desired.
Marigold, Mexican Marsh / *Tagetes lucida*	C,D,P	12" apart 2-3' tall	Feb.	Sept.	Easy to grow French tarragon substitute; lovely yellow to yellow orange bloom.
Marjoram (Sweet) / *Majorana hortensis* (*Origanum majorana*)	C,P (tender)	6" apart 8-10" tall	Mar., Apr.	Sept., Oct.	Killed by 20 degrees F or colder unless protected; cuttings root easily in fall; likes sun; keep blossoms picked.

HERBS

Key: C - Culinary; D - Decorative; I - Insecticidal; A - Annual; P - Perennial; B - Biennial

Common Name / Botanical Name	Key	Spacing/Height	Planting Time Spring	Fall	Varieties and/or Comments
Mint / *Mentha spp.*	C,P	6" apart 1-2' tall	any time except in freezing weather		Rich, damp soil, partial shade; very invasive; Varieties: spearmint, peppermint, pineapple mint (variegated), orange mint (heat resistant).
Oregano / *Origanum vulgare*	C,P,D blossoms	8-10" apart 2½' tall	Feb., Mar.	Oct., Nov.	Greek oregano superior flavor; full sun, well-drained soil; use leaves for seasoning; purple flowers dry very well for arrangements.
Parsley / *Petroselinum crispum*	C,B,D (border)	5-6" apart 6-8" tall	Feb., Mar.	Oct., Nov.	Soak seeds 24 hrs. to hasten germination; partial shade gives heat protection; Italian Parsley has superior flavor.
Rosemary / *Rosemarinus officinalis*	C,P,D (trailing)	6-8" apart 2-3' tall	Feb., Mar.	Oct., Nov.	Full sun, sweet soil; hardy to 15 degrees F; good drainage.
Rue (Herb of Grace) / *Ruta graveolens*	P,D	8-10" apart 18-24" tall	Feb., Mar.	Oct., Nov.	Bluish-green leaves, yellow flowers in June; reseeds readily; beautiful sub-shrub for landscaping; heat and drought resistant; a Shakesperian herb.
Sage / *Salvia officinalis*	C,P,D	8-10" apart 18-24" tall	Feb., Mar.	Oct., Nov.	Variegated and tricolor sage nice for landscaping; purple flowers in July, August; hardy, heat and drought resistant; full sun, prune drastically in the spring.
Salad Burnet / *Poterium sanguisorba*	C,P,D (border)	8-10" apart 6-8" tall	Feb., Mar.	Oct. Nov.	Hardy, evergreen, cucumber-like flavor; makes a charming border plant.
Santolina (Lavender Cotton) / *Santolina chamaecyparissus*	D,I,P	12" apart 10-12" tall	Feb., Apr.	Sept.- Nov.	Decorative, hardy herb, both gray and green; the backbone of a European knot garden; easily pruned, heat and drought resistant; also insecticidal.
Savory (Summer) / *Satureja hortensis*	C,A	No need to thin 10-12" tall	Mar., Apr.	X	Full sun, hot weather annual called by French the "Bean Herb"; also good in salads.

149

HERBS

Key: C - Culinary; D - Decorative; I - Insecticidal; A - Annual; P - Perennial; B - Biennial

Common Name / Botanical Name	Key	Spacing/Height	Planting Time Spring	Fall	Varieties and/or Comments
Savory (Winter) / *Satureja montana*	C,P,D	6-8" apart / 8-10" tall	Feb., Mar.	Oct., Nov.	Hardy evergreen, deep green leaves. Good soup and stew herb, also good with game.
Tansy / *Tanacetum vulgare*	D,I	12-24" apart / 2-5' tall	Feb., Mar.	Oct., Nov.	Excellent decorative plant for full sun; prized for fern-like foliage and late summer bloom.
Tarragon (French) / *Artemisia dracunculus*	C,P	8-14" apart / 6-8' tall	Feb., Mar.	Oct., Nov.	Morning and midday sun only; ample moisture; periodic feeding with fish emulsion, nothing stronger.
Thyme / *Thymus vulgaris*	C,P	12" apart / 6-12" tall	Feb., Mar.	Oct., Nov.	In humid climate, space widely; need ventilation and good drainage or will get fungal disease in heat; raised bed preferred.
Thyme, Lemon / *Thymus citriodorus*					As above; more heat resistant.
Wormwood / *Artemisia absinthium*	D,I,P	10-12" apart / 1-2' tall	Feb.-Apr.	Sept.-Nov.	Pretty, gray-green leaves, said to repel gnats if planted around pools and patios. Full sun, heat and drought resistant. Repels fleas if clippings are placed in dog's bed.
Yarrow / *Achillea millefolium*	D,P	8-10" apart / 1-2' tall	Feb.-Apr.	Sept.-Nov.	Hardy, heat-loving perennial; comes in gold, rose, pink and white; blooms June-July. Blooms dry well.

SALADINGS: A category of European Salad Greens, easily grown in our cool, wet springs and falls, and unavailable in the U.S supermarkets.

Common Name / Botanical Name	Key	Spacing/Height	Planting Time Spring	Fall	Varieties and/or Comments
Arugala / Roquette	C,A	Thin to 4" / 10-12" tall	Feb.	Sept.	Hardy, mustard-like salad green.
Mache / Cornsalad	C,A	Same as above	Feb.	Sept.	Sweet, cluster of small leaves.
Misticanza	C,A	Same as above	Feb.	Sept.	Mixture of small, colorful salad greens.

Vegetables

VEGETABLES

Vegetable gardening is one of the most soul-satisfying activities. No plant can be more beautiful than a ladened eggplant bush, profusely blooming peas or beans, or the lush, curly leaves and varied colors of garden lettuce. Vegetables can be planted in a plot or mixed with ornamentals as edible borders.

Vegetables bought in the supermarket may have been picked green and may ripen in the truck on the way from California or Florida. However, in your own garden you can choose the time of harvest. Nothing can rival the flavor of a vine-ripened tomato, or just-pulled sweet corn plunged into boiling water. An added advantage to having one's own garden is the control over the use of chemicals and fertilizers.

The temperature in our area is both a trial and a delight. We have approximately 270 frost-free days. The searing heat and humidity of summer, however, causes many limitations. The greatest advantage of our climate is that we can have both a spring and a fall garden, as well as the usual summer garden.

PREPARATION OF THE BED:

As our soil is usually acid and sandy, drainage is generally not a problem. Site selection for the vegetable garden should be made with care so that there is proper drainage and sunlight for at least six hours a day. A soil sample should be sent to your county agent's office to be analyzed, as most of our soil needs lime, nitrogen, phosphorus and potassium. The soil test will give a prescription for fertilizing and liming. Fertilizing can be done with inorganic or organic fertilizers, or both. Organic fertilizer is usually added as compost.

The compost pile is a vital tool of the successful vegetable gardener. Almost any organic matter can go into the compost pile: leaves, grass clippings, sawdust, manure, old hay and vegetable and fruit waste from the kitchen. The pile should be periodically turned and watered. Lime, soil, and inorganic fertilizer would benefit your compost. Experience will tell when the compost is "done." Both compost and inorganic fertilizer can be broadcast or banded in rows between the plants. Use the fertilizer recommended by soil analysis or a balanced fertilizer. Dolomitic lime should be used according to need as indicated by the soil analysis. Hydrated lime acts more rapidly but lacks magnesium and can cause burning.

The tilling depends on one's strength and the size of the vegetable plot. Hand tilling with a spading fork is satisfactory for a vigorous gardener with a small plot. Otherwise, some form of mechanical tiller is advised. These tillers are available from many manufacturers in various models. They may be purchased or rented. The rear-tined type is preferred.

SOURCES:

It is fun to start your own plants from seed. Garden supply stores, farm supply stores and department stores are sources of supply for seed, as well as plants, implements and fertilizer. The avant gardener, however, awaits the arrival of the seed catalogs. Cole crops (cabbage, broccoli, etc.), eggplant, tomatoes and peppers can be started in flats in a sunny window, greenhouse or improvised cold frame. They should be started around the first of February. If the plants are purchased, select with care to be sure that they are vigorous.

PLANTING:

After the last frost, plants should be set out with proper spacing and kept well watered until they are established. Direct seeding should be done in rows, however, lettuce, leaf and root crops can be lightly planted in 2 foot wide beds. The soil must be kept moist during the germination and early growth of any vegetable. Drip irrigation is extremely effective during the early period of germination. After germination, weeding should start immediately since tiny weeds can be gently pulled more easily than larger weeds.

SEASONS:

There is joy in the abundance of a southern garden almost every month of the year. The gardener will find that the cole crops, (cabbage, broccoli, cauliflower and brussels sprouts), and the root crops (potatoes, turnips, carrots, beets and onions), as well as English peas and snow peas, do best in early spring. Late spring and early summer bring forth squash, cucumbers, tomatoes and corn in abundance. The hot summer yields southern peas, okra, eggplant and peppers. The biggest bonus for the vegetable gardener in the lower south is the fall garden. Irish potatoes are a good fall crop. Plant late in August or early September. The usual spring or summer vegetables can be planted; snap beans do well; squash and cukes are iffy. The leaf and root crops are especially successful in the fall. Lettuce can be planted in late August in partial shade, later in full sun, broadcast lightly in 18 inch wide, raised beds every two weeks. Spinach needs cooler weather to germinate well. Mustard, collards, and turnips (plant white hybrids) do very well. Plant cabbage, broccoli and cauliflower plants rather than seeding directly. The late winter harvest depends, of course, on the weather. A warm winter can keep the table in fresh vegetables.

CARE:

The hoe, which has been with us for 5,000 years, is still the best weeder. The mechanical tiller or hand plow can also be used. Cultivation should be gentle and just deep enough to kill the weeds. Pull dirt onto the stems of plants, (i.e., mulch with dirt). Hand weeding may also be necessary.

Watering should be done after planting and about once a week if there is no rain. Seeds and seedling plants must be kept moist. Later in growth, watering should be thorough and deep, an inch of water once a week, or if very hot, as often as necessary. Drip irrigation is an efficient means of watering (see Garden Care under watering).

Vegetables can be divided into heavy feeders and light feeders. You should avoid over fertilizing, particularly with inorganic fertilizers, which should be placed near, but not on the plant. Small, frequent feedings are advised.

Mulching has distinct advantages as well as disadvantages. Mulching discourages weeds and conserves moisture, but it encourages fungus growth, a common problem in warm humid climates. Mulching can be done with black plastic, newspapers (only black and white, no comics, please), or organic material such as peanut hulls or hay.

PESTS AND DISEASE:

The vegetable garden has many enemies in the world of insects, viruses, fungi and bacteria. Two special problems are nematodes and fungi. The nematodes cause stunted small plants. Pull one up and the roots are stubby or have nodules. Fungi cause "dampening off" of seedlings. Seeds germinate but soon die. It is beyond the scope of this book to deal with the many specific problems. Always use the least toxic effective agent. Follow the recommendation of the county extension agent for insect and disease control. Before using any chemical, read and follow all directions. Chemicals come as either liquids or wettable powders for spraying, or powders for dusting. Don't forget the hand killing of insect pests in a small garden. Downy mildew and fungus diseases of tomatoes and cucurbits must be prevented, not treated. Therefore, regular, early spraying with a fungicide is recommended. Interplanting with marigolds may help the nematode problem.

GENERAL HINTS AND TIPS:

On peas and beans, use soybean inoculant for nitrogen-fixing bacteria. It can be obtained from farm supply stores.

Plant pea and bean crops thickly and do not thin them. Other crops should be thinned and carefully spaced, especially root crops.

Do not shade low-growing crops with tall ones.

Succession planting, to extend the season, is difficult in warm areas. The heat causes everything to mature together.

Do not over-water; do not under-water.

Do not over-fertilize; do not under-fertilize.

Companion planting of herbs and marigolds can discourage some pests.

If possible, plant several varieties of the same vegetable.

Pick produce when it is barely mature.

Keep vegetable picked; most plants stop producing when they have produced seeds for reproduction.

Watch your crop carefully for diseases and deficiencies.

Till spent crops and weeds, except tomatoes, into the earth immediately.

Replant southern peas after most spring crops.

Space your rows according to the requirement of the crop. Corn takes a lot of room and is for a big garden. Cucumbers can be raised vertically on a trellis. Stake your tomatoes; you will get more yield and they will take less room.

Separate cucurbits: squash, cukes, melons, etc. They will freely cross-pollinate.

Rotate crops to discourage disease.

The fall garden is tricky. Insect pests are prevalent in late August and September when most fall vegetables are planted.

Suggestions for a very small garden are lettuce, eggplant, tomatoes and a few squash.

Tomatoes and eggplant can be raised in pots or cans.

Consult your seed catalog for new varieties. The All American seed selections are excellent and reliable each year.

Keep a record of your successes and failures. Don't forget to plant your culinary herbs for seasoning.

THE SECRETS OF SUCCESSFUL TOMATOES:

Growing tomatoes in this climate requires special care. Because Verticillium and Fusarium wilt are problems, buy plants with resistance to the wilts labeled F and V. In addition blossom end rot and petal fall may be a problem. Adequate lime will prevent blossom end rot, but calcium may be needed as well. (Blossom end rot appears as a black spot at the blossom end of the tomato.) The plants should be planted deeply. Keep lower branches pruned, mulch well and stake the plants. Tomatoes are need regular fertilizer and moderate amounts of water. At the end of the season, destroy the plants and next year put your tomato patch elsewhere to avoid the wilts.

There are dozens of different cultivars. You may buy the plants at a garden supply store or raise them from seed. Tomatoes are either determinant, producing all at once, or indeterminate, producing all season. (See page159 for selections.)

VEGETABLES

Name	Days To Maturity	Varieties*	Planting Dates Spring	Fall	Seeds/Plants per 100 ft.	Distance Between Rows/Plants	Depth To Plant	Comments
Asparagus	3rd year	Mary Washington	Jan.-Feb.	Nov.-Dec.	50 roots	36"/24"	10"	Work rotted manure and a sprinkling of 5-10-15 into a trench 8" deep. Cover roots & mulch. Fertilize with 5-10-15 in Jan. Harvest lightly the 2nd year, only 1 month 3rd year, not at all before. Do not cut foliage back until killed by frost. Add compost annually.
Beans, Bush	50-60	Tendergreen, Harvester, Roma, Burpee, Brittle Wax (yellow), Fin de Bagnols (French), Blue Lake	Mar. 1-Apr. 15	Aug. 20-Sept. 20	½ lb.	24"	1-1½"	Make successive plantings for long seasons; plant thickly and inoculate seeds with soybean inoculate, a nitrogen-fixing bacteria. Keep picked regularly for maximum harvest.
Beans, Butter	65-75	Bush: Fordhook, Jackson Wonder. Pole: Burpee's Best, Carolina Sieva	Mar. 1-June 1	July 10-Aug. 1	½ lb.	24"	1"	Plant thickly; use inoculant.
Beans, Pole	60-75	Kentucky Wonder, Stringless Blue Lake, Burpee Golden, Romano	Mar. 1-Apr. 15	Aug. 20-Sept. 20	½ lb.	24"	1-1½"	Must be fenced or poled; use inoculant; will bear until frost with regular care.
Beets	55-65	Detroit Dark Red, Burpee Red Ball, Ruby Queen, Early Wonder	Feb. 15-Mar. 15	Sept.	1 oz.	18"/4"	1"	Thin carefully to 4"; pick when small.
Broccoli	60-80	Green Comet, Green Duke, DiCicco, Premium Crop	Feb. 15-Mar. 15	Sept.	100 plants	24"/10"	Cover roots	Start with plants; feed regularly with nitrogen while growing.
Brussel Sprouts	70-85	Jade Cross Hybrid	Feb. 15-Mar. 15	Sept.	100 plants	24"/10"	Cover roots	Keep picked; provide regular nitrogen.
Butterpeas	70	Dixiewhite	Apr. 1-May 1	July 10-Aug. 10	½ lb.	24"	1"	Plant thickly; use inoculant, keep picked; regular fertilizer.
Cabbage, Chinese	65-80	Round Dutch, Early Jersey Wakefield, Ruby, Pak Choy, Burpee Hybrid	Feb. 15-Mar. 15	Sept.	100 plants	24"/10"	Cover roots	Buy plants; provide regular nitrogen; pick when heads are firm.

VEGETABLES

Name	Days To Maturity	Varieties*	Planting Dates Spring	Planting Dates Fall	Seeds/Plants per 100 ft.	Distance Between Rows/Plants	Depth To Plant	Comments
Cantaloupe	80-90	Burpee Ambrosia Hybrid (by far the best for this climate)	Mar. 25-Apr. 20	X	1 oz.	60"/42"	1½"	Needs alkaline soil, add lime.
Carrots	70-80	Nantes, Chantenay, Danvers	Jan. 15-Mar. 20	Sept.	½ oz.	10"/4"	1"	Thin to 4 inches; keep weed-free or mulch; needs deep loose soil.
Cauliflower	55-60	Snow Crown, Self Blanche, Burpee Early White Hybrid, Snow Bird	Feb. 15-Mar. 20	early Sept.	100 plants	24"/10"	Cover roots	Buy plants; tie leaves over head when it starts to form if not self-blanching.
Collards	55-60	Georgia, Vates	Feb. 15-Mar. 15	Aug. Sept.	½ oz. or plants	24"/12"	1" or cover roots	Pick leaves from the bottom; better after frost.
Corn (sweet)	65-100	Silver Queen (white), Merit (yellow), Golden Bantam, Country Gentleman, Golden Queen, Truckers Favorite	Mar. 15-June 1	X	¼ lb.	24"/12"	½"	Plant several varieties & stagger planting; sidedress with nitrogen 2 times; keep weed-free until plants are up; plant in block for better pollination.
Cucumbers	50-55	Burpee Hybrid, Poinsett, Burpless Hybrid, Comichon (for pickling)	Mar. 15-May 1	Aug. 15-Sept. 15	¼ lb.	3-6 seeds in hills 3' apart	1½"	Keep picked; successive plantings.
Eggplant	75-90	Black Beauty, Ichiban Hybrid (Japanese), Dusky	Apr. 1-May 1	July 10-July 25	50 plants	36"/2"	Cover roots	Buy plants; sidedress with nitrogen; pick when small.
Leeks	110-130 from plants	Broad London, Titan	Feb.	Aug. 15-Sept. 15	300 plants	18"/4"	¾" for seeds	Plant in 4" deep trenches, cover seeds ¾", gradually draw in earth as plants grow; frost hardy, holds well in ground.
Lettuce	60-85	Looseleaf: Park's Master Chef Blend (mixture), Oakleaf, red & green, Romaine; Head: Burpee Bibb, Butter Crunch, Reinedes Glaces, Boston	Jan. 15-Apr. 15	Sept.	¼ oz.	18"/pick to thin	½"	Easy to grow except in extreme heat or cold; sidedress with regular nitrogen; pick to thin; plant several varieties; successive plantings; regular watering.

157

Name	Days To Maturity	Varieties*	Planting Dates Spring	Planting Dates Fall	Seeds/Plants per 100 ft.	Distance Between Rows/Plants	Depth To Plant	Comments
Mustard	40-50	Florida Broadleaf, Southern, Curled, Tender green Mustard, Spinach	Feb. 1-Apr. 1	Aug. 1-Oct. 15	½ oz.	18″	½″	Easiest green to grow; pick tender leaves, or pick to thin.
Okra	55-60	Clemson Spineless, Dwarf Green, Green Velvet	May 1-July 1	X	1 oz.	36″/12″	1″	Thin to 12 inches; keep picked; provide regular fertilizer and water.
Onions	42-55	Granax (Vidalia), Evergreen White Bunching, Spanish Yellow	Jan. 15-Mar. 25	Sept.-Dec.	300 plants	18″/24″	¾″	Buy plants or sets; pick at any time for tops or bulbs; heavy feeder; plant shallow; for mature onions, leave in ground until top dies.
Peas, Garden (green)	60-70	Early Alaska, Thomas Laxton, Wando	Jan. 15-Feb. 15	Sept.	1 lb.	24″	1½″	Plant thickly; use soybean inoculant; keep picked.
Peas, Snow	60-70	Sugar Snap, Sugar Bow, Sugar Bon, Dwarf Gray Sugar	Jan. 15-Mar. 1	Sept.	1 lb.	24″	1½″	Plant thickly; use soybean inoculant; keep picked.
Peas, Southern (summer)	60-70	Blackeye, Purple Hull, White Acre & many more	Apr.-Aug.	X	½ lb.	24″	1½″	Plant thickly; use soybean inoculant; plant several varieties.
Peppers, Bell	65-80	California Wonder (green), Golden Harvest (golden), Yolo	Apr. 1-June 1	X	50 plants	36″/2″	Cover roots	Buy plants; sidedress with nitrogen; superior flavor if left on the bush to yellow or red.
Peppers, Hot	65-90	Jalapeno, Cayenne & many more	Apr. 1-June 1	X	50 plants	36″/2″	Cover roots	Buy plants; sidedress with nitrogen; plant at distance from sweet peppers to prevent interbreeding.
Potatoes, Irish	70-90	Red Pontiac, White Kennebac	Jan. 15-Mar. 1	Aug. 10-Sept. 1	12 lbs.	24″/12″	5″ or plant on surface under mulch	Heavy feeder; likes acid pH; cut into chunks–each chunk must contain an eye; let pieces scab 24 hours before planting.
Potatoes, Sweet	90-150	Buy slips or tubers to cut up	Apr. 15-June 15	X	100 plants	24″/12″	Cover roots or plant 4″	As above.

VEGETABLES

Name	Days To Maturity	Varieties*	Planting Dates Spring	Planting Dates Fall	Seeds/Plants per 100 ft.	Distance Between Rows/Plants	Depth To Plant	Comments
Radishes	25-30	Cherry Belle, Scarlet Globe, French White	Jan. 15-Apr. 1	Sept.-Oct.	1 oz.	24"/1"	½"	Pick when small.
Rutabaga	40-65	Burpee Purple, Top Yellow	Jan. 15-Mar. 5	Aug. 1-Sept. 15	½ oz.	18"/4"	1½"	Thin to 6"; hard center means boron deficiency–add Borox.
Spinach	40-45	Bloomsdale, Melody Hybrid	Jan. 15-Mar. 15	Sept.-Oct.	1 oz.	18"	¾"	Feed regularly with nitrogen; provide regular moisture.
Squash, summer	40-55	Yellow Crookneck, Zucchini, Patty Pan, Scallopini	Mar. 15-May 15	Aug. 1-Aug. 20	1 oz.	36"/24"	1½"	Pick when small; keep picked.
Squash, Winter	85-100	Acorn, Butternut, Sweet Dumpling, Spaghetti Squash	Mar. 15-July 1	X	1 oz.	36"/24"	1½"	Leave on the vine until skin is hard; store in a dark, cool place; keeps all winter.
Swiss Chard	40-45	Burpee Fordhook, Rhubarb (red)	Jan. 15-Mar. 15	Sept.-Oct.	1 oz.	18"	¾"	Hearty, heat and cold-resistant green similar in flavor to spinach; feed regularly with nitrogen; provide regular moisture.
Tomatoes Determinate (bears for a limited time) Indeterminate (bears until frost with care)	70-90	Big Boy, Big Girl, Better Boy, Marglobe, Rutgers, Celebrity, Floramerica, Early Girl Roma, Cherry	April-July	Aug.	50 plants	48"/24"	Cover roots	Heavy feeder-regular fertilizer; moderate amount of water; see page 155 for more information.
Turnips	40-65	White Globe	Jan. 15-Mar. 15	Aug. 1-Sept. 15	½ oz.	18"/4"	1½"	Thin to 6"; hard center means boron deficiency-add Borox.
Watermelon	80-90	Burpee sugar Bush, Charleston Gray, Jubilee	Mar. 20-May 1	X	½ oz.	96"/96"	1½"	Plant in newly cleared soil, if possible.

*This is list of suggestions. There are a number of new improved varieties that come out each year. Always check the All-America selections. They frequently are a vast improvement over the old.

NOTES

Vines

VINES

The magical vine! It hides a multitude of sins: bad architecture in buildings, unsightly fences, compost piles, trash cans, fuel tanks and chimneys. It hides the harshness of wire fences and bare walls, shades patios and porches, and screens out unattractive views. It was used as camouflage in World War II because of its ability to grow back quickly. Vines can act as ground cover, holding soil and covering barespots where grass will not grow. Vining is no accident, but a trait that allowed plants to survive in the competitive world of vegetation.

Vines also add decorative planting, vertical interest, play of light and shadow, flowers, fruit, and texture. They are excellent for small gardens. They take so little space and give a mature appearance to a new garden.

It is most important to consider the exact reasons for using vines, and to select the ones that best suit your needs. Vines are most versatile, fast growing, and almost free of pests. They require a minimum of care and are easy to maintain, and rightly chosen, they can perform a valuable function. Wrongly chosen, they can become a nightmare. Know the characteristics of your vine choice in reference to its location, whether its a fast or slow grower, neat or rampant. Does it demand too much attention? Does it fit the space? A vine should be considered an accent plant unless it has some special function.

Most vines require sun and good soil, at least to get started. After being established, a perennial vine should be able to grow on its own with minimum care. It will grow in partial shade, but will not flower as it should.

Vines have several **methods of attaching** themselves. All should be given the proper means of support. They all grow by elongating their stems, some faster than others.

Trailing type (Cape Honeysuckle and roses) must be tied to a support to keep upright. Without this, they will trail on other plants.

Twining types (jasmine and wisteria) twine around objects for support.

Tendril type (grape and clematis) send out tendrils that grow from petioles, leaves, or stems to coil round and round the nearest vertical support.

Rooters (ivy) send out holdfasts or root-like structures to cling to surfaces. This group is tenacious, and can cause damage to stucco and wooden buildings especially, to window casings and eaves.

There are many attractive vines that we may enjoy. The list that follows includes some of the more useful.

VINES

Key: D - Deciduous; E - Evergreen; A - Annual; P - Perennial; N - Native

Botanical Name Common Name	Key	Exposure	Comments
Actinidia chinensis Kiwi	D,P	Sun, part shade	Delicious fruit in summer; requires plants of both sexes; luxuriant foliage; climbs rapidly (25 ft.) by twining; no pests; prune to maintain size; use for accent; texture coarse; moderately hardy.
Akebia quinata Five-leaf Akebia	P,E	Full Sun	Lovely, slender woody vine; delicate foliage; small, fragrant flowers in spring, clusters of purple in fall; well drained soil; grows to 30 feet.
Allamanda (See Patio Plants)			
Antigonon leptopus Coral Vine	D,P	Sun	Clusters of coral-pink flowers late summer until frost; climbs rapidly (40 ft.) by tendrils; flowers better in poor soil; prune hard, even to ground, in late fall; texture medium to coarse.
Aristolochia durior Dutchman's pipe	D,P,N	Full or semi-sun	Twining vine with small, brownish flowers, profuse in fall. Heart-shaped leaves to 1' long. Thrives in ordinary well-drained soil.
Bignonia capreolata Crossvine	E,P,N	Sun, part shade	Native; orange-red trumpet-shaped flower in spring, dark green foliage; grows rapidly (50-60 ft.) by tendrils which have adhesive discs; no pests; train on wire fences or walls.
Bignonia (See *Clytostoma*)			
Bouganvillea (See Patio Plants)			
Campsis radicans Trumpet Creeper	D,P,N	Full or semi-sun	Vigorous woody vine; orange trumpet-like flowers; prune in early spring to encourage flowering; climbs by aerial roots; needs support; may cause dermititis.
x tagliabuana Madame Galen			Vigorous hybrid with larger flowers in scarlet and orange.
Clematis armandii Armand Clematis	E	Sun	Showy white flowers, spring, on previous year's growth; grows rapidly (15-20 ft.) climbing by twisting petioles; shade roots from summer sun with mulch or bricks; prune after bloom to control size and shape; use on trellis as accent.
Clematis x Jackmanii Large-flowered Clematis Cultivars	D,P	Sun	Large showy flowers - white, purple, pink in summer; must be provided with protection from our summer afternoon sun; roots shade; roots shade; roots must be cool, use mulch or bricks to cover roots; restrained growth; climbs by twining (5-30 ft.); likes lime; use as accent on wall, post or shrub.

163

VINES

Key: D - Deciduous; E - Evergreen; A - Annual; P - Perennial; N - Native

Botanical Name Common Name	Key	Exposure	Comments
Clematis paniculata Sweet Autumn Clematis (Japanese Clematis)	D,P	Sun	Showy display of small fragrant white flowers in early fall; vigorous growth (30 ft.); climbs by twining; dense growth, prune out old wood yearly - blooms on current season's growth; use as decorative screen.
Clerodendrum (See Patio Plants)			
Clytostoma callistegioides (*Bignonia speciosa*) Argentine Trumpet Vine	E	Sun	Flowers purplish mauve with white throat and two purple lines running to each petal; profuse blooming through late spring and summer; climbs by tendrils; may be top damaged in severe freeze.
Euonymus fortunei Wintercreeper	E,P	Sun, shade	Dark green foliage with whitish veins; growth moderate - 3-6 ft.; climbs by aerial roots; watch for scale; use as screen in shade.
Euonymus fortunei radicans Common Wintercreeper	E,P	Sun, part shade	Good evergreen vine for color; clings by tiny roots; pests - Euonymus scale.
X*Fatshedera lizei* (*Fatsia x Hedera*) Tree Ivy	E,P	Part shade, shade	Dark green, large ivy-like leaves; requires support to climb; prune to train; rapid growth (8-9 ft.); watch for aphids; use as espalier in narrow or broad strips against a wall.
Ficus pumila Climbing Fig (Fig Vine)	E,P	Part shade, shade	Light green foliage, climbs by aerial roots to 30 ft., leaves are held flat against the wall; rapid growth; trim young erect growth and old main stems; keep thinned to prevent insects; use to cover masonry walls; fruiting branches hang out; may be damaged by severe cold.
Fig Vine (See *Ficus*)			
Gelsemium sempervirens Carolina Jessamine	E,P,N	Sun, shade	Native; display of yellow fragrant flowers early spring; growth rapid to 20 ft., climbs by twining; prune to control after flowering; no pests; good screen on fences and trellises; poisonous.
Gloriosa Lily (See Bulbs)			

VINES

Key: D - Deciduous; E - Evergreen; A - Annual; P - Perennial; N - Native

Botanical Name / Common Name	Key	Exposure	Comments
Hedera canariensis / Algerian Ivy	E,P	Part shade, shade	Glossy dark green foliage forms mass of trailing vine, climbs by aerial roots to 30 ft., texture coarse; prune only to control; use over walls; 'Canary Cream' - green leaves with cream colored margins; moderately heavy.
Hedera helix / English Ivy	E,P	Part shade, shade	Dark green leaves; climbs by aerial roots to top of support then trails over; rapid growth to 50 ft.; medium to coarse texture; varieties available are small leaved and variegated; do not allow to climb valuable trees; very hardy; very invasive; should be used in containers.
Honeysuckle (See *Lonicera*)			
Ipomoea alba (*Calonyctium aculeatum*) / Moon Flower	D,A	Sun, part shade	Wonderful large white flowers midsummer until frost, flowers open at night; climbs rapidly to 40 ft. by grasping; use for summer bloom on fence or wall; the opening bloom delights young children; large seeds easy to gather and restart.
Ivy (See *Hedera*)			
Jessamine (See *Gelsemium*)			
Jasmine, Star (See *Trachelospermum*)			
Jasminum floridum (See Shrubs)			May be used as espalier; train against wall.
Kiwi Vine (See *Actinidia*)			
Lantana montevidensis / Trailing Lantana	D,P,N	Sun	Flower clusters - rosy, lavender, white - spring until frost; rapid growth to 3-4 ft.; easily rooted; use as trailer, in pots, and as ground covers.
Lathyrus latifolia / Everlasting Sweet Pea	P	Sun	Climbing vine - flowers are many colors.
Lathyrus odoratus / Sweet Pea (See Annuals)			
Lonicera / 'Dropmore Scarlet'	E,P	Sun	More orange than scarlet. Very hardy hybrid of *L. hirsuta* x *L. sempervirens*.

VINES

Key: D - Deciduous; E - Evergreen; A - Annual; P - Perennial; N - Native

Botanical Name / Common Name	Key	Exposure	Comments
Lonicera x heckrotti Everblooming Honeysuckle	E,P	Sun	Carmine and gold flowers throughout summer; medium texture; climbs to 12 ft., twining; use for detail interest on fence or trellis. Occasional pruning and fertilizer will keep it blooming.
Lonicera sempervirens Trumpet Honeysuckle	E,P,N	Sun, part shade	Native; gold to scarlet red tubular flowers spring through summer, red berries in fall; rapid growth to 50 ft., twining; prune to control size; best flowering in sun; use on trellis or fence. 'Sulphurea' - yellow.
Lygodium japonicum Japanese Climbing Fern	D,P	Shade, part shade	Lacy, delicate foliage; climbs by twining to 8-10 ft.; prune off old fronds each year before growth appears; use on low fence, post; naturalized.
Mandevilla (See Patio Plants)			
Parthenocissus quinquefolia Virginia Creeper	D,P,N	Sun, shade	Rampant growth hard to contain; reddish new growth, blue berries and brilliant scarlet color in fall; excellent ground cover for slopes, attracts birds.
Passiflora incarnata Passion Vine	P,N	Sun	Bright green leaves; flowers exotic, 3" in diameter, pinkish-lavender with delicate fringe, opens in the morning, closes at night; *P. incarnata* 'Alba' white, rare form.
Polygonum aubertii Silver-lace Vine, Chinese Fleece Vine	D,P	Sun, shade	Fast, twining 20' vine; fragrant, small pinkish-white flowers in clusters late summer into fall; must be pruned severely in small gardens.
Rosa banksiae Lady Banks Rose	E	Sun, part shade	Little maintenance required if given enough room; no pest problems; several varieties available with white or yellow flowers; blooms March to April, single or double multiflowered clusters; massive growth; may reach 20 ft.
Rosa laevigata Cherokee Rose	E	Sun, part shade	Georgia state flower. Very aggressive with sharp thorns; rampant growth unless frequently pruned; white 2½" blooms in April; climbs to considerable height when growth is unchecked.
Roses (See Rose chapter)			
Solanum jasminoides Jasmine Nightshade	E,P	Sun, part shade	Clusters of small white flowers late summer until frost; climbs by twining 10-15 ft., fine texture; requires little care; use for screen; top damaged in cold winters; poisonous.

VINES

Key: D - Deciduous; E - Evergreen; A - Annual; P - Perennial; N - Native

Botanical Name / Common Name	Key	Exposure	Comments
Stauntonia hexaphylla Japanese Staunton Vine	E,P	Shade	Splendid evergreen vine with fragrant white male flowers and purplish female flowers on same plant; rich, moist soil; somewhat acid pH.
Stephanatis (See Patio Plants)			
Tecomaria capensis Cape Honeysuckle	E or D,P	Sun	Scarlet, trumpet-shaped flowers, summer until frost, flowers on new growth so prune after flowering; slow grower to 8 ft.; attractive foliage, use for ornamental value; may be pruned as shrub; top tender.
Thunbergia alata Black-eyed Susan Vine	D,A	Sun	Golden flowers with brown center; brilliant display all summer; may survive mild winter with mulch; use also on patio as pot plant or hanging basket; other Thunbergia species offer different colors.
Trachelospermum asiaticum Japanese Star Jasmine (Asiatic Jasmine)	E,P	Sun, part shade	Yellow-white flowers seen when climbing high, climbs by twining to 12 ft.; dark green, glossy foliage; use for interest on fences and walls; may be used as ground cover.
Trachelospermum jasminoides (Rhynchospermum) Confederate Jasmine	E	Part shade, shade	Covered with white fragrant flowers late spring; climbs by twining to 15 ft.; prune to control and make bushier; excellent screen; variegated form available; may be damaged in severe freeze.
Wisteria floribunda Japanese Wisteria	D,P	Sun	Fragrant, violet-blue, long pendent clusters in spring; aggressive, rampant grower to 30 ft. climbs by twining; medium texture; prune aggressively to train and control; use on trellises or pergolas; white variety available; invasive.
Wisteria frutescens American Wisteria	P,N	Semi-sun	Small 3"lavender blue blooms; rich soil; blooms later. Var. 'Nivea' - White - Very rare. May be pest because of root sprouts; native, not invasive.
Wisteria sinensis Chinese Wisteria	D,P	Sun	Pendent clusters of violet-blue flowers in spring before leaves; aggressive twining growth habit but may be trained as above or as tree; rampant growth can girdle trees. This is the most widely planted wisteria; white variety available; spread by stolons above and below ground may make this a pest; invasive.

NOTES

Ground Covers

GROUND COVERS

Ground covers are prized not only for their decorative effects, but also for the artistic freedom they give to the gardener to create both pleasing lines and large areas of mass planting. Combining ground covers with each other and with other plants results in striking visual effects. By contrasting textures, leaf shapes, colors and heights the gardener/artist has limitless materials with which to create his or her own imaginative garden.

Before choosing a ground cover, one should consider environmental factors. Some think ground covers are damaging around the bases of trees or shrubs. Invasive vines may smother larger plants. Make sure that growth habits and mature size are appropriate to the site. This will prevent either sparse planting or eventual overgrowth of space. Plants designated in the comments as 'invasive' may become pests unless properly controlled.

In this climate, gardeners usually select evergreen ground covers in preference to deciduous ones. The evergreens provide various hues of green or variegated foliage all year. Some, including the deciduous plants, supply seasonal interest from fruits or flowers. There is a great variety of ground covers with which to work. Some need sun while others prefer shade. Many are colorful the year round. The list comprises herbaceous perennials, herbs, low growing shurbs, sprawling vines, ornamental grasses and succulents. For more information on these species, please refer to the appropriate chapters.

PREPARATION:

Since little can be done to the soil after the ground cover is established, initial preparation is of the utmost importance. If the area to be planted is infested with perennial weeds, and the area cannot be spaded, use a biodegradable weed killer. Be careful not to damage permanent shrubs and trees. Add well-rotted manure and a good basic fertilizer and work into the soil. Three pounds of fertilizer per one hundred square feet should be adequate. Before planting it is a good idea to check the pH and make any needed adjustments. A mulch may be applied before planting. For continued weed control, any of a variety of mulching materials may be used. Wood chips, pine straw and bark have the advantage of giving a newly planted garden a "finished" look as well as holding in needed moisture.

PLANTING:

In temperate zones, most ground covers should be planted in the fall. Cool weather helps the plants recover from the shock of transplanting with the advent of spring, their root systems are already established and the plants begin to cover the ground area quickly. Rows can be either straight or staggered. The staggered rows are especially advantageous on slopes where the cover helps to prevent erosion of the soil. The plants will benefit from being set in slight depressions that catch the water.

MAINTENANCE:

While most ground covers are considered low-maintenance plants, they are not 'no' maintenance plants. During the first year, even the hardiest of covers will benefit during the hot summer from weekly deep waterings. Wherever the ground cover develops thatch or the leaves begin to lose their luster, it is time to prune. The stray tendril or branch will have to be pruned, and in many cases the entire area will be much enhanced by a shearing or mowing (eg. liriope) during the early spring. A light, yearly application of fertilizer will result in lush and vigorous growth.

GROUND COVERS

Key: E - Evergreen; D - Deciduous; N - Native

Botanical Name Common Name	Key	Height	Space Apart	Exposure	Comments
Ajuga reptans Bugleweed Carpet Bugle	E	4-6"	8-12"	Sun, shade	Small spire-like blooms in spring may form a carpet of blue; foliage deep green to bronze; stoloniferous; may be invasive; needs moisture; may develop crown rot; good low ground cover; variety 'Alba' (white flowers).
Artemisia abrotanum Southernwood	E	3-4'	12-15"	Sun	Foliage grey-green, fine feathery texture; leaves scented; prune annually to maintain shape; drought resistant; good in mass as groundcover.
Aspidistra elatior Cast-iron Plant	E	1-2'	12"	Shade	Dark green, wide bladed leaves arising directly from soil; spreads slowly by rhizomes, very tolerant of all conditions; may be grown in narrow soil strips and under roof overhangs; variety 'Variegata' (variegated), both valuable in flower arrangement.
Asplenium platyneuron Ebony Spleenwort	E,N	6"-1'	12"	Shade	Perky fern; slender fronds 2" wide.
Bugleweed (See *Ajuga*)					
Cephalotaxus harringtonia 'Drupacea'	E	3'	3-4'	Part shade, shade	Drooping branches with needle-like leaves, grows slowly; female plants bear drupes.
Chaenomeles speciosa 'Nana' Jet Trail	D	12"	12-18"	Sun, part shade	Everblooming white; blooms on bare branches in winter and early spring.
Chrysogonum virginianum Goldenstar	E,N	6"	8"	Part shade	Bright yellow daisy-like flowers in spring; likes sandy loam with drainage; native; blooms over a long season.
Cyrtomium falcatum Holly Fern	E	1-2'	3'	Part shade, shade	Arching stems form compact clumps; glossy dark green foliage; coarse texture; remove damaged fronds in spring; good ground-cover or accent plant.
Daylily (See *Hemerocallis*)					
Dianthus plumarius Cottage Pinks		2-12"	6-8"	Sun, part shade	White, pink or red flowers in spring; bluegreen grassy foliage; lovely with annuals or bulbs; likes lime.

GROUND COVERS

Key: E - Evergreen; D - Deciduous; N - Native

Botanical Name / Common Name	Key	Height	Space Apart	Exposure	Comments
Galium odoratum Sweet Woodruff	E	3-4″	6″	Shade	Tiny white flowers late spring; needs moist, acid soil; good with bulbs.
Ginger, Wild (See *Hexastylis*)					
Hedera canariensis Algerian Ivy	E	12-18″	18″	Shade, part shade	Green leaves or variegated variety 'Canary Cream'; shear annually to 6″; keep out of trees.
Hedera helix English Ivy	E	12-18″	18″	Shade, part shade	Glossy green leaves; sheer annually; many small-leaved varieties available; invasive; use only in containers.
Helleborus orientalis Lenten Rose	E	12-15″	12-15″	Shade	Handsome foliage; cream to dull rose flowers; drought resistant.
Hemerocallis hybrida Daylily	D or E	18″	18-30″	Sun, shade	Many varieties of many different colors - yellow to orange to corals; there are those that bloom early (April-May), mid-season (June-July), and late (August-September). Select evergreen when possible. Requires little care, but blooms better when fertilized.
Hexastylis (Asarum) arifolium Wild Ginger	E,N	6-10″	12″	Shade, part shade	Small maroon flower early spring; kidney-shaped leaf; needs moist, highly organic soil; native; forms clumps; stands deep shade.
Holly Fern (See *Cyrtomium*)					
Hosta lancifolia Narrow Leaved Plantain Lily	D	18-24″	18″	Shade, part shade	Lilac flower spikes in August; handsome lance-shaped leaves; low maintenance perennial; watch for slugs; other Hosta species and varieties are available; top kills in winter.
Hosta ventricosa Blue Plantain Lily	D	18-24″	18″	Shade, part shade	Blue or white flower spikes to 2-3′ in early summer; watch for slugs; needs moisture; flowers better with some sun; top kills in winter.
Ivy (See *Hedera*)					
Juniperus conferta Shore Juniper	E	16″	3′	Sun	Rich blue-green foliage; likes sandy soil; drought resistant; salt tolerant; watch for mites; 'Blue Pacific'–low trailing habit, blue-green color; 'Compacta'–light green.

GROUND COVERS

Key: E - Evergreen; D - Deciduous; N - Native

Botanical Name Common Name	Key	Height	Space Apart	Exposure	Comments
Juniperus horizontalis Creeping Juniper	E	4-6"	3'	Sun	Heat resistant; silver blue color; fast growing, excellent ground-cover. 'Wiltoni' (blue rug) flat trailing habit.
Juniperus procumbens 'Nana'	E	6"	4-6'	Sun	Cascades gracefully; mounding growth habit.
Liriope muscari Big Blue Lirope	E	12"	12"	Sun, shade	Dark green grass-like leaves recurving toward ground; blue spike blooms in August; tolerant but invasive ground cover. 'Big Blue,' 'Evergreen Giant,' 'Monroe White,' 'Webster's Wide Leaf.'
Liriope spicata Lirope	E	10"	12"	Shade, part shade	Grass-like leaves recurving toward ground; covers more rapidly than *L. muscari*.
Mazus reptans	E	2"	12"	Sun, part shade	Forms a mat with lilac flowers; good in moist soil, for paving and for overplanting bulbs.
Pachysandra terminalis Japanese Pachysandra	E	4"	5"	Shade, part shade	Handsome green or silver edged leaf.
Mitchella repens Partridge Berry	E,N	2-3"	4"	Shade	Native; red berries in fall; spreads as a trailer.
Mondo (See *Ophiopogon*)					
Ophiopogon jaburan Snakebeard	E	6"	4-6"	Sun	Sunproof
Ophiopogon japonicus Mondo, Monkey grass	E	6"	4-6"	Shade, part shade	Dark green grass-like leaves; requires little care and is tolerant; variety 'Nana' is smaller and less invasive.
Partridge Berry (See *Mitchella*)					
Periwinklke (See *Vinca*)					
Phlox divaricata	E,N	8"	6"	Sun, part shade	Blue flowers spring; use in small areas; susceptible to nematodes.
Phlox pilosa Downy Phlox	E,N	15"	6"	Sun, part shade	Similar to *p. divaricata*; bears pinkish-blue or, rarely, white flowers.

GROUND COVERS

Key: E - Evergreen; D - Deciduous; N - Native

Botanical Name Common Name	Key	Height	Space Apart	Exposure	Comments
Phlox stolonifera Creeping Phlox	E	6-12"	6"	Sun, part shade	White, blue, pink flowers in spring; good bulb cover.
Phlox subulata Moss Phlox, Thrift	E,N	4-6"	4"	Sun, part shade	Violet, blue, white flowers; spring blooming.
Pinks (See *Dianthus*)					
Polystichum *acrostichoides* Christmas Fern	E,N				Lacy, evergreen fronds
Star Jasmine (See *Trachelospermum*)					
Stokesia laevis Stokesia	E,N	12-18"	12"	Sun, part shade	Lavender flowers in May; native.
Thymus serpyllum Mother of Thyme	E	1-2"	8"	Sun, part shade	Tiny fragrant flowers; blooms in June; charming for small edging or hardy enough to plant between stones in a path.
Trachelospermum *asiaticum* Japanese Star Jasmine	E	8-12"	3'	Shade, part shade	Small, creamy fragrant flowers late spring; but may not bloom here; forms dense screen of dark green; may be invasive.
Vinca major Big Leaf Periwinkle	E	8-12"	12"	Shade, part shade	Blue flower in spring; rapid growing and should be confined; thrives in shade.
Vinca minor Common Periwinkle	E	5-8"	8-12"	Shade, part shade	Blue flower in spring; wide spreading with stems rooting along ground; non-climbing; rapid growing; excellent under trees or on banks; not as heat tolerant as *V. major*.
Viola affinis Brainard Violet	E,N	6-8"	8-10"	Shade, part shade	Blue flowers in spring, can be invasive; prefers rich, moist but well drained soil; becomes semi-dormant during long, hot summers; sometimes susceptible to viral disease.
Viola lanceolata Lance Leaved Violet	E,N	6-8"	8-10"	Shade, part shade	White flowers, narrow leaf, not as invasive but otherwise as above.
Woodruff (See *Galium*)					

175

NOTES

Native Plants

THE VALUE OF NATIVE PLANTS

Louise G. Smith
Birmingham, Alabama

The southeast is blessed with a rich and varied flora. The early naturalists who explored the region were captivated by the beauty of flower and foliage. They sent seed and slips abroad for cultivation. Gardeners have long appreciated the native dogwood *(Cornus florida),* magnolia *(Magnolia grandiflora)* and holly *(Ilex opaca),* and have made them an integral part of the landscape. Nevertheless, we have largely ignored hundreds of garden worthy native trees, shrubs and flowers. Fortunately, this neglect is beginning to be overcome as gardeners become increasingly sophisticated and environmentally concerned. This great wealth of plant material is truly a part of our natural heritage which should be cherished and protected.

There are native species appropriate for every niche of the home landscape. Evergreen and deciduous materials abound that are adaptable to sun or shade and to wet or dry conditions. These materials range in size from the mighty oak to the diminutive bluet. Because of the lack of both demand and interest, very few of these treasures have been available to the gardening public. For most of the 20th Century, if you wanted to grow native azaleas *(Rhododendron spp.),* silverbell *(Halesia carolina),* mountain laurel *(Kalmia latifolia),* oakleaf hydrangea *(Hydrangea quercifolia)* or any number of other beautiful native trees and shrubs, you either dug from the wild or did without. Unfortunately, wild-dug material was often scraggly, had a very poor root system and was slow or almost impossible to reestablish. Consequently these wonderful and decorative plants were dismissed as being too difficult to grow.

The good news is that an ever increasing number of native trees and shrubs are being commercially propagated and container grown for ease of transplanting. Many are now regularly available in neighborhood garden centers and as demand grows so will the variety offered. With well grown material at hand, the landscaper need only give attention to the optimum habitat in order for each species to achieve a high rate of success. When natives are used, more research to determine proper location is necessary, but the rewards will be great both for the health of your tree or shrub and for your own appreciation of your floral heritage. Once properly placed and carefully planted, your native should need no extra coddling.

Wild flowers have a reputation for being difficult, and some truly are. Trailing arbutus *(Epigaea repens)* and native orchids, among others, give the experts no end of trouble and should certainly be avoided by the novice. However, many perennial, biennial and annual southeastern species are easily grown and with time will colonize a substantial area.

Far more than trees and shrubs, wildflowers have suffered from the hands of collectors. Roots, rhizomes and tubers have traditionally been dug by the thousands from the wilds of the southeast, shipped to brokers for storage, and months later, mailed to the customer. Often, these plants never developed a good root system, frequently were dug at the wrong time and had numerous opportunities to dry out before reaching your doorstep. It is small wonder that most died and gardeners were disenchanted.

While you will not yet find many of these wildflowers at your local garden center, there are an increasing number of small mail-order nurseries throughout the southeast that specialize in native plants. Be sure that you are getting nursery propagated and grown material and that instructions for cultivation are included.

Woodland plants, which bloom before the trees leaf out, are especially appealing as harbingers of spring. They enjoy humus, deep shade and, for summer coolness, combine well with ferns or low-light non-natives like hosta and caladiums.

Many of the sun loving natives that brighten our roadsides and fields make tough, long blooming additions to the perennial border. With their bright colors, heat tolerance and low fertility requirements, they are well suited to low maintenance gardening. Commercial growers are now selecting the better clones for distribution to the home gardener and even to the cut flower trade.

Native plants offer variety and beauty. They are adapted to our fluctuations in winter temperature and summer moisture. As more and more of their natural habitats are destroyed, give them a refuge in your garden. You won't be sorry.

The following Native Plants are listed in this book in the specific chapters:

TREES:

Acer floridanum (Florida Maple)

Acer rubrum (Red Maple)

Aesculus pavia (Red Buckeye)

Amelanchier canadensis (Shadblow Serviceberry)

Betula nigra (River Birch)

Carpinus carolinia (American Hornbeam)

Cercis canadensis (Eastern Redbud)

Chionanthus virginicus (White Fringetree)

Cornus florida (Flowering Dogwood)

Fagus grandiflora (American Beech)

Franklinia altamaha (Franklinia)

Fraxinus pennsylvanica (Red Ash)

Gordonia lasianthus (Loblolly Bay)

Halesia carolina (Carolina Silverbell)

Ilex cassine (Dahoon Holly)

Ilex decidua (Possumhaw)

Ilex opaca (American Holly)

Ilex vomitoria (Yaupon Holly)

Juniperus virginiana (Eastern Red Cedar)

Kalmia latifolia (Mountain Laurel)

Liriodendron tulipifera (Tulip Tree)

Magnolia grandiflora (Southern Magnolia)

Magnolia virginiana (Sweetbay Magnolia)

Malus angustifolia (Southern Crabapple)

Myrica cerifera (Southern Wax-myrtle)

Osmanthus americanus (Devilwood)

Ostrya virginiana (American Hophornbeam)

Persea borbonia (Red Bay)

Pinckneya pubens (Pinckneya)

Pinus elliottii (Slash Pine)

Pinus glabra (Spruce Pine)

Pinus palustris (Longleaf Pine)

Pinus taeda (Loblolly Pine)

Prunus angustifolia (Chickasaw Plum)

Prunus caroliniana (Carolina Cherry-laurel)

Quercus alba (White Oak)

Quercus falcata (Southern Red Oak)

Quercus laurifolia (Laurel Oak)

Quercus phellus (Willow Oak)

Quercus virginiana (Live Oak)

Sabal palmetto (Cabbage Palmetto)

Sassafras albidum (Sassafras)

Stewartia malacodendron (Silky Stewartia)

Styrax americanus (American Snowbell)

Taxodium distichum (Common Bald Cypress)

Ulmus parvifolia (Chinese Elm)

Vaccinium arboreum (Farkleberry)

SHRUBS:

Small

Euonymus americanus (Strawberry Bush)

Fothergilla gardenii (Dwarf Bottlebrush)

Leucothoe axillaris (Coastal Leucothoe)

Lyonia lucida (Fetterbush)

Yucca filamentosa (Adam's Needle)

Medium

Callicarpa americana (American Beautyberry)

Calycanthus floridus (Sweetshrub)

Clethra alnifolia (Sweet Pepperbush)

Hydrangea quercifolia (Oakleaf Hydrangea)

Ilex glabra (Inkberry)

Itea virginica (Virginia Sweetspire)

Lantana camara (Lantana)

Rhus aromatica (Fragrant Sumac)

Yucca gloriosa (Spanish Dagger)

Large

Aesculus parviflora (Bottlebrush Buckeye)

Aralia spinosa (Devil's Walking Stick)

Baccharis halimitolia (Groundsel Bush)

Cephalanthus occidentalis (Button Bush)

Cliftonia monophylla (Black Titi)

Cyrilla racemiflora (Red Titi)

Elliottia racemosa (Georgia Plume)

Illicum floridanum (Florida Anise Tree)

Illicum parviflorum (Star Anise)
Leucothoe populifolia (Florida Leucothoe)
Lindera benzoin (Spicebush)
Myrica cerifera (Southern Wax-myrtle)
Petlea trifoliata (Hop Tree)
Styrax americanus (American Snowbell)
Viburnum nudum (Possumhaw Viburnum)
Viburnum prunifolium (Blackhaw Viburnum)
Yucca aloifolia (Spanish Bayonet)

AZALEAS

Rhododendron alabamense (Alabama Azalea)
Rhododendron arborescens (Sweet Azalea)
Rhododendron atlanticum (Coastal Azalea)
Rhododendron austrinum (Florida Azalea)
Rhododendron canescens (Piedmont Pinxter)
Rhododendron prunifolium (Plumleaf Azalea)
Rhododendron serrulatum (Hammock-sweet Azalea)
Rhododendron speciosum (Oconee Azalea)
Rhododendron viscosum (Swamp Azalea)

ANNUALS

Coreopsis tinctoria (Calliopsis)
Daucus carota (Queen Anne's Lace)
Gaillardia pulchella (Blanket Flower)
Phlox drummondii (Annual Phlox)

PERENNIALS

Achillea millefolium (Yarrow)
Amsonia tabernaemontana (Blue Star)
Aquilegia (Columbine)
Asclepias incarnata (Swamp Milkweed)
Baptisia alba (Wild Indigo)
Belamcanda chinensis (Blackberry Lily)
Boltonia asteroides
Calopogon barbatus (Grass-pink)
Coreopsis auriculata
Coreopsis lanceolata
Echinacea purpurea (Purple Coneflower)
Epigaea repens (Trailing-arbutus)
Eupatorium purpureum (Joe-Pye-Weed)
Euphorbia corollata (Flowering Spurge)
Gaura lindheimeri
Hedyotis crassifolia (Bluets)
Hibisus moscheutos (Rose Mallow)
Lantana camara (Lantana)
Lantana montevidensis (Trailing Lantana)
Liatris elegans (Blazing Star)
Lobelia cardinalis (Cardinal Flower)
Phlox maculata (Wild Sweet William)
Sisyrinchium atlanticum (Blue Eyed Grass)
Solidago (Goldenrod)
Spiranthes gracilis (Slender Ladies'-tresses)
Tiarella cordifolia (Foam Flower)
Tradescantia virginiana (Spiderwort)
Trillium cuneatum (Sessile Trillium)

Verbena canadensis (Rose
　Verbena)
Verbena tenuisecta (Moss
　Verbena)
Viola (Violet)

BULBS
Amaryllis belladonna
Belamcanda chinensis
　(Blackberry Lily)
Hymenocallis caroliniana
　(Spider Lily)
Iris cristata (Crested Iris)
Iris laevigata
Iris virginica
Zephyranthes atamasco
　(Rain Lily)

VINES
Aristolochia durior
　(Dutchman's Pipe)
Bignonia capreolata
　(Crossvine)
Campsis radicans (Trumpet
　Creeper)
Lantana montevidensis
　(Trailing Lantana)
Lonicera sempervirens
　(Trumpet Honeysuckle)
Parthenocissus quinquefolia
　(Virginia Creeper)
Passiflora incarnata (Passion
　Vine)
Gelsemium sempervirens
　(Carolina Jessamine)
Wisteria frutescens (American
　Wisteria)

GROUND COVERS
Asplenium platyneuron (Ebony
　Spleenwort)
Chrysogonum virginianum
　(Goldenstar)
Hexastylis arifolium (Wild
　Ginger)
Phlox divaricata
Phlox pilosa (Downy Phlox)
Phlox subulata (Moss Phlox)
Polystichum acrostichoides
　(Christmas Fern)
Viola affinis (Brainard Violet)
Viola lanceolata (Lance Leaved
　Violet)

Ornamental

Grasses

THE CASE FOR ORNAMENTAL GRASSES

Thomas Angell
Walterboro, South Carolina

Grasses are without a doubt some of the most diverse and useful of all plant groups. Man's very existence, as well as that of the majority of the domesticated animals on which he depends, owe their sustenance to the productive capabilities of grasses. Not only do grasses provide us with the principal grains of the world, but they also furnish us with such necessities as sugar, hats, baskets and beer; not to mention that most revered element of the American landscape, the lawn. It is, however, not their indisputable utility, but their often-overlooked decorative qualities, which are enticing people to use them increasingly in their landscapes.

The subtle beauty, graceful forms and the easy care of ornamental grasses are now winning them a well-deserved niche in our modern planting palette. As innovative gardeners and garden designers search for new freedom and individualism in garden expression, they often seek to create a landscape which acknowledges the ecological nuances of site diversity through a more naturalistic approach. The many representatives of the families of grasses, sedges and rushes, especially the natives, provide an almost boundless list of possible plant combinations for our most difficult gardening situations. The majority of these grasses tolerate a wide variety of soils and temperature conditions and are nearly insect and disease free. There are grasses suitable for use in sun or shade, as well as wet or dry garden conditions. They have a diversity of size, form and color, both of leaf and of flower and thus lend themselves to a rich variety of design applications

Ornamental grasses integrate effectively with annuals and perennials, as well as wildflowers and indigenous plantings, to offer a cyclical brocade with continual season interest. When many of our common garden bloomers have lost their charm toward late summer and fall, the beauty of these grasses comes into play as their colorful plumes and wavy foliage change to tones of amber, beige and tan that continue their striking presence into winter. The exciting range of colors of the decorative grasses is rivaled only by their tremendous diversity of form. In addition to extremes of blue, cream, red and yellow, there are countless hues of green, which can become the perfect foil for otherwise monotonous evergreens. The scale of these plants spans the gamut from the diminutive and delicate to the giant and thus could find a place in a tiny courtyard or large estate.

Swathes of meadow consisting predominantly of native grasses can be useful as a dynamic transition from an open space to the typical mixed shrub and tree margins of a property. Most native grasses are best used en masse, such as native love grass or little bluestem, but some such as tall switch grass or plume grass work well as striking accents in a mixed border or perennial bed, either planted singly or in clumps of three to five each. Care is limited to once annual mowing or burning in late winter with minimal use of fertilizer or pesticide.

Some of the best and most useful native grasses, such as sweet grass and switch grass, are becoming popularized in garden centers and home landscapes. Plant breeders have responded to the demand by selecting various named cultivars for increased bloom, fall color, uprightness or compactness. While most native grasses enjoy medium to high sunlight and are three to four feet high at maturity, there are shade tolerant and lower-height species such as slender spike grass and river oats. Some of the more moisture-loving species such as the sedges and rushes are only beginning to become available in the trade.

Ornamental grasses are the perfect plants to loosen up our plantings and inject an element of whimsy or wild nature into our sometimes overly manicured residential landscapes. Gardeners in the south are becoming increasingly aware of a new trend in American gardening, which encourages a more diverse but well planned harmony of perennials and herbs, fruits and vegetables, and native plantings to complement our old favorites. The increasing popularity of ornamental grasses reflects our desire to create and live in diverse gardens which provide year round interest, yet are low maintenance. Ornamental grasses are endearingly easy to grow and can be a dramatic addition to any garden.

ORNAMENTAL GRASSES

*native
The dead foliage is attractive in winter, cut back early spring. Multiply by division.

Botanical Name Common Name	Height/Spread	Exposure	Comments
Acorus gramineus Japanese Sweet Flag	6-12"/6"	Sun, part shade	Moist areas, bog gardens. 'Variegatus'-white striped, 'Ogon'-gold striped.
Andropogon glomeratus Bushy Bluestem	3'	Sun	Blue green grass with 7' tall whitish tufted top; moist soil.
Carex conica	8"/6"	Part shade	Evergreen, moist areas. 'Variegata.'
Carex Morrowi	12"/8"	Part shade	Evergreen; moist areas. 'Albomarginata'-striped white.
**Carex platyphylla* Blue Satin Sedge	6"-12"	Part shade, shade	Glaucous blue leaves 1" wide; spreading; use as groundcover.
**Chasmanthum* *latifolium* Inland Sea Oats	3'/2'	Sun, part shade	Fine texture; tolerant of various soils; attractive seed heads from July until fall.
**Chasmanthium laxum* Slender Spike Grass	2'	Part shade, shade	Flat leaves and panicles of flat seed heads of 2 to many florets.
Cortaderia sellolana Pampas Grass	8-10'/5-6'	Sun	Giant plumes (fuller on female plant) prominent late summer, early fall; leaf margins very sharp; grows very large and is difficult to control in landscape. 'Rubra'-reddish, pink plumes.
'Pumila' Dwarf Pampas Grass	3-4'/3-4'	Sun	More manageable in landscape.
Elymus glaucus Blue Lyme Grass	3-4'/3-4'	Sun	Outstanding blue-gray foliage; spreads by underground rhizomes; attractive in groups or as ground cover.
**Elymus virginicus* Virginia Wild Rye	2'	Sun, shade	Erect inflorescences; glaucous nodes and clustered seed heads.
**Eragrostis spectabilis* Lovegrass	2'	Sun	Dense clump with airy flower plumes from July to October.
**Erianthus giganteus* Plume Grass	4'	Sun	Moist soil; tall plumes to 6'-8'.

ORNAMENTAL GRASSES

*native
The dead foliage is attractive in winter, cut back early spring. Multiply by division.

Botanical Name / Common Name	Height/Spread	Exposure	Comments
Miscanthus sinensis / Japanese Silver Grass	5-6'/3-4'	Sun	All miscanthus have prominent white midrib. This one has a wider blade and, therefore, medium texture. Handsome winter color, magenta plumes.
'Gracillimus' / Maiden Grass	4-5'/3-4'	Sun	Graceful; fine texture; green in summer, almond in winter; may be used in more formal setting.
'Variegatus' / Variegated Japanese Silver Grass	4-5'/3-4'	Sun	Vertical white variegation; fine texture.
'Zebrinus' / Zebra Grass	4-5'/3-4'	Sun	Yellow or white horizontal bands.
Muhlenbergia capillaries / Sweet Grass	2'	Sun	Haze of deep pink flowers covering the plant may be stunning; narrow glossy green leaves.
Panicum amarum 'Dewey Blue' / 'Dewey Blue' Beach Grass	4'	Sun	Blue green-silver foliage, light airy tan plumes all winter.
Panicum virgatum Switch Grass Cultivars			
'Heavy Metal'	3'-4'	Sun	Steel blue foliage; dark burgundy seed heads.
'Northwinds'	3'-4'	Sun	Wide olive-green foliage; attractive narrow plumes September; upright habit.
'Prairie Sky'	3'-4'	Sun	Powdery blue foliage; billowing plumes of amber brown late September.
'Cloud Nine'	6'	Sun	Vertical clumps of metallic-blue foliage topped by giant reddish-brown cloud like plumes.
Pennisetum alopecuroides / Rose Fountain Grass	4'/3'	Sun	Fine texture; beautiful flower spikes July.
'Moudry'	1½-2'	Sun	Beautiful, almost black, flower spikes.

187

ORNAMENTAL GRASSES

*native
The dead foliage is attractive in winter, cut back early spring. Multiply by division.

Botanical Name / Common Name	Height/Spread	Exposure	Comments
Pennistum setaceum Fountain Grass	4'/3'	Sun	Treat like an annual; rose colored foliage and flowers.
'Autrosanguineum'	4'/3'	Sun	Beautiful purple foliage and flowers.
'Rubrum' Crimson Fountain Grass	4'/3'	Sun	Crimson or burgundy foliage and flowers.
Schizachyrium scoparium Little Bluestem	1'-2'	Sun	Powder blue foliage; narrow willowy plumes to 3'; foliage russet-red in autumn.
Sorghastrum nutans 'Sioux Blue' 'Sioux Blue' Indian Grass	2'-3'	Sun	Copper seed heads, metallic blue foliage, upright growth.
Sporobolus heterolepis Prairie Dropseed	1'-2'	Sun	Medium green, narrow foliage; flowers August until frost; drought and heat tolerant.
Sporobolus junceus Pineywoods Dropseed	1'-2'	Sun, part shade	Pink and brown tinted flowers August until frost.
Tridens flavus Purpletop	2'-4'	Sun, part shade	Purplish inflorescence that turns black.
Tripascum dactyloides Eastern Gamma Grass	3'-4'	Sun, part shade	Forms a good hedge or screen; orange-pink plumes in fall; moist soil.

Lawn

LAWN

While homeowners have had a long love affair with their lawns, they are beginning to realize that beautiful lawns have an ecological impact. Because lawns remain an intrinsic part of the American landscape, we must consider the environmental effects of our lawn maintenance practices. By making some simple changes, we can save money and time, as well as preserve our natural environment. Too often we are careless with water, fertilizer and other chemicals to the detriment of the health of our families, our pets and the planet. While we encourage the use of lower maintenance plantings, the appropriate warmer season grasses are centipede, St. Augustine, zoysia and bermuda.

Centipede Grass: Centipede *(Eremochloa ophiuroides)* is the most frequently used grass. It is a light green and the blade is of medium width. Its advantage is relative ease of upkeep. The surface runners (stolons) are easily controlled around walks and beds. During the growing season it may be mowed every 7 to 10 days. It must be fed judiciously as overfeeding will cause decline. Centipede prefers a pH of 5.0 to 6.0. Thatch can be a problem. Centipede is not tolerant of heavy shade but grows well under the high shade of pine trees. It may be planted by seed, sprigs or sod.

Zoysia Grass: Zoysia *(Zoysia spp.)* is a dark green, coarse to fine-bladed grass. It tolerates shade and may be mowed every 7-10 days. Unfortunately, it is not at all tolerant of drought and is quite prone to pests and disease. It requires a rich soil for good growth and heavy fertilization to keep it thick. It grows by underground rhizomes and is therefore difficult to control in beds. Zoysia is usually established by sprigs, plugs, or sod. It tends to grow slowly.

St. Augustine Grass: St. Augustine *(Stenotaphrum secundatum)* is a dark blue-green, wide or coarse bladed grass. Its major advantages are its relative shade and salt tolerance. St. Augustine requires medium to high fertility and a pH of 6.0 to 6.5 It grows by above-ground stolons and is, therefore, easy to control in beds. It is susceptible to winter injury and to chinch bugs. St. Augustine does not produce seeds and so is planted vegetatively.

Bermuda Grass: Bermuda grass *(Cynodon spp.)* is an aggressive grower, requiring mowing every 5 to 7 days. It also requires heavy fertilization and a pH of 6.0 to 6.5. It not shade tolerant. It grows aggressively into flower beds, and is difficult to control because of underground rhizomes. For these reasons, it is not for the average homeowner. Its tolerance to traffic makes it ideal for athletic fields and golf courses. It may be used on sandy banks for erosion control. The common variety may be seeded, Improved varieties are planted vegetatively.

PREPARATION AND PLANTING:

As for any other successful planting, first the soil must be adequately prepared. Make sure you have adequate drainage. A pH of 6.0 to 6.5 is desirable, except for centipede which prefers a pH of 5.0 to 6.0. Have your soil tested through the county extension agent (see Soil and Its Improvement), and be prepared to add lime as recommended. When making a new lawn, remove all debris and dig the earth to a depth of 6 to 10 inches. Be careful not to damage trees by destroying their roots. Add topsoil if necessary. Turn in fertilizer and organic material.

Zoysia, centipede, and St. Augustine are established by sprigging, plugging, or sodding. Centipede may also be seeded. While sodding is the most expensive, it provides an "instant" lawn. With sprigging, the lawn will cover faster than with plugging. Competition from weeds may become a problem. With reliable seed, a beautiful centipede lawn may be produced from seed in about 4 months.

After planting, make sure the lawn is adequately watered, fertilized, and mowed until it is established.

RENOVATION OF AN OLD LAWN:

First, you will need to assess the problems. Your county extension agent can help you with this. A soil analysis will determine the pH and nutrition requirements. Often the soil will be compacted and will need to be aerated. (Done with coring machine or spiking equipment.) Is there evidence of disease or pests? Look for the holes and tunnels of mole crickets. Check for weeds and thatch. Are bare spots under trees where there is either root competition, or too much shade, especially for centipede?

When the problems have been identified and dealt with, planting may be done. Bare areas will have to be cultivated, debris removed and organic material added. You may plant by sprigs or plugs, or if using centipede, by seed.

You may find a mixture of grasses, especially Centipede and St. Augustine, in some old lawns. Additionally, you may find in a relatively good centipede lawn that the bare spots are in areas of shade. St. Augustine will do well in that shade, while centipede will not. While it is considered unorthodox, it is possible for grasses to coexist. Centipede may be damaged by over fertilization and over watering. St. Augustine requires more of both. A balance can be achieved so that a lush green lawn results.

FERTILIZATION:

Do not over fertilize. Apply fertilizer in recommended amounts to prevent injury to the grass. Centipede is particularly susceptible to overfeeding. Apply when the grass is dry and water well.

Many formulations of fertilizer may be used successfully to fertilize your lawn. A soil analysis should be done. If the specific formulation is not readily available, substitutes may be used. One should try to get close to the ratio recommended, and at least one-half of the nitrogen should be in a slow release form. Products made especially for the lawn may contain herbicides. These work well, but must be used carefully. Use the amount of fertilizer recommended in the analysis or as recommended on the bag for your type of lawn. After that you may cut

191

back to find the minimum amount required.

Centipede may be fertilized in early spring only, or the amount may be divided into two applications (early spring and midsummer). St. Augustine needs at least two monthly applications. Some like to fertilize again in the fall. Ask your county extension agent or a reputable professional for further advice.

When using a spreader, measure the correct amount for the square footage. Set the spreader setting low and cover the area repeatedly in different directions until the proper amount is applied. This is more accurate than the spreader settings as walking speed will vary.

WATERING:

Water when needed as indicated by a silvery color in the leaf blades. Soak the soil to a depth of 6-8" inches. This will require about 1 inch of water. Do not over-water or allow the soil to become soggy. Deep infrequent watering promotes a deeper root system and, therefore, a healthier lawn. If one uses an automatic watering system, it should be set for a weekly, early morning soaking to about one inch (1½ to 2 hours). In hot weather, watering may be required twice a week.

MOWING:

Mow high–to 1½ to 2", or even 3". Mow often–never remove more than one-third of the grass blade at one cutting. Use a sharp mower, and mow when the grass is dry. Mowing high encourages deep roots and tall grass shades the roots (conserves moisture) and shades out weeds.

Grass clippings, if the above rules are followed, should be left on the lawn to act as a mulch. This also recycles the nutrients so that fertilizer needs may be decreased. If more than one-third of the blade is cut at one time a mulching mower should be used so that the clippings are chopped several times.

THATCH:

Thatch is a layer of accumulated dead plant material at the soil surface. It prevents penetration of water into the soil, harbors pests and disease spores, and leads to a weak, shallow-rooted grass. To prevent thatch accumulation greater than ½ inch, remove the dead grass before "green up" in the spring. To do this, mow the lawn in two different directions with a low blade setting then rake off the dead grass. If heavy thatch has already accumulated, a dethatching machine may be used.

PESTS AND DISEASE:

A properly cared for lawn will be relatively resistant to insects and disease. If problems appear, seek help from your county extension agent or a reliable garden center. A description of the symptoms will help them advise on treatment. Always use pesticides as directed on the label.

Major problems include:

FUNGUS: Especially brown patch *(Rhizoctonia solani)* and dollar spot *(Sclerotinia homeocarpa)*. Both kill the grass in a circular pattern.

192

The circles of brown patch are a few inches to several feet in diameter; those of dollar spot are only a few inches in diameter, though the circles may run together. In dollar spot, the dead areas may begin on one edge of the blade, then advance across the blade. Control of both includes adequate, but not excessive, nitrogen. Watering in the morning helps as the foliage has time to dry before evening. Fungicides may be used; follow directions carefully.

MOLE CRICKETS: Mole crickets are usually recognized by the problems they cause. Walking over an infested area one may sense a fluffiness of the soil. Examination of the dying grass will reveal partially destroyed root systems. There may be holes in the ground about the diameter of a pencil surrounded by small mounds of dirt. These are the entrances and exits to the mole cricket tunnels. (Holes and mounds alone without the tunnels may be those of earthworms.) Older infestations appear as bare depressed areas with the holes and tunnels.

The mole crickets themselves are 1 to 1.5 inches long and are a light brown.

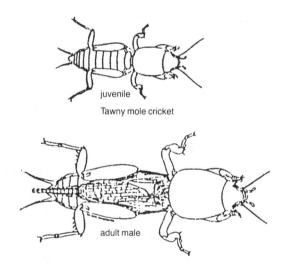

juvenile

Tawny mole cricket

adult male

Mole crickets may be controlled; eradication is difficult. Request information from your county extension agent or garden center on specific insecticides and time to apply. Follow the directions carefully as to timing of application and whether or not to water.

WEEDS:

The best control for weeds is a healthy, well cared for lawn. If the weed problem is too extensive to handle by hand, pre and post emergent herbicides are available. Identify the problem by taking the weed to the county extension agent or your garden center. Use the herbicide according to directions. Remember that the herbicide may be harmful to the roots of nearby shrubs and trees.

NOTES

Seashore Gardening

SEASHORE GARDENING

Gardening at the seashore provides its own pleasures and problems. A little shade or a colorful bloom will soften the summer, sun-drenched view. There are a few plants which will thrive despite salt spray and strong winds off the ocean. Sandy soil and scorching are other hurdles which must be overcome.

By using tolerant plants to provide a windbreak, and by digging organic matter into the sand, one can provide conditions suitable to both tolerant and semi-tolerant plants.

Fully tolerant plants are indicated by the symbol FT, natives by the letter N. More information on these plants may be found in the lists at the end of the respective chapters.

VINES AND GROUNDCOVERS

Artemesia abrotanum (Southern Wood)

Clematis paniculata (Sweet Autumn Clematis)

Fatshedera lizei (Bush Ivy)

Ficus pumila (Climbing Fig)

N *Gelsemium sempervirens* (Carolina Yellow Jessamine)

Hedera caraniensis (Algerian Ivy)

Juniperus conferta (Shore Juniper)

Juniperus horizontalis 'Wiltoni' (Blue Rug Juniper)

Lantana

Lonicera sempervirens (Trumpet Honeysuckle)

Liriope muscari (Lily-turf)

Ophiopogon jaburan vittata (Snakebeard)

Ophiopogon japonicus (Mondo Grass)

Ophiopogon japonicus 'nana' (Dwarf Mondo Grass)

N *Parthenacissus quinquefolia* (Virginia Creeper)

N *Phlox subulata* (Thrift)

Rosa banksiae (Lady Banks')

Rosa laevigata (Cherokee Rose)

Tecomaria capensis (Cape Honeysuckle)

Trachelospermum asiaticum (Asian Jasmine)

Vinca minor (Periwinkle)

SHRUBS

Agave americana (Century Plant)

Bambusa multiplex (Fern leaf Bamboo)

Callistemon lanceolatus (Bottle-brush)

Chaenomeles speciosa (Flowering Quince)

Chamaerops (Chamaerops Palm)

Cleyera japonica (Cleyera)

Cuphea hyssopifolia (Mexican Heather)

FT *Eleagnus pungens 'Fruitlandii'* (Thorny Eleagnus)

Euonymus japonica (Japanese Euonymus)

Fatsia japonica (Japanese Fatsia)

Feijoa sellowiana (Pineapple Guava)

FT *Nerium oleander* (Oleander)

Hibiscus syriacus (Shrub Althea or Rose of Sharon)

FT *Ilex vomitoria* (Yaupon Holly)

Juniperus chinensis (Chinese Juniper)

N *Lantana spp.* (Lantana)

Ligustrum lucidum (Waxleaf, Glossy or Chinese Privet)
Ligustrum japonicum 'Recurvifolia' (Japanese Privet)
N,FT *Myrica cerifera* (Wax Myrtle)
FT *Opuntia compressa* (Prickly Pear)
Palmetto (Palmetto Palm)
FT *Pittosporum tobira* (Japanese Pittosporum)
Plumbago capensis
Podocarpus macrophyllus maki (Yew)
Pyracantha coccinia
Pyracantha koidzumi
Raphiolepis indica (Indian Hawthorn)
Rosa rugosa
Santolina chamaecyparissus (see Herbs)
Santolina virens
Serissa foetida
FT *Viburnum suspensum* (Sandankwa Viburnum)
FT *Viburnum tinus* (Laurustinus)
N,FT *Yucca aloifolia* (Spanish Bayonet)
FT *Yucca filamentosa* (Adam's Needle Yucca)
FT *Yucca gloriosa* (Mound-lily Yucca)

TREES
Butia capitata (Jelly Palm)
Eriobotrya japonica (Loquat)
N *Ilex opaca* (American Holly)
Juniperus chinensis 'Torulosa' (Hollywood Juniper)
Juniperus virginiana (Eastern Red Cedar)
Lagerstroemia indica (Crape Myrtle)
N *Magnolia grandiflora*
FT *Myrica cerifera* (Wax Myrtle)
Parkinsonia aculeata (Jerusalem Thorn)
N *Pinus elliotii* (Slash Pine)

N *Pinus palustris* (Longleaf Pine)
N *Pinus taeda* (Loblolly Pine)
Pinus thumbergiana (Japanese Black Pine)
N *Prunus caroliniana* (Carolina Cherry Laurel)
Punica granatum (Pomegranate)
N,FT *Quercus virginiana* (Live Oak)
N *Sabala palmetto* (Cabbage Palm)
Sapium sebiferum (Chinese Tallow Tree or Popcorn Tree)
Trachycarpus fortunei (Windmill Palm)

FRUITING SHRUBS AND TREES
Diospyros kaki 'Tane Nashi' (Japanese Persimmon)
Diospyros kaki 'Fuyugaki' (Japanese Persimmon)
Ficus carica 'Celeste' (Sugar Fig)
Ficus carica 'Brownturkey' (Sugar Fig)
Pyrus communis (Pear)
Vaccinium ashei (Rabbiteye Blueberry)
Vitis rotundifolia (Muscadine)

GRASSES
Cortaderia selloana (Pampas Grass)
Miscanthus sinensis (Japanese Silver Grass and varieties)
Pennisetum setaceum (Fountain Grass and varieties)

LAWN GRASS

Sod with St. Augustine only. You may seed with centipede or Bermuda grass.

FLOWERS

All annuals if protected. (Special favorites are gaillardia, lisianthus, marigold, zinnia, portulaca, sweet allysum, vinca and petunia.)
Daffodils
Hemerocallis hybrida (Daylily)

Container

Gardening

CONTAINER GARDENING

Container gardening is an art and can be a feature in your garden as important as any other landscape element. Containers make it possible to locate plants where other plantings are not possible and create visual interest in virtually any setting.

Container gardening has a broad appeal in today's fast paced society. Anyone can do it and do it well. In small courtyards a grouping of containers harmoniously arranged by size, shape, color, or medium creates a garden unto itself. A single outstanding container, such as an urn or large Italian terra cotta pot, can serve as a focal point beckoning one into a garden "room" or may brighten up a dark corner of your yard.

Container plantings can be functional as well as pretty. In our mild winter climate what could be more cheery on your patio than a tub of lettuces, parsley and mustards, or one of the winter hardy herbs, or a Meyer Lemon tree covered with fruit?

Containers make perfect statements on patios, porches and pool surrounds. Large ones can be incorporated into your garden beds to provide a focal point, continuity of color among perennials and annuals, or simply color interest and height among your evergreen shrubs where there is a gap. Hanging baskets are always attractive on summer porches or suspended from tree limbs, creating different height interests. Containers of all kinds have the potential to add great depth to your garden, as well as emphasizing various architectural aspects of your house, garage or driveway entrance. Nothing is more inviting than to be met at a front door or garden entrance by groupings of flowering plants or, more formally, by a matched pair of topiary evergreens.

Plants can be grown in almost anything you can imagine: an elegant lichen covered terra cotta pot, a rustic hollowed out tree stump, a stone trough, a beautiful cast iron urn, a paint bucket, a tin can, or even your grandmother's kitchen sink. Containers, however, should always reflect the character of your house and garden. A whiskey barrel, although perfect in a rustic setting marking an entrance drive by a split rail fence, would be out of place on the porch of a Georgian style home, as would a Grecian urn against a weathered fence. Just make sure the container provides adequate drainage.

To plant a wonderfully successful container, one must incorporate both artistic and horticultural aspects that are the result of thoughtful planning. Some containers may be planted with one special plant, a tall standard, a favorite-colored plant, an unusual succulent, or a fragrant plant located by a much-used path to your front door. Some of the most satisfying plantings are seasonal mixes. Whatever your choice, first and foremost, choose plants suited to your site. Consider the sun or shade level as well as the wind exposure. Be sure to look at plant label specifications for growing conditions as well as heat and cold hardiness. Avoid planting cool weather annuals, such as pansies, petunias or snapdragons, in the late spring because they will not withstand the imminent summer's grueling heat.

Matching your container to its occupants and to its surroundings, as well as choosing an aesthetically pleasing association of plants in a mixed container, takes into consideration the basic elements and principles of design required of any art form.   Primarily these include proportion and scale, balance, form, contrast, texture and color.   The mass of plant material should not be too large for the container or too small.   For instance, a large evergreen standard clipped into a ball at the top should be in the right proportion to its container. If the container seems too small, it may be corrected with a planting of flowers to create weight at the bottom.   Conversely, a planting of tiny forget-me-nots would not be the right scale for a half whiskey barrel.   A giant red mustard or acanthus leaf should not be planted next to a tiny viola or alyssum. Not only do the leaves mask and shade the smaller plant, the disparity of scale has a displeasing effect.

Visual interest in mixed containers comes from contrasting textures, shapes and sizes: lacy to broad, rough against smooth and glossy.   In a shade loving container a combination of ferns with different textures and colors can be just as interesting and beautiful as a floral combination.   For example, a planting of Bird's Nest Fern, Tassel Fern and variegated Korean Fern makes an interesting statement of varying textures and shapes and is also winter hardy in our zone.

A consideration of color combinations, although somewhat a marker of personal taste, is more pleasing when colors are blended harmoniously.   Avoid too many colors.   There are certain combinations that always work such as hot pink with an all green planting or with silver such as silver leaf Artemisia or Dusty Miller.   Silver foliage is very versatile as it can contrast or harmonize with almost any color.   Light colors and white, such as white impatiens, can successfully brighten a dark corner while purple flowers will disappear.

Planting a container requires several steps.   Of course, the larger the container, the happier your plants will be.   Roots will have more running space; water retention will be better; there will be less temperature change and more space for mixtures of plants.

Planting tips:
1. If planting a large container, plant on site.
2. For improved drainage always put terra cotta chards, gravel or Styrofoam peanuts in the bottom of the pots.   Mixed annuals only require about 12" of soil for root growth.
3. Use only the finest potting soil, usually found in the best nurseries.   Your soil should hold moisture, but also allow water to pass through it easily. Heavy, inexpensive varieties will not do this.
4. If using moisture-absorbing crystals, incorporate them into the soil according to the instructions.   There is some debate as to their effectiveness.
5. Fill the container to about one inch below its rim taking particular care to pat down the soil near the sides of the pot where heat and cold are closest to your plants.
6. If your container is to be placed in a bed, put it on a firm flat base such, as bricks or a flagstone, to keep it level.
7. Water and fertilize regularly. Incorporate slow release fertilizer at the time of planting and afterwards use a liquid fertilizer weekly. Containers dry out

more quickly than surrounding garden plants, so do not allow planters to dry out to the point of stressing your plants. In the heat of our summers, some containers may require twice daily watering.

Container gardening is demanding and requires almost daily commitment, but the results of your labor can provide satisfaction and pleasure year round--more than anything else in your garden. Because you will give your container more attention than your garden plantings, you can pack your plants tightly together for instant gratification. It is not necessary to leave space for the individual plants to grow.

Deadheading your flowering plants, as well as pinching back the scraggly leggy ones, will keep blooms coming longer and create bushier, healthier looking containers. To achieve perfection with your containers, adjustments are always necessary. Be prepared to change out plants periodically and be prepared to have a few spare plants available to replace any unhealthy or dead ones. You might have to move a container to find better light or a more protected spot.

For seasonal plantings there are generally two planting times in the lower south: winter to spring, and summer to fall. At the onset of winter, sometime in November, you can plant what you may have considered to be traditionally spring plants--pansies, violas, petunias, dianthus, snapdragons, many herbs, lettuces and vegetables. Although these plantings will not thrive during our coldest times, they will look presentable through the winter and will be better established for bursting forth at the first of spring, and will last until the first heat of summer. In early May, however, you will want to replant your annual containers with heat tolerant plants that will last throughout the summer until first frost.

Becoming a container gardener can add a fascinating and wonderful dimension to life. Try to create plantings, whether a series of pots of single specimens or just one large mixture, that are works of art. Avoid the boring, predictable, mass-produced plants. Take advantage of the locally owned, specialty nurseries that can guide you and teach you what is possible during the two planting seasons. Use resources available on the Internet for new plants and ideas of planting combinations. Visit the website for the University of Georgia's experimental gardens, www.uga.edu/athensselect to be informed of what's new and recommended for our climate.

Sometimes the secrets of plant combinations for any particular environment may only be revealed by trial and error. You may have the right microclimate to grow something your neighbor cannot grow. So be adventurous, have fun, and have the courage to fail.

Gardening for

Pollinators

GARDENING FOR POLLINATORS
Butterflies, Bees and Hummingbirds

In our climate, observation of wildlife, especially pollinators, in our gardens can provide immense entertainment for two-thirds of the year. Whether we're watching a hummingbird in stationary flight over a trumpet vine or a swallowtail resting on a black-eyed Susan, gardeners derive great satisfaction from the behavior of these seasonal visitors. They provide color, grace and industrious activity.

In addition to enhancing the enjoyment of our gardens, pollinators are essential for plant reproduction. Worldwide, over ninety percent of all flowering plants need either an insect or animal to distribute pollen so that the fruit or seed will set. We would not enjoy common foods such as squash, citrus, or berries or even cotton fabric without pollination.

Unfortunately, the population of pollinators has declined dramatically due to habitat loss, pesticide use, diseases and insects. For example, the honeybee population has dropped drastically in the past decade due to a parasitic mite.

How can we as gardeners help pollinators?

Gardeners can be proactive locally by creating food and habitat for them. Planting nectar rich flowering plants for the butterflies and hummingbirds, as well as host plants for butterfly caterpillars are the two most important steps we can take. A listing of appropriate nectar and host plants is printed at the end of this section.

Providing trees for perches and shrubby plants for shelter from wind and predators, as well as for nesting sites, are other helpful actions. Butterflies must warm up their wings each day before they can begin any activity, so placing a wide flat stone in a sunny location is appreciated.

Have you ever observed butterflies grouped around mud puddles? "Puddling" is their way of obtaining essential minerals from the soil. A good substitute is a mixture of sand (one gallon) and salt (1/2 cup) moistened and placed near the nectar plants in a shallow container.

Gardeners may also offer clean water in birdbaths and additional food in special feeders. Soft rotten fruit such as bananas and watermelon, as well as hummingbird nectar are favorites.

Finally, gardeners should try to avoid or minimize the use of pesticides and herbicides toxic to bees and other beneficial organisms. Insecticidal soaps and horticultural oils are less harmful. Their use should be confined only to those areas where the pests are located. Also nothing should be sprayed on open blossoms when pollinators are present.

Good nectar plants have flowers with a sweet fluid and either a short tubular structure for long bills (hummingbirds) or large, flat open-faced petals for landing (butterflies). Generally a large mass of a single color or closely related colors is more attractive to pollinators than an assortment of colors.

Providing a succession of blooming plants from early spring to late fall ensures food for these seasonal visitors. A mixture of trees, shrubs, vines, perennials and annuals will be most successful.

Good host plants for larvae are plants that caterpillars will eat. Often they have specific limited choices. An adult butterfly usually lays her eggs on the plant that the young will eat since baby caterpillars cannot travel far. When the appropriate plants are not available, their population declines.

The Most Common Butterflies in the Southeast and A Few Suggested Host Plants for their Caterpillars:

Buckeye –Petunias, snapdragons, verbena
Cabbage White – Mustard family including cabbage, nasturtium, cleome
Eastern Tailed Blue - Clovers
Eastern Tiger Swallowtail – Cherry, wild plum, ash, tulip tree
Gray Hairstreak – Clovers and others of pea family, rose of Sharon
Great Spangled Fritillary – Lantana, Joe-pye weed, pentas
Gulf Fritillary – Passion flowers
Monarch – Milkweed (Asclepias) species (the only plant the Monarch butterfly uses to lay its eggs.)
Orange Sulphur – Pea family ,clovers
Pearl Crescent – Asters, daisies, zinnia, mint
Question Mark – Elms, nettles, sugarberry
Red-spotted Purple – Cherries, willow
Sleepy Orange – Wild sennas
Silver-spotted Skipper – Wisteria, pea family, native grasses
Spring Azure – Blueberry, cherry, dogwood, holly, viburnum
Viceroy – Elms, willows, cherry

Nectar Plants for Butterflies, Bees and Hummingbirds:
* indicates top attractors

Shrubs and Trees
Abelia x grandiflora (Glossy Abelia)
Aesculus pavia (Red Buckeye)
Amelanchier (Shadbush)
*Buddleia davidii (Butterfly Bush)
Cercis canadensis (Redbud)
Chaenomeles spp. (Flowering Quince)
Clethra alnifolia (Sweet Pepperbush)
Illex vomitoria (Yaupon Holly)
Itea virginica (Virginia Sweetspire)
Kolkwitzia (Beautybush)

Lirodendron tulipifera (Tulip Poplar)
Persea borbonia (Redbay)
Philadelphus (Mock-Orange)
Quercus virginiana (Live Oak)
Rhododendron spp. (Azalea)
Sabal palmetto (Cabbage Palm)
Vaccinium arboretum (Blueberry)
Vitex agnus-castus (Chaste Tree)
Viburnum spp. (Viburnum)
Yucca spp. (Yucca)

Perennials
Achillea millefolium (Yarrow)
Allium sphaerocephalum
   (Ornamental Garlic)
Aquilegia canadensis (Wild Columbine)
Aralia spinosa (Devil's Walking Stick)

*Asclepias tuberosa (Butterfly Weed)
*Aster spp. (Aster)
Ceratostigma plumbaginoides
   (Blue Plumbago)
*Coreopsis spp. (Tickseed)

205

Dianthus spp. (Pink)
Dianthus barbatus (Sweet William)
Dicentra spectabilis (Bleedng Heart)
*Echinacea purpurea
   (Purple Coneflower)
*Eupatorium purpureum
   (Joe-Pye Weed)
Helenium autumnale (Sneezeweed)
Hemerocallis (Daylily)
Iris virginica (Blue Flag Iris)
*Lantana camara (Lantana)
*Liatris spicata (Gayfeather)

Lilium spp. (Lily)
Lobelia cardinalis
   (Cardinal Flower)
*Monarda didyma (Bee Balm)
Phlox spp.
*Rudbeckia hirta
   (Black-eyed Susan)
Salvia spp.
Solidago spp. (Goldenrod)
Verbena spp. (Verbena)

Annuals

Antirrhinum majus (Snapdragon)
Cassia (Cassia)
Cosmos bipinnatus (Cosmos)
Delphinium elatum (Delphinium)
Digitalis (Foxglove)
Gaillardia pulchella (Blanket Flower)
Gomphrena globosa (Globe Amaranth)
*Helianthus annuus (Sunflower)
Heliotropium arborescens (Heliotrope)
Impatiens spp. (Impatiens)

*Pentas lanceolata (Star Flower)
Petunia (Petunia)
Tagetes (Marigold)
Tithonia rotundifolia
   (Mexican Sunflower)
Tropaeolum majus (Nasturtium)
*Verbena spp. (Verbena)
Viola (Pansy)
Zinnia (Zinnia)

Corms, Grasses, Ground Covers and Vines
Aguga (Bugleweed)
Bignonia capreolata (Cross Vine)
Campsis radicans (Trumpet Creeper)
Chasmanthium latifolium (Inland Sea Oats)
Crocosmia (Montbretia)
Ipomoea spp. (Morning Glory)
Lonicera sempervirens (Trumpet Honeysuckle)
Panicum virgatum (Switchgrass)
Passiflora incarnata (Passion Vine)

Citrus for the

Lower South

CITRUS FOR THE LOWER SOUTH

Growing citrus fruit in the lower south can be successful, as well as decorative and delicious. The trees are evergreen, and the fragrance from the blossoms and the abundant fruit make them a welcome addition to any garden.

When purchasing your citrus tree, the first factor to consider is cold hardiness. Many varieties cannot tolerate any frost, but others will do quite well in most of our winters. Be sure to do proper research or use local nurseries. Dwarf plants are a good option for the smaller garden. They do well in containers; the size may vary from 4 to 10 feet.

The location of your planting is critical. Select a sunny, wind-free spot. In front of a south facing wall or a stand of trees may be just the spot. In addition, they may do very well in a container on a patio where you can enjoy the fragrance. The container can be moved when there is a heavy freeze.

Citrus require good drainage and rich, slightly acid soil. The soil should be kept moist but not soggy; watering deeply about twice a week in the spring and summer should suffice. Keep your citrus well fertilized with any brand of citrus fertilizer until September. The leaves will turn yellow if the plant does not have enough fertilizer. Keep any growth below the graft (swelling toward bottom of trunk) pruned away to keep the suckers from overwhelming the growth.

Pests are definitely a problem – including aphids, whiteflies and scale. Keep an eye out for problems and treat accordingly.

Depending on the age of your tree when you buy it, you can harvest fruit in a couple of years.

PLANTING TIPS:

- Plant in full sun if possible, because more sun means more fruit.
- Do not plant too deeply. Root ball should be just above the level of the ground.
- Do not mulch or sod under citrus trees, because mulch promotes root rot.
- Start using dry citrus fertilizer in March to promote new growth. Fertilize each month until September
- Young trees are helped by the addition of liquid fertilizer, between applications of dry fertilizer, during the growing season.
- Remove young fruit from the trees for the first 2 or 3 years to promote growth and stronger trees except for lemons, limes and kumquats.
- Do not let trees dry out during winter. **Most citrus trees that die during the winter are killed by the lack of water, not the cold temperatures.**

(tips courtesy of Flying Dragon Citrus Nursery, Jacksonville, FL)

Below is a brief list of citrus cultivars that are cold hardy and have been successful in the lower south. Many more are available and new cultivars are regularly introduced, so be open to new possibilities.

Grapefruit:

Dwarf Star Ruby – Sweet flavor; large fruit; deep red flesh.

Kumquat:
  Meiwea - Large and round; sweet with few seeds.
  Nagame – oval; most common in U.S.
Lemon:
  Meyer Lemon – Some are hardy to 20 °; has lower acidity than other lemons.
Orange:
  Amber Sweet – Most cold hardy; sweetest and juiciest; vibrant orange.
  Hamlin – More tart; pale yellow to green; seedless.
Mandarin:
  Satsuma – Ripe in fall; peels easily; most cold tolerant.

NOTES

Gingers

GINGERS
John McEllen

The old-fashioned stalwart, white butterfly ginger has been joined by a host of outstanding new cultivars in many colors and sizes, filling many niches in the southern garden. Gingers are wonderful garden plants for our warm humid climate in which they thrive. Many are good for pot cultivation. They include tall plants, short plants, plants with ornate foliage and with sweet fragrance. There are plants for sun and shade, and flower color ranges from soft lavender blue to bright red, orange, pink, purple, yellow, gold, white and shades in between.

Gingers prefer moist organic soils, but certainly are not temperamental. While they generally die down in the winter, full growth is achieved when days become longer and warmer. They bring a welcome vitality to the garden in the long, hot, humid days of summer. For the most part, gingers are disease and pest resistant and, as long as soil is good and moisture adequate, little fertilization is needed. Ginger flowers and foliage are great for flower arranging and the plants are deer resistant.

The list of available gingers is increasing every year with new hybrids and new discoveries. Catalogs and Internet sites, along with local nurseries, offer many cultivars.

Gingers – Zingiberacae

Alpinia – Roots hardy to 15 °; partial sun to light shade; grown more for foliage than for flower

Alpina zerumbet (Shell Ginger) - 8' to 9'; dark green 2' long, 5" wide leaves; waxy white or pinkish shell-like flowers on pendant clusters; remove canes that have flowered

Alpina zerumbet 'Variegata' – very attractive gold striped leaves; 3'-4' tall; excellent in large containers

Costus – Spiral gingers; shade to light shade; rhizomatous perennials; hardiness of other available cultivars is questionable

Costus malortieanus (Spiral Ginger) – 6'- 8'; the leaves lance shaped, mid green, and a distinct spiral growth habit; terminal buds are orange with yellow bracts but true show is the spiral growth

Curcuma – Light shade to shade; makes larger and larger clump; fleshy roots and thick aromatic rhizomes; leaves are narrowly ovate to oblong; cone-like terminal inflorescences are formed from colorful bracts; genus of 40 species and more becoming available each year – great additions to our summer gardens for foliage and flowers

Curcuma alismatifolia (Pink Tulip) – 2'; long narrow stiff leaves; pink inflorescence which resembles a tulip

Curcuma rocoeana 'Jewel of Burma' – 2'-3'; 6"-8" bright orange cone with yellow flowers

Dichorisandra thyrsifolia – 3' to 5'; not a true ginger but actually a member of Wandering Jew family (Tradescantia); 3"-4" erect fleshy stems; spirally arranged lance shaped, lustrous dark green leaves, 8"-12" long; dense terminal racemes 5"-8" long of an intense blue in autumn.

Elaftavia cardamomum (Cardamom) – Evergreen perennial for shade; rhizomatous; fruits provide spice

Globba (Dancing Girl Gingers) – About 70 species; rhizomatous herbaceous perennials from SE Asia; bear 3 petaled tubular flowers on slender branched stalks in terminal pendant racemes from autumn to winter
  Globba schomburgkii – yellow inflorescence followed by formation of many bulbils; becomes rampant ground cover in shady areas
  Globba wintii – (Mauve Dancing Girl) - 2' tall with 6" to 8" pendant inflorescence of long lasting purple bracks; perennial; a less reliable white form is 'White Dragon'.

Hedychium (Butterfly Gingers) – About 40 species
  Hedychium coronarium (White) – old-fashioned southern favorite; many new varieties and hybrids are becoming available
  Hedychium coronarium (Orange) – 12" –18" spikes of orange flowers
  Hedychium 'Dr. May' – 4' blue-green foliage with fragrant yellow flowers
  Hedychium 'Elizabeth' – 6'-8'; dark green foliage; raspberry scented flowers
  Hedychium 'Pink Flame' – 5'; white butterfly-like blooms with deep rose flame-like spots on lips; fragrant; grow in sun to partial shade; great in mixed borders; late summer fall bloom; excellent cut flowers

Kaempferia (Peacock Gingers) – Very attractive patterned leaves; use as you might hosta; deciduous in winter; new introductions and hybrids are coming to market each year; purple flowers in most varieties but grown for foliage; outstanding addition to our summer shade gardens
  Kaempferia 'Alva' – 10"-12" large leaves with brushes in patterns of maroon and green edged in white
  Kaempheria atrovirens 'Silver Peacock'– bold silver patterned leaves
  Kaempheria 'Grande' 2'-3' green, white and bronze pattern on upper side of leaf, maroon underside
  Kaempheria afflactica 'Brush Strokes'– 5"; large red markings; 'Satin Checks' glossy, dark markings

Zingiber daceyi – (Pine Cone Ginger or Shampoo Ginger) - basal cone shaped with white flowers with a fragrant watery sap which can be used for washing; excellent cut flower

NOTES

Invasive Plants

of the Southeast

INVASIVE PLANTS OF THE SOUTHEAST
THE WAR OF THE WEEDS

Invasive, non-native organisms pose a threat to our natural environment by displacing native species, destroying natural habitat and choking waterways. Because they are free of the parasites, diseases and herbivores present in their native lands, invasives experience rapid and unrestricted growth, costing our country billions annually to control. The unrestrained growth of these invaders can result in extinction of rare species and threaten the populations of many of our valuable native plants which define the foundation of our American landscape. Due to the fact that the climate of the southeastern United States is similar to portions of China and Japan, where many of these exotics originate, the southeast is particularly vulnerable to destructive invasive species from those regions.

In your garden, invasives will be easy to combat by following a few simple rules:

* Seek information on species invasive in your area from botanical gardens, and government agencies such as your county extension agent.
* Ask for only non-invasive species when you acquire plants. Ask your nursery retailer not to sell invasives and to offer native or other non-invasive alternatives.
* Wherever possible, remove invasives from your garden or manage them to prevent spread. Management may include pruning away flowers, removing seeds, mowing or herbicide use.

The following are among the most invasive species of the southeast:

1. Chinese Privet, *Ligustrum sinense*
2. Nepalese Browntop, *Microstegium vimineum*
3. Autumn Olive, *Elaeagnus umbellata*
4. Chinese Wisteria, *Wisteria sinensis*, & Japanese Wisteria, *W. floribunda*
5. Mimosa, *Albizia julibrissin*
6. Japanese Honeysuckle, *Lonicera japonica*
7. Multiflora Rose, *Rosa multiflora*
8. Hydrilla, *Hydrilla verticillata*
9. Kudzu, *Pueraria Montana*
10. Golden Bamboo, *Phyllostachys aurea*
11. English Ivy, *Hedera helix*
12. Chinese Tallow, *Sapium sebiferum*

Source: Georgia Exotic Pest Plant Council — www.gaeppc.org

Note: Not all "exotics" are invasive. Many introduced or non-native plants are easily controlled, especially in restricted garden spaces and can be elegant and rewarding ornamentals. They can have great economic value and do not disrupt our natural ecosystems or threaten biological diversity.

Culture

BASIC ORCHID CULTURE
Gail Matthews

Orchids have become extremely popular, both in home decor and in home gardens. The appeal of orchids is probably due to the length of bloom time on some varieties and the discovery that they are not difficult to grow. Orchids are the largest group of flowering plants in the world and they grow almost everywhere, from near Arctic to near desert environments. Because of this wide range of habitats, there are no rules that fit all orchids. As a matter of fact, the closest to an absolute in orchid culture is that "for every rule there is an exception".

There are seven basic needs: water, light, temperature, fertilizer, humidity, air movement and support. Ideally, all of these factors should be kept in balance. When one need goes up, all needs should go up, and likewise when one need goes down, all needs should go down. In summer light intensity goes up, so should water, fertilizer, humidity, etc. In the gray days of January, when there is less available light, water and fertilizer needs are less. The one exception here is air movement, which especially is needed when light and temperature go down.

Over watering kills more orchids than anything else. The exception here is that while too much water will kill an orchid, one should never water "just a little". When you do water, water copiously. The visible roots should turn green. Then don't water again until the plant is almost dry. When in doubt, wait to water. It takes much longer to kill an orchid by under watering than by over watering. An easy way to see how dry it is down inside the pot where the roots are (without sticking your finger down there and destroying your manicure), is to stick the blunt end of a wooden shish kabob skewer down into the media about midway between the plant and the outside edge of the pot. After about thirty minutes, remove the skewer. The color of the wood will tell you how wet the plants roots are.

Light is the most critical factor in blooming. If you do everything else right and don't give your orchid enough light, you will not get any blooms. About ninety percent of the time that orchids don't re-bloom, lack of sufficient light is responsible. Leaves should be a bright, almost lime green. Nice dark leaves mean you are growing a nice foliage plant, and probably aren't going to have any flowers. More information on proper light levels appears under the various genera.

Temperature is pretty easy. Most orchids like the same temperatures we do. When we are too hot, so are they, and likewise with the cold. They generally quit growing at 85 degrees, but will tolerate higher temperatures. Lows tolerated range from 28 to 60 degrees. More specifics will be covered under the various genera.

For fertilizer, remember the old sayings of "weakly weekly" and "what kind is less important than using SOME kind". Bloom booster (with a higher number in the middle of the three numbers) should be used once the leaf growth is complete. Switch to a higher nitrogen fertilizer (the first of the three numbers) after your plant has bloomed.

Humidity should ideally be between 40% and 70% and that amount is pretty hard on your furniture and walls. Consider putting your plants outside for the summer where they will love our high humidity. Grouping plants will also increase the humidity in an area.

Air movement helps orchids in many ways; it cools the leaves and reduces the chance of bacteria and fungi forming on the leaves of wet or crowded plants. The amount of movement needed is enough for gentle movement of the leaves. Ceiling fans or a small oscillating fan should do the trick.

Support is what the orchid grows in or on. With so many orchids available from so many sources, you may find them bare root or in what appears to be soil. Bare root means you can water daily, or even several times a day. The media, that appears to be soil, must be allowed to completely dry before watering.

COMMONLY GROWN ORCHIDS:

Phalaenopsis and paphiodilums are very similar in their requirements. Grow them in medium light and don't allow them to get completely dry. Phalaenopsis may need a cooling off period in the fall to know that it is time to bloom. Let their temperature go down into the fifties, but not below, for a couple of weeks.

Dendrobiums, oncidiums, and cattleyas all need more light than the phalaenopsis and paphiodilums, and also need to be slightly drier between waterings. Dendrobiums (especially the phalaenopsis type) like more fertilizer (try giving them a slight top-dressing or timed release fertilizer in the spring); water them more during high light and high temperatures, and they should reward you with flowers twice a year. The dendrobiums do not like temperatures below 60 degrees, while the oncidiums and cattleyas will tolerate fifties or even upper forties.

Vandas come in lots of bright, beautiful colors and require very high light and daily watering. Sprinkler systems work well for busy growers. When given high light, watered daily and fed at least weekly, they will bloom multiple times each summer.

Cymbidiums really don't like our summers, but they love our winters. High light levels are needed, but provide some shade during the hot summers. They do well from 28 degrees up to 80 degrees. Grow them outside as long as the temperatures are above the upper twenties; move them inside on the occasions that nighttime temperatures fall below 28, and back outside when it warms up slightly. Give them a generous sprinkling of slow release fertilizer in the spring and feed them additionally any time you are feeding anything else. A top dressing of dry manure is good. When the temperatures rise in the summer, they will appreciate having their foliage cooled off with water daily, but not enough to over-wet the pots. Stop all nitrogen in August and give them a liberal dose of super phosphate. Do not bring them inside to enjoy the flowers until the flowers open. An abrupt change in temperature and humidity can cause the buds to drop. This sounds like a lot of trouble, but they can be magnificent with multiple spikes of 15 or more flowers that last for months.

A few additional tips:

- Plants brought back from Hawaii in mesh bags are usually babies and will take up to seven years to mature and bloom.
- If you are an overwaterer, try planting your orchid in a clay pot, which dries out quicker than a plastic pot.
- If you tend to under water, use plastic pots.
- Hold your hand about 12 inches above your plant during the brightest part of the day.
- A fuzzy shadow is enough for phalaenopsis and some paphiodilums. A sharp shadow is enough for dendrobiums and oncidiums. Exception: watch leaf color.
- Orchids are the original survivors: tough plants that are hard to kill.
- Find a local retailer and ask questions.
- Join your local orchid society.
- Orchids can be addictive! Like potato chips, one is not enough!

Designing a Landscape

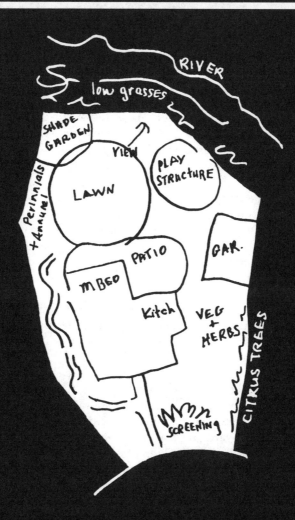

for Your Home and Garden

DESIGNING A LANDSCAPE FOR YOUR HOME AND GARDEN

Kathrine Clark
Savannah, Georgia

A home landscape and garden is your personal outdoor environment. As such, it is important to give proper consideration to its plan. Your garden will envelop your home, give shelter to you and your family, provide habitat for a wide assortment of wildlife, and represent who you are to the general public.

Before designing your garden you should take an inventory of the elements within the space that may affect your design. Note the locations of trees, power lines and other utilities, water spigots, walkways, driveways, and places that people generally walk through and enter your house. The orientation of your area is also important as it will influence the amount and intensity of sun it will receive. On the north side of any structure or feature, shadows will fall. In the summer they will be shorter, but in the winter shadows will be much longer. This will have a direct effect on what you can and cannot grow, especially if you want to grow winter flowering annuals. Likewise, a west-facing location is the hottest in summer and many delicate woodland specimens may not survive.

Ideally, you will be creating a space for human comfort and enjoyment. Many unpleasant aspects of a space can be improved by proper landscape design, such as adding canopy trees for shade or hiding unpleasant views with a screen of shrubs. Likewise, attractive areas may be enhanced or highlighted by proper framing and colorful accents.

Make a list of what you would like to achieve through your design. Do you want a place for entertaining, an inviting entrance, or a place for thought and reflection? Although some of your ideas may seem abstract, there is often a way to achieve an effect if you can articulate your desire. Consider where you live, the style of your home and surroundings, and where you are: in the city, suburbs, or in the country.

Walk around your neighborhood or one with landscapes that you admire. Try to identify as many of the plants and landscape elements that you can. Pay attention to where they are placed and how tall they are. Take notes or photographs if necessary. Don't be shy about saying hello to someone if you see them working in their yard. It's not as common to talk to strangers these days, but most good gardeners enjoy talking about their favorite pastime.

Also, visit a few nurseries and garden shops in your community. Get to know the people who work there. Buy a few small plants for your patio from time to time and soon you have started a relationship that may last for years.

Why is this important? A landscape evolves and changes from season to season and over the years. Once you plant a shrub or a tree, or even a flower, it continues to grow and eventually dies. Also, it is a rare person who can achieve a total home landscape instantly. Even if it were completely installed by a crew of professionals, the work would not be finished. There's always a need for fine tuning, maintenance, and changes. Essentially, your landscape will become part of your life.

As delightful as the vegetative world can be, a large part of the success of your landscape will be based on the structure or bones of your design. Structure is simply the organizing element of the plan. Often the structure relates directly to the architecture of your home. Usually there is a clear geometric or simple curvilinear layout to the overall design. It is frequently reflected in the shape of the lawn and patio, the arrangement of planting beds, the location of walkways, trees, walls, hedges, and smaller features. Staying true to the theme will give a feeling of correctness and logic that a more haphazard approach will not.

Because almost all shrubs, trees and other ornamentals have general habits of growth, you can approximate the effect they will have on your plan with very little artistic training. These forms can be used together to create an interesting composition that will complement the architecture of your home and environment.

For instance, take a digital photo of your home or proposed garden area. Print out several copies on ordinary bond paper. Try drawing simple plant forms, ovals, smaller circles, long soft horizontal shapes, and spiky grasses directly on top of an area you would like to change. You can quickly see what effect a new shrub or tree will have before you even make your purchase.

For some people it is easier to visualize a landscape from an aerial perspective, known simply as a plan view. For large projects, a plan is essential for coming up with an accurate count of the plants you will need to purchase, as well as the correct spacing for them. Correct spacing of new plant material is essential to the success of your design. Please consult your plant lists to determine the mature size and spacing recommendations for your selection. If you plant closer than you should, not only will you have to spend more time on maintenance, but you may also be setting yourself up for unhealthy-looking, diseased plants.

If you have access to an accurate survey of your property and a house plan, your job is halfway done. If not, you will need to create a measured drawing of the area for which you are designing. For foundation planting, draw the outline of your home and show the location of your windows, doors, walkways, driveway, trees, and any other physical elements which could affect your design. Draw the outlines of your planting beds; let them reinforce the structure of your design. Make them wide enough to accommodate at least three rows of shrubs. Keep them simple and clean.

Carefully estimate the width of each shrub form you have drawn on your photograph. Using a circle template or a ruler, mark out the width of that shrub and draw a light circle in the approximate location you have selected. Stagger your rows of plants rather than lining them up like a grid. This locks the forms together into a unified and surprisingly natural looking mass. Likewise, when you place the second and even third row of smaller plants in front, they will not only be shorter in height, but will also look best if their positions are locked into the design by staggering them into the gaps behind them.

Generally speaking, it is best to use larger groups of a few shrubs rather than a multitude of individuals. By varying the form, texture, or color of the groups a surprisingly interesting effect will often occur. Alternating or repeating elements, such as small groupings of tall shrubs with larger groupings of lower species and back again, creates a rhythm which will supply both unity and interest. Layering lower growing plants in front of the taller ones behind them also adds sophistication and depth to the design.

If you plan your garden so that it is beautiful in winter when most of the leaves and flowers are gone, it will be fabulous in springtime.

Xeriscaping

XERISCAPING

The goal of xeriscaping is to reduce the amount of water the lawn, garden and landscape need to remain healthy. Xeriscaping (from the Greek word for "dry") is the creative use of plants that are drought-tolerant and sustainable and can encompass the use of many plants, not only cacti and other desert varieties. Since native plants have had centuries to adapt to local weather patterns, it is preferable to use these, as they rarely need extra water once they've become established in the first year of planting.

During the summer, nearly 50% of total water consumption is used to irrigate yards and landscapes. About half of that is applied unnecessarily or is wasted. (It is a fact that there is little correlation between the amount of water a plant actually needs and that which is applied.)

SOME SUGGESTIONS:

Soil Improvement: Organic matter added to soils improves the water-retention capacity.

Modify the Lawn Area: Reduce lawn area where possible. Include more drought-tolerant groundcovers wherever possible. There are over 30 million acres of grass lawn in the US and each 25-40 foot section requires 10,000 gallons of water a summer.

Surface Mulches: With proper mulches applied at the appropriate depth, the soil moisture percentage can be kept twice as high as compared to bare soil.

Zoned Irrigation: Most plants, including turf grasses, develop deeper root systems and tolerate drought better if watered infrequently, but deeper.
  a) Retrofitting an existing landscape to make it more water-efficient also provides considerable economic benefits. Group plants with similar watering needs.
  b) Use efficient watering systems such as drip irrigation or soaker hoses.

As gardeners, we can learn how to lower our water use and stop run-off, thereby protecting our rivers and streams.

Succulents

SUCCULENTS

Many cacti and succulents are quite tough and therefore much easier to grow than people suspect, either as potted plants in a bright window or as interesting contributions to a protected spot in the garden.

Succulent plants, including the cactus family, have a highly specialized anatomy to enable them to survive prolonged drought. Because of their ability to survive, succulents are successful plants, both for containers and for protected and dry locations, to add interest and variety to our gardens during summer's heat and drought.

Many cacti and succulents will survive the winter in our coastal south but are less hardy inland, where the temperatures are lower. However, all are extremely easy to propagate, and when threatened with sub-freezing temperatures, it is simple to take cuttings for rooting indoors. When preparing cuttings to root, it is important to leave them unpotted at room temperature for several days to harden off before placing them in soil in a pot.

Recommended:

Aeonium – Pale green, fleshy leaves

Agave – Many sizes and colors; often terminal thorns

Aloe – Leaves reputed to contain healthful juice

Crassula – A large family containing plants with many variations, most with fleshy leaves

Delosperma cooperi – Low, freely branching with purple flowers; an excellent ground cover in a dry sunny spot

Dudleya – Often rosette form

Echeveria – Also beautiful rosettes

Euphorbia – A large, varied family, one of the more frequently seen is the Crown of Thorns; recently hybridized

Gasteria – Low, stemless plants with opposite leaves

Haworthia – Stemless rosettes

Kalanchoe – Varied blooming and non-blooming cultivars; often used in containers

Sedum – Largely small ground covers; often hardy; in many colors

Sempervivum – Rosettes of varying sizes and colors; generally hardy

Senecio – Usually tender; of many varieties; often used for containers

PLANT NOMENCLATURE

Why bother with proper botanical names? They are frequently difficult to pronounce and are written in such different ways that it is confusing. On the other hand, once understood, botanical nomenclature is a language used around the world and is a standard to be used to make certain you obtain the plant that you want. For instance, you tell your nurseryman you want a "Grancy Greybeard." He may not know that is another common name for a "Fringe Tree," but the botanical name *Chionanthus virginicus* is unmistakable.

Although the nomenclature seems confusing, it need not be if one understands the basics. The binomial system of nomenclature was developed by Linneaus in 1753. Each plant has at least two names which indicates its genus and species. Genus refers to a broad group of plants which share similar physical characteristics and are more like each other than any other group. Thus, the genus *Ilex* is a group of 400 different plants known commonly as hollies.

As we all know, there are a number of different types or species of Ilex. A species is marked or distinguished by specific features which continue from generation to generation. The species name completes the binomial name. Thus, we have the *Ilex cornuta,* commonly known as the Chinese Holly. Note that the genus is capitalized and that both names are generally italicized or underlined.

A variety is another subdivision of a species. Varieties are found in nature. *Ilex cornuta burfordii,* Burford holly, is a variety of *Ilex cornuta.* The leaf of the *I. cornuta* is square or oblong with at least 3 stout spines. *Ilex cornuta burfordii* may have one or no terminal spine. Otherwise plant characteristics are similar.

A cultivar is essentially a cultivated variety. It has been developed by selection or by hybridization. If propagated from seed, it will not be true to the parent. *Ilex cornuta burfordii* 'Avery Island' is a yellow fruited cultivar of *I. cornuta.* Note the single quotes. Also it is not italicized or underlined. Many are not in Latin form.

In review:

Genus	Species	Variety	Cultivar	Common Name
Ilex	*cornuta*			Chinese Holly
Ilex	*cornuta*	*burfordii*		Burford Holly
Ilex	*cornuta*	*burfordii*	'Avery Island'	Burford Holly 'Avery Island'

Hybrid is used to designate the offspring that result from a cross between two species of genera. It may occur in nature through horticultural engineering to create plants of increased hardiness or yield. Hybrids are identified by the use of an X.

Many of the Greek and Latin words used describe some aspect of the plant.

229

leaf (-folius, -phyllus)
   heterophyllus–having 2 or more kinds of leaves
   microphyllus–small-leaved
flower (-anthus, florus)
   floribundus–free-blooming
   grandiflorus–large flowers
   pleniflorus–double-flowered
size
   humilis, nanus–dwarf
   altus–tall
   micro–small
   macro–large
color
   rubrus–red
   albus–white
   flavus–yellow
   chrysanthis–golden flowered
   pallidus–pale
   argenteus–silvery
   violaceus–violet
   virens–green
habit of growth
   prostratus–lying on ground
   repens–creeping
   divaricatus–spreading
   cristatus–crested
   fastigiatus–branches erect
origin
   chinensis, sinensis–China
   japonica–Japan
   orientalis–old world
human value
   edulis–edible
   officinalis–medicinal

Other names may be reminiscent of mythology (Narcissus). Some are commemorative (Franklinia). Perhaps learning the origin of the name can help you remember it.

Trustees' Garden Club

S	M	T	W	T	F	S
			1	2	3	4
5	6	7	8	9	10	11
12	13	14	15	16	17	18
19	20	21	22	23	24	25
26	27	28	29	30	31	

Savannah, Georgia

JANUARY

January is the month to get a head start on spring. There is plenty of work to be done both inside and out. Arbor Day is the third Friday of the month.

PLAN: On days too cold for anything else, you can learn from garden **catalogs** (see section on Sources). Plan your garden for a succession of blooms and vegetable harvests. Try a few new plant selections as well as old favorites. The nurseries will have lovely bedding plants later in the spring, but it is fun to try something different.

PLANT: Shrubs and **trees** may be planted or transplanted this month. Dig a large enough hole, add organic material such as peat or compost, if needed, and water well to eliminate all air pockets. Shrubs and trees like to be planted no deeper than the original soil line. Leave at least one inch of dirt ball exposed to allow for settling. When transplanting, head (prune) back one quarter of the growth to overcome the loss of roots.

Annuals and **perennials** that may be sown into the ground at this time include poppies and larkspur, but most think that they do better with a fall sowing.

Tulips should be planted this month. They should have been in the refrigerator for about two months prior to planting. Daffodils may still be planted.

Sow, outside, seeds of parsley, and perennial **herbs** such as thyme, sage, and rosemary. Also sow, outside, the seeds of cold weather annuals such as chervil and coriander. Start basil inside. Put in perennial plants.

The following **vegetable** seeds may be sown outside in January: English peas, edible pea pods, collards, spinach, lettuce, leeks, and mustard. Sow seeds of carrots and beets in late January. Put out broccoli, brussel sprout, and cauliflower plants and onion sets.

For an early start, sow peppers inside for transplanting.

PRUNE: Pruning tools should be sharpened and oiled so they will be ready for the spring.

Unless there has been a severe freeze, you may begin removing **diseased** and **injured limbs** from trees. Make a clean cut with the newly sharpened tools. Remove unsightly shoots and **crossing branches.**

FERTILIZE: Make beds ready by digging and adding organic matter. Add lime and other nutrients as indicated by your soil analysis from the county extension agent. In beds where you intend to interplant, scratch in the organic material, fertilizer, and lime. Be careful not to disturb shallow rooted plants.

Ideally, you have had a soil analysis done in the fall and have applied the lime as recommended. If not, you may apply **lime** now to all plants except acid loving plants as azaleas, camellias, Japanese iris, Siberian iris, and blueberries. Lime takes several months to activate so it is best to apply it early. Gerbera daisies bloom more profusely if given lime.

MISCELLANEOUS: Pull **seedling trees** from beds and borders while they are easy to see and before they get larger.

Throw coffee grounds on **acid loving plants** as azaleas and camellias.

In case of a **hard freeze**, place Spanish moss over pansies and other tender plants. It is easy to remove as it begins to warm.

Mark the handles of your **tools** with bright orange or yellow tape so they don't get lost in the beds.

Clean up garden **debris** in which many insects and some diseases will be wintering.

Take **hardwood cuttings** for propagating difficult to find shrubs and trees. There can be great satisfaction in growing a tree from a stick and, certainly, it is cheaper. The following is a very simple method: Dig peat into the earth about one foot deep in a sheltered location. Cut ten inches of last year's growth from the desired plant. Dip the cutting in rooting hormone and place gently into the loose earth, keep watered. Roots should be well established by May or June. Deutzia, crape myrtle, buddleia, kerria and hypericum are a few of the more easily rooted plants.

Force **flowering branches** inside for spring color. Select the branches with care. Consider that you are pruning the plant so look at the form of the tree. Consider also the shape of the tree. Are there crossing branches or inward directed branches that need to be removed? Cut the branch, selecting for shape and buds. Place it in warm water and store in a cool, dimly lit room. Keep the water clean by changing it about once a week or add a handful of charcoal to the water. As the buds swell bring the branches into more light. Mist to prevent drying. Arrange as the buds begin to open.

YOUR COLORFUL GARDEN

Trees and Shrubs:

Burford Holly	Flowering Quince
Camellia japonica	Taiwan Cherry
Daphne odora	Winter Honeysuckle
Flowering Apricot	

Bulbs, Annuals and Perennials:

Crocus	Pansy
Iris unquicularis	Scilla
Narcissus	Snowflake

FEBRUARY

Soil preparation and pruning should be completed in February to be ready for spring. This is an important month for planting trees, shrubs and roses.

PLANT: Trees and **shrubs** are best planted now. This will allow roots to become somewhat established before top growth begins. Always dig a hole much larger than the roots. Work in organic matter if needed. If the plant is bare rooted, place the roots over a cone of dirt. Never place the plant too low. Fill in with soil and water well. Shrubs and trees should be mulched following planting.

Flowering plants, both **annuals** and **perennials,** may be put in the ground as they become available in the nurseries. For variety and to get the colors you want, you might wish to grow from seed. Try gaillardia, nemophilia, gloriosa daisy and many others. Experiment! Begin seeds of tender annuals indoors. Nasturtiums may be sown in the soil where they will grow. They like poor soil.

Roses should be planted this month. You must have a well drained, sunny location, and you must prepare the ground adequately with organic material, fertilizer and lime. Proper preparation will ensure years of pleasure.

Rapid maturing, cool season **vegetables** as lettuce, garden peas, edible pea pods, radishes, carrots, spinach, mustard and potatoes may still be sown outside this month. Plants of cabbage and cauliflower, onions and broccoli may be put out. Do this early in the month so they will produce before hot summer weather arrives.

For an early start, begin seeds of warm weather vegetable as tomatoes, peppers and eggplant inside, so they will be ready for placing out after the danger of frost.

Continue to plant perennial herbs and cool weather annual herbs. Now is a good time to sow dill. Tulips still may be planted.

DIVIDE: Divide and replant **perennials, ferns** and **ground covers.** Share what you cannot use with other gardeners or potential gardeners.

PRUNE: H eavy pruning for size and shape may be accomplished this month on all but spring flowering **shrubs** and **trees.** Prune out all dead, injured and diseased branches. Remove unsightly shoots and suckers at the base. Prune out long branches deep within the body of the plant to obtain a natural look. Vitex, crape myrtle, and others that bloom in the summer should be pruned this month. They bloom on new growth and will benefit from a good winter pruning including removal of all old flowerheads. Prune out old canes on oleander. Top the other canes to control size. Prune *Camellia sasanqua*, Prune spring flowering plants as azalea, spirea and dogwood after they bloom.

There are two methods of pruning large, overgrown shrubs. This should be done now for maximum regrowth in the growing season. The first method requires selective removal of three to four old canes or large stems and a modest cutback of others. A few more canes should

234

be removed each year until the shrub is the desired size. It may be kept in bounds by judicious pruning each year.

Another popular method of pruning badly overgrown shrubs is to cut all branches back to within 10 to 12 inches of the ground. The vigorous new growth must be lightly pruned and reshaped in June. This method is easier than the other, but it leaves an unsightly mess for several months.

Prune **fruit trees** and **vines** this month.

Roses, except climbers, should be pruned. Cut canes on a slant. Get rid of older stems to promote vigorous new growth.

If there has been severe **winter damage** it may be wise to delay pruning until the new growth begins to show to indicate where to cut. Prune back about one inch below the damage line or further for shape.

Cut or mow established **mondo** and **liriope** before new growth appears. Use hand clippers, a string trimmer or set mower to three inches. In about two months you will have a fresh green border.

FERTILIZE: Use **wood ashes** from your fireplace in your garden. The wood ashes contain 5-25% potassium. The potassium needs of the soil will be supplied by one half cup per square yard.

Shade trees and **flowering trees** are fertilized this month. Scatter a balanced fertilizer beneath and slightly beyond the spread of branches. Water in well.

Sprinkle a balanced fertilizer around **bulbs** as they begin to sprout. Be careful not to get the fertilizer on the foliage. Fertilize iris also.

SPRAY: Lime sulphur may be applied to roses and other plants to kill dormant insects and disease spores. Spray around the mulch as well as the plants. Lime sulphur may be combined with a dormant oil spray.

MISCELLANEOUS: Cuttings to root new plants may now be taken from house and patio plants you have kept inside for the winter (e.g. hibiscus, geranium, allamanda.)

All pruning cuts of any size should be on a slant to shed water. Sealing of pruning cuts is mainly cosmetic.

YOUR COLORFUL GARDEN

Trees and Shrubs:

Camelia japonica
Daphne odora
Forsythia
Flowering Apricot
Flowering Quince
Saucer Magnolia
Mahonia beali

Star Magnolia
Taiwan Cherry
Tea Olive
Winter Honeysuckle
Wintersweet

Bulb, annuals and perennials:

Calendula officinalis
Daffodil
Hyacinth

Pansy
Snowflake

MARCH

March is a wonderful month for color in the garden as well as a busy month of garden care. The average last frost date for the coastal area is March 15.

PLANT: Continue planting as in February. Nurseries are well stocked with everything from trees to bedding plants. It is preferable to plant trees and shrubs sooner than later, though it can be done at almost any time in the spring, winter or fall, as long as the soil is properly prepared and watering adequate. Much planting is done in the spring as plants tend to be more available. It is also wise to see the bloom of the plant so there will be no surprises.

Summer blooming **annuals** as zinnias, portulaca, salvia and cleome may be started from seed inside to be put out at the end of the month as it begins to warm, or they may be sown where they are to grow. Sow nasturtiums where they are to grow; they like poor soil and full sun. Zinnia seeds may be sown at intervals through August for bloom and cut flowers into the fall. Petunias, lantana and hollyhock may be put into the ground as soon as the danger of frost is over. In the shade, try begonias, impatiens, ageratum and *Phlox divaricata* among ferns or hostas. For bushier plants pinch off terminal growth as you plant the annuals.

Perennial bedding plants may also be put out now. Try gerbera daisies, pinks, shasta daisies, stokesia, coreopsis and perennial salvia. Pansies may be put in now if they were not planted in the fall.

Plant summer flowering or foliage type **bulbs** and **tubers.** These include caladium, canna, gloriosa lily, tulbaghia, agapanthus, montbretia and gladiola. If gladiola corms are planted every two weeks until July, they will provide a continual source of bloom.

Cool season **vegetables** may still be planted, but it is also time to plant summer vegetables: corn, beans, squash, etc. Seeds of tomatoes and peppers may be started inside to be transplanted in early April.

Continue planting perennial and cool weather annual herbs and start planting summer annuals: dill, basil, savory.

DIVIDE: Perennials in overcrowded clumps may be divided. These include daylilies, hostas, shasta daisies, gerbera daisies, and coreopsis. Replant the divisions as soon as possible or share with a friend. Daylilies may be divided at any time of the year as long as the ground is not frozen.

PRUNE: Complete heavy pruning begun in February. Delay pruning of azaleas and spring blooming shrubs until after bloom. If shrubs have been badly damaged by cold, be patient. When new growth begins to appear you will know how much of the plant actually needs to be cut. Even if the entire plant appears to be dead, wait to replace it. Many will grow back from the crown.

FERTILIZE: Shrubs, trees, ground covers and **vines** should be fertilized now, in May and again in July. Ideally, you had a soil sample analyzed in the fall so you know exactly what is required. If not, use a general purpose well balanced fertilizer for most trees and shrubs. Use one tablespoon per foot of height for shrubs and one cup per inch of trunk diameter for trees. Spread it evenly beneath and beyond the spread of branches where there are feeder roots. It is not necessary to wait until after bloom to fertilize **azaleas** and other spring blooming plants. Water well to wash the fertilizer into the soil. Trees may also be fertilized by the use of a tree spike fertilizer which is driven into the ground around the dripline.

Begin rose fertilization program.

SPRAY: Dogwoods often develop a fungal disease called anthracnose. It causes the blooms to be twisted and disfigured and the leaves to have black or rust colors spots. This may be controlled with a spray program using a fungicide. The fungicide should be applied first when the flower buds begin to open, again a week later, and a third time when the leaves begin unfolding.

This is a good time to apply a **dormant spray** to shrubs and trees. use an oil mixed with an insecticide to prevent and treat scale on camellias, hollies, gardenias and other susceptible plants.

Roses may be sprayed or dusted every ten days during the growing season. Use a combination of an insecticide and a fungicide to control aphids and spider mites as well as black spot and mildew.

LAWN: Begin your lawn program early this month with application of a pre-emergent **herbicide.** Fertilization may begin about two weeks after general green-up of the lawn. A light fertilization several times during the growing season is preferable to heavy fertilization which may injure the grass. Use herbicides to kill the weeds, but use very carefully as directed to prevent injury to shrubs and trees as well as the lawn.

If your permanent lawn is over planted with **rye**, cut it close so that the sunshine can penetrate to the permanent grass.

Centipede and St. Augustine can be **sprigged** in new lawns or to renovate old lawns.

MISCELLANEOUS: Water in the morning so that the leaves can dry off before nightfall. Moisture promotes the development of fungus.

Use a waterproof closable container to store **fertilizer.** Otherwise, it will absorb moisture and form a hard cake.

YOUR COLORFUL GARDEN

Trees and Shrubs:

Azalea	Pearlbush
Banana Shrub	Purpleleaf Plum
Camellia japonica	Quince
Crabapple	Raphiolepis
Dogwood	Red Tip Photinia
Flowering Almond	Spirea
Flowering Apricot	Wisteria
Forsythia	

Bulbs, Annuals and Perenninals:

Ajuga	Gerbera Daisy
Carolina Jessamine	Heuchera
Columbine	Iris
Daffodil	Johnny Jump-up
Daylily	Pansy
Forget-me-not	Tulip

APRIL

April is still a busy month in the garden both for bloom and for work. Fortunately the weather is glorious making it easier to get out.

PLANT: This is the opportune time to plant warm season **annuals, perennials, shrubs** and **trees.** It is beginning to get late in the spring to plant bare-root stock. Try new varieties and new color combinations each year. To achieve what you want, you may wish to order varieties unavailable locally from some of the wonderful catalogs. (See section on Sources.) Don't be afraid to try seeds. They may be started outdoors now, indoors under lights, or may be sown where they are to grow. Keep them moist for germination. Seeds are not as costly as plants and you can share the excess with friends.

The planting area must always be well prepared. With hot weather coming, attention must be given to keeping new plants well watered.

Seeds of heat loving **annuals** as zinnia, marigold, portulaca, rudbeckia, gloriosa daisy and celosia may be sown where they are to grow, or plants from garden centers may be planted. In the shade try begonias, impatiens, ageratum and *Phlox divaricata* among ferns or hostas. Water well unless rainfall is adequate. You will have bushier, stronger plants if you can make yourself pinch off all blooms and buds from the new plants at planting time.

Start **hanging baskets** early in April. Impatiens, begonias and caladiums do well in the shade. For sunny locations try verbena, trailing lantana, dwarf marigold, annual vinca and petunias. Portulaca is wonderful in baskets as it tolerates hot sun and drought. To have a bushier basket, keep the tips of the plants pinched. Also start pots for your patio or porch.

Chrysanthemums should be rooted and replanted or divided. When new shoots have reached five inches long, cut below a leaf node. Remove the lower leaves and dip the stem in rooting hormone. Place in builders sand or sterile potting medium up to, but not touching the top leaves. These should root in ten to twenty days. After that, plant in your garden and fertilize every two weeks. Pinch for bushier growth when six inches tall and continue pinching until August 1. Though this is standard practice, some gardeners in our area note two to three bloom periods if the chrysanthemums are allowed to bloom. Cut back after flowering each time and keep the plants fertilized.

Dahlias and **canna lilies** may be planted this month for summer bloom. In full sun, dahlias will give rich color well into the fall. Newly introduced varieties of cannas are very attractive.

Continue planting **gladioli** every two weeks for cut flowers.

Caladiums may be started from tubers as the soil warms.

Keep rapidly growing cool weather **vegetables** regularly fertilized and watered. Put out tomatoes, eggplant, squash, cucumbers and other summer vegetables. Plant tall tomato plants within six inches of the first leaves, burying roots and stems. They will put out new roots all along the stem that is underground.

Plant basil, dill and other annual **herbs.**

DIVIDE: Daylilies may still be divided. Divide other **perennials** as well (e.g. phlox, coreopsis).

PRUNE: Azaleas can be pruned after they have bloomed. To keep at present height, prune back about one third. If they are overgrown cut back two or three of the largest stems to the base. Prune other stems to just below the desired height. Prune forsythia, quince, spirea and other **spring flowering shrubs** in the same way. Never shear the shrubs as it destroys their natural graceful growth pattern.

Pyracantha is prized for its winter berries and the birds it attracts, including flocks of Cedar Waxwings. Its growth, however, may be difficult to contain. Protect yourself from the thorns using good heavy gloves. Prune out all long and wayward shoots now, so that the remaining limbs will develop the colorful berries.

Shear hardy candytuft, alyssum and lobelia after blooming. This makes it look neater and provides a succession of bloom. Remove spent flowers from snapdragons for another crop of flowers. The blooms will not be as large but they do provide garden color. Continue this procedure along with fertilization for repeat bloom, until the plants are killed by warm weather.

Cut back the stems of **daffodils** so the flowers do not produce seed. Do not cut back the foliage as it is now storing food for next year's bloom.

FERTILIZE: If you have not fertilized your azaleas, you must do so now. Use azalea-camellia special on **azaleas, camellias,** and **daylilies.** Use one tablespoon per foot of plant height. Spread it lightly beneath and beyond the branches. Do not throw it at the base. Water well. You will repeat this again in May and then in early July.

After planting **annuals, perennials** and **vegetables** fertilize monthly. This will keep bloom on the flowers and maximize vegetable production.

SPRAY: You may still spray **shrubs** for tea scale, but be sure to do it before temperatures go above 80°. Use a mixture of Volck oil and an insecticide as recommended by the county extension agent or nurseryman. This spray will also control other scales as well as red spider. It may be used on most garden shrubs, but should be used particularly on azaleas, camellias, yaupon, boxwood, hollies and gardenias as they are more susceptible to scale. Systemic insecticides may be used at any temperature, but not plants grown for fruit or vegetable.

LAWN: Begin a lawn fertilization program this month after greenup. See section on Lawns for specific directions.

MISCELLANEOUS: To revitalize your **house plants** move them out under the trees for the summer. This is a desirable time to repot container plants.

YOUR COLORFUL GARDEN

Trees and Shrubs:

Azalea
Banana Shrub
Calycanthus
Camellia japonica
Conradina canadensis
Deutzia
Dogwood

Lady Banks Rose
Oakleaf Hydrangea
Pomegranate
Roses
Spirea

Bulbs, Annuals and Perennials:

Alyssum
Amaryllis
Bignonia
Columbine
Coreopsis
Dianthus
Forget-me-not
Geranium
Gerbera Daisy
Honeysuckle
Iris

Johnny-jump-up
Lantana
Larkspur
Nasturtium
Pansy
Petunia
Phlox
Poppy
Snapdragon
Stokesia
Violet

MAY

May begins to get a little warm and planting slows down. Care and feeding become of great importance.

PLANT: Warm weather **annuals** may still be planted for summer color. Set out those you have started on the window sill. Buy others from the nursery. You may continue to plant zinnia seed at intervals for cut flowers until frost. Overplant bulb beds with annuals using seeds or transplants. Use care not to injure the bulbs while planting.

Plant rooted **chrysanthemums** where you wish them to bloom in the fall. Stem cuttings may still be rooted if you did not do it in April.

Daylilies are beginning to bloom. Make your selections and plant them this month. Clumps are easily lifted, divided and transplanted now.

To move **bulbs** as daffodils and lycoris, dig when the foliage dies down. Store in a dry place until time to replant in the fall.

Caladium tubers like the warm ground. Plant them now. **Dahlias** also may be planted at this time.

Plant warm weather **vegetables** as beans, squash, tomatoes, melons and eggplant if not planted in April. Plant summer peas, okra and butter beans.

PRUNE: Prune spring flowering **shrubs** as soon as the blooms fade. Not all of them will need to be pruned. Prune to control size, or to remove an awkward limb. Always remove damaged or diseased branches.

Azalea pruning must be completed as flowers will begin to set in July for next spring. To encourage branching and to keep the plants from becoming too large, trim the spring growth as it matures. This will promote a good growth habit and appearance through the fall and winter.

Remove seed pods from **daylilies** unless you want to use the dried pods for arrangements. Most daylilies are hybrids so the seeds will not come true.

Shear candytuft and alyssum.

Remove spent blooms from **roses.**

FERTILIZE: Shrubs need the second application of fertilizer now. Use a balanced fertilizer, one tablespoon per foot of height for shrubs or one cup per inch of trunk diameter for trees as you did in March.

Give **daylilies** a light application of fertilizer as the buds begin to appear. Flower substance and bloom will be improved with irrigation in the absence of rainfall.

After blooming, fertilize **iris** with a balanced fertilize or well rotted cow manure. The fertilizer should not touch the rhizome.

Annuals and **perennials** need regular fertilization every four to five weeks. Use a complete fertilizer.

Crape myrtles may be fertilized now if not done earlier. Use one half cup per inch of trunk diameter spread beneath and beyond the branches.

Fertilize **gloriosa lilies** when they are well started.

Continue fertilization of **roses**. Use one fourth cup per plant monthly. Begin in a ring six inches out from the stem and extend out to eighteen inches.

SPRAY: Keep your eyes open for signs of **insects** and be prepared to spray. Yellow foliage may be caused by **lace bugs** and **spider mites.** A brownish deposit on the underside of leaves and a small insect with lacy wings indicates lace bug. A fine webbing can suggest spider mites. **Aphids** are tiny round, usually green insects found on new growth. Most insects may be controlled with an insecticide spray or dust. Use carefully according to manufacturer's directions. Use a commercial type sticker-spreader, or a small amount of detergent in the spray so that the spray will not be washed off with the first shower. **Spider mites** may be more difficult to control. Junipers are especially susceptible to these. A miticide must be used for control. A hard spray of cold water also dislodges them.

With high humidity **fungal** diseases may become a problem. They may be controlled with a fungicide.

If using a program of regular spraying, keep **roses** sprayed at seven to ten day intervals. Use a dust or spray especially formuated for roses. It should contain a fungicide to control blackspot as well as an insecticide.

If your **camellias** are heavily infested with scale (indicate by a white deposit on the underside of the leaves), they may be drenched or sprayed every six weeks with a systemic insecticide as currently recommended. Follow directions carefully. The oil you used earlier in the spring will prevent but not control; treat the problem completely.

LAWN: Look for lawn **diseases** on St. Augustine and centipede. Brown patch is apt to appear at this time of the year. When viewed early in the morning, the brown circular or irregular areas may appear sunken with a dark purplish ring on the outer edges. The disease will spread rapidly if not treated. The entire area should be sprayed with a fungicide at the rate recommended by the manufacturer. This should be repeated in seven to ten days.

MISCELLANEOUS: If there is not adequate rain, **water** your beds and lawn well once a week applying at least ½ to 1 inch of water. Measure the amount delivered by placing a wide mouthed container under the spray. Early watering is preferred so that the leaves will dry before nightfall. Residual moisture promotes the growth of fungus.

To conserve moisture and decrease weeds, **mulch** shrubs and flowers. Use pinestraw, hay, oak leaves or compost to a depth of two to three inches. Mulch all plants except some iris (bearded, tectorum, and cristata species).

Cover the roots of **clematis** with bricks to keep the ground cool in the hot sun.

Sink your **houseplants** in the earth in their pots in a shady location to decrease tending for the summer.

YOUR COLORFUL GARDEN

Trees and Shrubs:

Azalea

Butterfly Bush

Honeysuckle

Ligustrum

Magnolia

Oakleaf Hydrangea

Pomegranate

Rose

Bulbs, Annuals and Perennials:

Blue Salvia

Columbine

Cosmos

Dianthus

Forget-me-not

Gaillardia

Gerbera Daisy

Gloriosa Lily (Rothschildiana)

Gloriosa Daisy

Impatiens

Iris

Larkspur

Pansy

Poppy

Shasta Daisy

Snapdragon

Stokesia

Tiger Lily

Verbena

Yarrow (pink)

JUNE

You should have completed all your major spring planting and pruning. Results of your earlier efforts should be visible by June.

PLANT: Continue to sow seeds of **zinnias** and **marigolds** for cut flowers into the fall. Put out **gladioli** bulbs. They only require nine weeks to bloom.

You may still take cuttings of **chrysanthemums** in early June to put out later in the month. Plant chrysanthemums from the nursery as they become available. Plant eighteen inches apart for growing space.

Dahlia tubers may still be planted for fall bloom. Place them six to eight inches deep and three to four feet apart.

Plant more summer peas in the vegetable garden and enjoy the harvest of most **vegetables.**

PRUNE: Continue to prune **shrubs** as they finish blooming. Finish pruning **azaleas.** Cut out dead or damaged limbs. Cut back to limit size where necessary. Try not to alter the plant's growing habit. For instance, spirea has graceful weeping branches. To prune, thin out limbs in the center of the plant. Do not shear.

As foliage begins to mature, it may be pinched back to encourage branching. This will result in a bushier plant.

Prune the aggressive shoots of such plants as pyracantha and elaeagnus as they come out. It will be much easier now.

It is a good idea to remove **spent blossoms** on annual flowering plants as much as possible. This encourages further blooming rather than seed production. Exceptions to this rule are for seed collectors and those who want to keep the dried seed pods for arrangements. In most cases, seed collectors should keep spent blossoms until the end of the blooming season when the last few blooms may be kept for seed. Seeds of hybrids should not be kept as they will not reproduce the parent plant. Daylily seeds, for instance, do not come true, but often the seed pods are allowed to dry for arrangements.

Prune out tips of **chrysanthemums** every three weeks until mid August for bushier growth and more bloom. Do the same with **dahlias.**

FERTILIZE: For heavier bloom apply an extra application of fertilizer to **crape myrtles** this month.

Use a complete fertilizer on annuals every four to five weeks.

Yellow leaves on azaleas may indicate a nutrient deficiency. Nitrogen deficiency is indicated by a yellowing of old leaves. This should be corrected by application of an acid forming fertilizer (the standard azalea-camellia fertilizer will do). If the leaves are yellow with green veins (chlorotic), the plants have an iron deficiency. This deficiency will be corrected by application of an iron chelate solution unless the soil pH is too high for the plant to utilize the iron. To detect acid or alkaline pH a soil test is required. The county extension agent will have this test performed for you.

SPRAY: A black coating like soot on leaves (especially gardenia and crape myrtle) indicates infestation with **white flies** or **aphids.** A black fungus lives on the sticky honeydew secreted by the insects. The insects may be controlled with an insecticide or with the new insecticidal soap.

Downy mildew causes a white or gray coating of the leaves (especially on crape myrtle). It may be controlled with a fungicide.

Use an appropriate insecticide to control **lace bug** on azaleas and pyracantha. The lace bug may cause the leaves to become yellow gray in appearance.

Repeat insecticide spray monthly to treat **scale** on camellias and hollies.

Continue spraying **roses** regularly or as needed.

LAWN: Mole crickets in your lawn may become evident this month. Dead and dying grass with the root system destroyed, fluffiness in the grass when walked upon, and small pencil sized holes marked by mounds of coarse earth are all signs of this lawn pest. As with so many pests and diseases, control, not elimination, is the goal. Control of the mole cricket (a fat brown version of the better known cricket) requires using both bait for the adult and an insecticide for the larvae at various intervals. Please discuss with the county extension agent or your nurseryman the newest recommendations as they change frequently.

MISCELLANEOUS: Continue to **water** weekly to ½ to 1 inch if there is not a good rain.

Complete **mulching** of beds with pine straw. Mulch Louisiana iris with dried manure.

If your **hanging baskets** are outside, remove the saucers so that the roots do not become water logged and rotten.

Indoor plants will appreciate some time out of doors. To prevent leaves from scorching move gradually from dense to light shade.

Cuttings of new growth should be taken from shrubs for **propagation.** Please see chapter on Propagating.

YOUR COLORFUL GARDEN

Trees and Shrubs:

Althea	Mock Orange
Bottlebrush	Oakleaf Hydrangea
Butterfly Bush	Oleander
Crape Myrtle	Pomegrantate
Gardenia	*Rosa rugosa*
Magnolia	Rose

Bulbs, Annuals and Perennials:

Ageratum	Gloriosa Lily
Amaryllis	Hosta
Blue Salvia	Impatiens
Butterfly Weed	Lantana
Canna Lily	Marigold
Clematis	Petunia
Cleome	Phlox
Coreopsis	Queen Anne's Lace
Cosmos	Shasta Daisy
Crinum Lily	Snapdragon
Dahlberg Daisy	Stokesia
Dahlia	Sunflower
Daylily	Verbena
Forget-me-not	Yarrow (gold, white, pink)
Gaillardia	Zinnia
Gerbera Daisy	

JULY

Despite warm weather and vacations there are still a few things to keep the gardener busy.

PLANT: Zinnias may still be planted or seed sown for bloom until frost. **Caladium** may also be set out, and **gladioli bulbs** may be planted every ten days until the end of this month for a succession of bloom and cut flowers into the fall.

Plant your second crop of summer **vegetables,** or begin your first. Tomatoes, squash and summer peas may still be planted. Suckers from tomato plants may be rooted to started new plants for continued fruit production. Rooting may be done in soil, sand, vermiculite or even water. Dip the end in a rooting hormone, place in the medium and keep moist. The plants may be transplanted into the garden in 3-4 weeks, but you must protect them from the hot sun for a few days after planting.

DIVIDE: Daylilies may be divided and transplanted year round except during freezing periods. Divide to suit scale of garden. Water well until established. Cut off the seed pods.

PRUNE: Remove dying flower heads and cut back leggy **annuals** especially salvia. They will put out new growth and ultimately will bloom more profusely into the fall.

Cut back **herbs,** including mint, oregano and basil, to keep plants more compact. This will also keep them from going to seed too soon.

Continue to pinch back the growing tips of your **chrysanthemums.** If this is not done, the plants will have spindly, sprawling branches with fewer flowers, but then again, you may see more than one period of bloom.

Prune all summer flowering **shrubs** after flowering. Revitalize old bushes by cutting the heaviest canes to the ground.

Buds for next year's bloom on **azaleas** will begin to set in July so pruning should be completed.

For a second flowering on **crape myrtle,** cut off spent blossoms.

FERTILIZE: Fertilize **annuals** every four to five weeks. Use one teaspoon of a complete fertilizer per square foot. Fertilize **daylilies** again this month. Fertilize **clematis** and water in well. Be sure to wash any fertilizer off the leaves.

Give **shrubs** their last fertilization of the season. Spread one tablespoon per foot height of plant around the drip line. Use a balanced fertilizer for all but the acid loving shrubs. On those (azaleas, camellias) use acid forming azalea-camellia special unless your soil analysis recommends otherwise.

Continue fertilizing **roses.**

SPRAY: Watch for insects on **vegetables** and **flowers.** Aphids will be seen first on new growth. Leaf hoppers leave a hole in the leaf. Spray at first sign of these insects to control them. Use topical or systemic insecticides, the insecticidal soap or products recommended by your nurseryman. Be careful to follow the manufacturer's directions, in particular those regarding harvest and spray times.

Sooty mold may still appear if humidity is high. See June for cause and control.

The presence of **slugs** may be suspected when the bottom leaves are chewed around the edges. There are several favorite methods for capturing slugs. Stale beer may be placed in a shallow bowl which is sunk into the ground. (Drowned slugs in the morning!) They may be captured by putting one half a grapefruit rind upside down in the garden. The slugs will be underneath in the morning and may then be killed by spraying with a vinegar and water (1:1) solution. (They are pickled on contact!) Last, and easiest, when it works, slug bait may be spread around the garden when the slugs are doing their damage.

Continue to watch for problems on **roses.**

LAWN: Refertilize your lawn this month.

Raise the cutting edge of the **mower** one half to one inch. This will keep the roots cooler and conserve moisture.

You may **sprig** or plug grass in bare spots to repair the lawn. Remember to keep well watered.

MISCELLANEOUS: Keep vegetables and flower beds **weeded.** Mulch to decrease weed growth and conserve moisture.

Water regularly and adequately. It is preferable to water early in the day so that the foliage will dry. The moisture on warm nights will promote the growth of fungus. Water until at least one half inch has been delivered. A light sprinkling will bring the roots to the surface.

Cuttings may still be taken from shrubs to make new plants. Layering is an easy way to get more of some favorites. (Please see chapter on Propagation.)

Before going on **vacation** put your garden in order. It is discouraging to return to a ruined garden after so much spring work. Cut back annuals. They will put out new growth and be ready to bloom again when you return. Pinch out growing tips of chrysanthemums and dahlias. Cut off any buds that will bloom while you are gone. Spray with an insecticide and fertilize one last time. Give a deep watering to everything. Harvest vegetables. Mow lawn. If you will be gone longer than two weeks you should have a neighbor water well at intervals. Arrange to have the lawn mowed as well.

YOUR COLORFUL GARDEN

Trees and Shrubs:

Abelia	Hypericum
Althea	Magnolia
Butterfly Bush	Oleander
Crape Myrtle	Yucca

Bulbs, Annuals and Perennials:

Blue Salvia	Lisianthus
Butterfly Weed	Marigold
Cleome	Moon Vine
Cosmos	Montbretia
Dahlia	Petunia
Daylily	Phlox
Dill	Physostegia
Fennel	Plumbago
Forget-me-not	Portulaca
Four o'clock	Rudbeckia
Gaillardia	Stokesia
Gerbera Daisy	Sunflower
Gladiolus	Tulbaghia
Gloriosa Lily	Vinca
Hosta Lily	Wooly Lamb's Ear
Impatiens	Yarrow (golden)
Lantana	Zinnia
Liatris	

AUGUST

Since August is too hot for much outdoor gardening, plan to do what is necessary early in the morning.

PLAN: Order spring flowering **bulbs** and **perennial** seeds and plants now for fall planting. Plan to order wildflower seeds also. Some **annuals**, such as poppies and sweet peas, will also need to be planted in the fall. The nurseries will have some stock come in for fall planting, but it is fun to try something a little different. Plan for fall vegetables.

PLANT: Plant **lycoris** bulbs the depth of the bulb. The flower stalks will come up and will bloom in the fall. These bulbs resent being moved.

You may continue to plant cucumbers, summer squash and snapbeans for fall picking. Suckers from tomatoes may be rooted in sand or soil for harvest until frost. Plant potatoes, snapbeans, turnips, winter greens, etc. in the **vegetable** garden.

PRUNE: Continue to pinch back the growing tips of **chrysanthemums** until August 1. At this time the buds will begin to set. Buds appearing before that time may be removed for better ultimate bloom.

Prune **hydrangeas** that have finished blooming.

Rejuvenate the garden for fall by cutting back straggly plants. Many **blooming plants** (geraniums, impatiens, begonias, marigolds, blue salvia) will bloom again if fertilized. Cut back hanging baskets as well.

Overly aggressive summer growth of **shrubs** may be cut back and hedges trimmed for appearance. Otherwise shrubs should not be pruned now.

FERTILIZE: Continue to fertilize **chrysanthemums** and **dahlias** every three to four weeks until color shows. Fertilize **caladiums.**

Continue to fertilize **annuals, perennials** and **vegetables** on a regular schedule.

If **shrubs** have a light green color in the new growth (chlorosis), use chelated iron in the amounts indicated on the label.

Continue to fertilize **roses.**

SPRAY: Look for **aphids** on crape myrtle and gardenia. Control of aphids will prevent sooty mold. Sooty mold may be caused by aphids, mealy bugs or whiteflies. Control with an insecticide or use an insecticidal soap spray.

In dry, hot weather **spider mites** may become a problem on ornamentals, foliage plants, and on vegetables. The insects are difficult to see, but their presence may be indicated by light webbing on the underside of leaves. To control, apply a miticide according to label directions. The spider mites tend to become resistant to the controlling agents very rapidly. It is therefore a good idea to use different agents at intervals. A hard spray of cold water will also help to control these pests.

Remember to look for problems on **roses** and spray regularly or as needed.

MISCELLANEOUS: Continue to **water** regularly and thoroughly. Keep beds **weeded.**

If your **soil** has not been tested in more than two years, prepare soil samples and take them to your extension agent for testing. Place about a pint of soil, dug from several locations in your bed, in a bag and take to the county extension agent. They will perform an analysis and advice will be given regarding pH and nutritional level of the soil.

Begin collecting **dried plant materials** for winter arrangements. In the fields look for yarrow, cattails, oats and wild grasses. From the garden collect rosehips, celosia, okra pods, daylily seed pods, and garlic and chive flowers. Pick before completely dried and hang upside down in a well ventilated room.

YOUR COLORFUL GARDEN

Trees and Shrubs:

Abelia	Hypericum
Althea	Oleander
Butterfly Bush	*Rosa rugosa*
Crape Myrtle	Yucca

Bulbs, Annuals and Perennials:

Basil, Opal	Lisianthus
Blackberry Lily	Marigold
Blue Salvia	Montbretia
Cleome	Phlox
Cosmos	Physostegia
Dahlia	Plumbago
Gaillardia	Pineapple Sage
Gerbera Daisy	Portulaca
Gloriosa Lily	Rudbeckia
Hosta Lily	Tulbaghia
Impatiens	Zinnia
Lantana	

SEPTEMBER

Gardening picks up again in September. Fall is an important planting time.

PLAN: Make certain you order or buy your seeds and bulbs for fall planting. Be adventurous and try something new.

PLANT: Start seeds of hardy **annuals** now to transplant into the garden in October. Fall **bedding plants**, especially chrysanthemums, should be planted now.

Plant paperwhite narcissus, snowflakes (*Leucojum vernum*), Easter lilies, Madonna lilies and the bearded and Louisiana iris.

Plant fall **vegetables** using both bedding plants and seed. Collards, beets, carrots, mustard, kale, turnips, radishes, lettuce, onions, spinach and parsley are some that may be planted in the fall garden. As in the spring, prepare the beds by digging deeply and adding plenty of fertilizer and organic material to replenish nutrients.

DIVIDE: Divide and replant **perennials** that have finished blooming. **Daylilies** should be dug and separated by pulling apart or dividing the large clump with a shovel or two spading forks. Cut the leaves back to twelve to fourteen inches. They should then be replanted to the same depth and watered well.

Iris should be separated at this time. After digging the iris, cut the foliage back to three inches and allow the rhizome to dry in the sun a few days. Use only the outside rhizomes. Plant in full sun. Prepare the soil by working in bone meal. Plant the rhizome practically on top of the soil spreading the roots out on both sides in small trenches. Pack soil around the roots firmly. Usually the clumps may be left undisturbed for three to four years.

Separate and transplant overgrown **liriope** clumps.

PRUNE: Prune scraggly **shrubs.** Do only cosmetic pruning. You do not want to promote new growth that will not mature before cold weather.

Remove spent **flower heads** and **seed pods.** Save for dried arrangements if you wish.

Root prune shrubs and small **trees** that you plan to move later while dormant. Cut a circle around the base of each plant just outside the dripline. This will stimulate new root growth so that there will be healthy ball or roots when moved. Keep the plant well watered.

Prune **climbing roses** after they bloom.

FERTILIZE: Stop fertilizing **chrysanthemums** when the buds show color.

Gerberas and **clematis** would especially appreciate a few tablespoons of lime worked into the soil around the base.

Keep **tomatoes** in production by feeding with a complete fertilizer. Continue fertilizing **roses.**

SPRAY: With cool damp nights and warm days, watch for **mildew** especially on squash, crape myrtle, zinnias, dahlias and roses. Use a fungicide and spray the top and the bottom of the leaves covering thoroughly.

MISCELLANEOUS: For larger bloom and earlier flowering of your **camellias, gib** them now with gibberellic acid (see Camellias). Remove a vegetative bud from next to a flower bud. Place a drop of the solution in the remaining bud cup.

September and October tend to be dry months. Continue **watering** regularly. Lawns must be protected from drought, if they are to recover well the following spring.

Continue collecting **dried materials** from field and garden for winter arrangements.

Stake **chrysanthemums** and **dahlias** if necessary.

Begin to prepare **house plants** for their return to the house. First check for pests, spray if necessary. Turn the pots where they sit to break up roots that have gone through the bottom. Move them to a semi-shaded porch or carport for a week or so; next move them inside to a well lighted window and then to less illuminated spots if necessary. This slow transfer to the ultimate winter home will allow the plants to acclimatize and will reduce leaf drop.

YOUR COLORFUL GARDEN

Trees and Shrubs:

Abelia	Crape Myrtle
Butterfly Bush	*Rosa rugosa*
Cassia corymbosa	Rose

Bulbs, Annuals and Perennials:

Ageratum	Gloriosa Lily (Superba)
Basil, Opal	Ginger Lily
Blackberry Lily	Hosta
Blue Salvia	Impatiens
Butterfly Weed	Lantana
Canna	Ligularia
Cardinal Flower	Lycoris
Chrysanthemum	Marigold
Cleome	Plumbago
Dahlia	Zinnia
Gerbera Daisy	

OCTOBER

As the days begin to cool we should develop a gardening desire usually associated with spring. Many plants would do better if planted at this time of the year. **Fall is for planting.**

PLANT: Perennials, biennials and **hardy annuals** should be sown or planted now through November. Root growth will proceed well through the winter months. The plants will branch more freely and bloom more profusely in spring when planted in the fall. Plants to be put out now include aquilegia, perennial candytuft, dianthus, shasta daisy, hosta, liatris, snapdragons, pansies, stock and many others. Sweet peas, larkspur and poppies should be sown where they are to grow. If the plants you want are not available in the nursery, order and grow from seed. It is very rewarding to grow your own. Pansies and calendula should be planted early for fall bloom.

Sow **wildflowers** now.

Begin planting spring flowering **bulbs.** Include something new. Try iris, anemones, narcissus, hyacinths, lilies, ranunculus as well as others. Mix bonemeal in the hole in which the bulb is to be planted. Refrigerate tulips for at least six to eight weeks. They should be planted in late December or January.

Plant parsley and perennial **herbs** as sage, thyme and rosemary.

As soon as it begins to cool, begin fall planting of **trees** and **shrubs.** Fall planting allows good winter root growth before new growth in the spring. Root prune small trees and shrubs that you expect to move later in the season.

Transplant **magnolias** now.

DIVIDE: Divide and transplant daylilies, liriope, ajuga, iris and other perennials as required.

PRUNE: Cut back bearded **iris** foliage when it begins to flop over.

On evergreen **shrubs,** prune out long irregular shoots to shape. No major pruning is done until early next spring.

FERTILIZE: Fertilize **pansies** and **calendula** at planting and 3 to 4 weeks later. Use a balanced fertilizer.

SPRAY: To combat the **scale** on camellias and holly, spray with a mixture of oil emulsion (Volck) and an insecticide. Make certain that you cover the underside of the leaves. It is also important to await cooler temperatures. Daytime temperatures should be below 85° F. Night time temperatures must be above 40° so don't wait too long. Systemics may be used at any temperature.

LAWN: For a green carpet all winter, the lawn may be overseeded with annual rye grass. Use five pounds per 1000 square feet of grass. Keep damp until the seeds germinate. Be very careful not to seed too thickly and keep it mowed, as competition with the permanent grass may be a problem. Used annually it will ruin a centipede lawn.

Do not fertilize warm season grasses in the fall.

MISCELLANEOUS: Keep every thing well **watered** if the fall is dry.

Mulch tender shrubs and plants (cassia, brunfelsia, amaryllis). Do not mulch perennials deeply as it may cause them to rot.

When they finish blooming, hibiscus, allamanda, bird of paradise and other **patio plants,** that are not tolerant of cold weather, may be brought into a garage or other sheltered area for a rest. Cut back if necessary. They will require little water over the winter.

Take **cuttings** of impatiens and geraniums to carry over the winter. Geraniums should be cut at about five to six inches and allowed to dry a few days. Dip the cut end in rooting hormone and place in sand or peat. Keep in shade and keep moist.

Collect and dry seeds of cassia, hosta, blackberry lily and herbs for planting next year.

Collect dried grasses and flower heads for winter arrangements.

YOUR COLORFUL GARDEN

Trees and Shrubs:

Butterfly Bush	Rose
Cassia splendida	Tea Olive

Bulbs, Annuals and Perennials:

Ageratum	Ligularia
Blue Salvia	Marigold
Chrysanthemum	Phlox
Cosmos	Plumbago
Dahlia	Portulaca
Gerbera Daisy	Rudbeckia
Gloriosa Lily	*Sedum spectabile*
Impatiens	Zinnia
Lantana	

NOVEMBER

November continues to be a busy month for completing fall planting and fall chores.

PLANT: Trees and **shrubs** do well when planted in the fall. They send out new root growth in winter so that they are well established by spring. When planted in the fall, water loss is not as great and survival rate is improved. The advantage of spring planting is the ability to see the bloom before buying. When planting trees and shrubs, dig a hole larger than you think you need. Work peat into the soil if needed, place plant in hole making certain that it is no deeper than the original soil line, and water well.

Small trees and shrubs may be transplanted when cold weather begins. Prune to compensate for root loss.

Continue planting **perennials** and **hardy annuals** either by sowing seed or buying available plants.

Spring blooming **bulbs** may still be planted. Work bone meal into the soil where planting. Store tulips in the refrigerator for six to eight weeks to be ready for planting in December or January.

DIVIDE: Perennials, iris and **daylilies** may still be divided and transplanted.

Divide and replant **dahlias** after the first killing frost. They do not require winter storage in our climate.

PRUNE: Pinch back fall planted **snapdragons** when they are five inches high. Do this several times for bushier plants.

When **chrysanthemums** have finished blooming cut back stems to within five inches of the ground. If the clump is to be transplanted to make room for other plants, do that now while the plants are dormant. Remove to an out of the way sunny location to save for cuttings next spring. Apply a light mulch.

Prune **shrubs** and **trees** only to remove overly vigorous shoots.

SPRAY: Spray to prevent **tea scale**, if you have not already done so.

LAWN: If **artichoke weed** is a problem, it may be sprayed with an appropriate herbicide. Contact your county extension agent for current recommendations.

MISCELLANEOUS: Check **mulch.** Its depth should not exceed two inches. Mulch tender plants to protect from cold weather.

Dig and store **caladium bulbs** before frost. Remove foliage, dust with a fungicide and store in a stocking or onion bag (for air circulation) where the temperature is near 60 F.

When **frost** comes, wash the frost crystals off the leaves of tender plants before the sun comes up to prevent damage by scorching.

Consider forcing **bulbs** for indoor winter bloom. (See Bulbs)

Remove dead **annual plants** and cut off tops of **perennials.**

Keep watering, if we do not get a weekly inch of rain.

YOUR COLORFUL GARDEN

Trees and Shrubs:

Abelia

Camellia japonica

Camellia sasanqua

Cassia splendida

Rose

Tea Olive

Bulbs, Annuals and Perennials:

Blue Salvia

Canna

Chrysanthemum

Dahlia

Gerbera Daisy

Impatiens

Lantana

Plumbago

Nasturtium

Violet

DECEMBER

If you have done the planting, mulching and spraying recommended in October and November, you may enjoy holiday preparations with little gardening care.

PLANT: Tulips may be taken out of the refrigerator and planted this month, or early in January. It is not too late to plant other spring flowering **bulbs.**

Hardy **annuals** and **perennials** may still be planted out. It is a little late for the seeds of poppies, sweetpeas and larkspur but it may be worth a try. Give a light mulch of pinestraw.

Shrubs and **trees** may still be planted. Keep well watered to protect from freezing temperatures. Established plants, including those from the woods, may be moved this month. They should have been root pruned in the fall.

MISCELLANEOUS: Remember to keep **watering** weekly.

If a **freeze** is forecast, water well to prevent damage. Susceptible plants may be covered with plastic or heavily mulched, but the covering should be removed as it begins to warm, lest further damage occur from the rapid warming.

Poinsettia should be placed in good light out of the way of drafts. They should be watered well about twice a week (when the dirt feels dry). For ease in watering and better drainage the foil wrap should be removed and a saucer or decorative pot placed under the plant. The color may last for months with this care. Poinsettias may be used as cut flowers. The leaves should be stripped and the cut stem placed in hot water for conditioning. When the plant has finished blooming it may be planted outside on the sunny southside of the house. In this location it will bloom each year.

The purchased **Christmas tree** will last longer if a fresh cut is made off the trunk before putting it in water.

Magnolia leaves will turn a beautiful rich brown and keep indefinitely, if the branch stem is stood in a solution of 1/3 glycerine and 2/3 water for three weeks, or until enough of the glycerine has been absorbed to make the leaves soft and pliable.

YOUR COLORFUL GARDEN

Trees and Shrubs:		Bulbs, Annuals and Perennials:
Ardesia	Nandina	Alyssum
Camellia japonica	Pyracantha	Gerbera Daisy
Camellia sasanqua	Poinsettia	Impatiens
Foster Holly	Rose	*Iris unguicularis*
Ilex vomitoria	Tea Olive	Paperwhite Narcissus
Savannah Holly		

INDEX

261

262

Garden Guide to the Lower South
Trustees' Garden Club • P.O. Box 24215
Savannah, Georgia 31403-4215

❏ AmEx ❏ Discover
❏ Visa ❏ MasterCard

Please send me _____ copies of your garden book at $19.95 per copy plus $4.00 postage and handling. (Georgia residents include 6% sales tax.) Enclosed is my check or money order made payable to Trustees' Garden Club for $ _____

Name _____
FOR CHARGE ORDERS, PRINT NAME AS IT APPEARS ON CARD

Address _____

City _____ State _____ Zip _____

Account No. _____ Exp. Date _____

Signature _____

Garden Guide to the Lower South
Trustees' Garden Club • P.O. Box 24215
Savannah, Georgia 31403-4215

❏ AmEx ❏ Discover
❏ Visa ❏ MasterCard

Please send me _____ copies of your garden book at $19.95 per copy plus $4.00 postage and handling. (Georgia residents include 6% sales tax.) Enclosed is my check or money order made payable to Trustees' Garden Club for $ _____

Name _____
FOR CHARGE ORDERS, PRINT NAME AS IT APPEARS ON CARD

Address _____

City _____ State _____ Zip _____

Account No. _____ Exp. Date _____

Signature _____

Garden Guide to the Lower South
Trustees' Garden Club • P.O. Box 24215
Savannah, Georgia 31403-4215

❏ AmEx ❏ Discover
❏ Visa ❏ MasterCard

Please send me _____ copies of your garden book at $19.95 per copy plus $4.00 postage and handling. (Georgia residents include 6% sales tax.) Enclosed is my check or money order made payable to Trustees' Garden Club for $ _____

Name _____
FOR CHARGE ORDERS, PRINT NAME AS IT APPEARS ON CARD

Address _____

City _____ State _____ Zip _____

Account No. _____ Exp. Date _____

Signature _____

Reorder Additional Copies